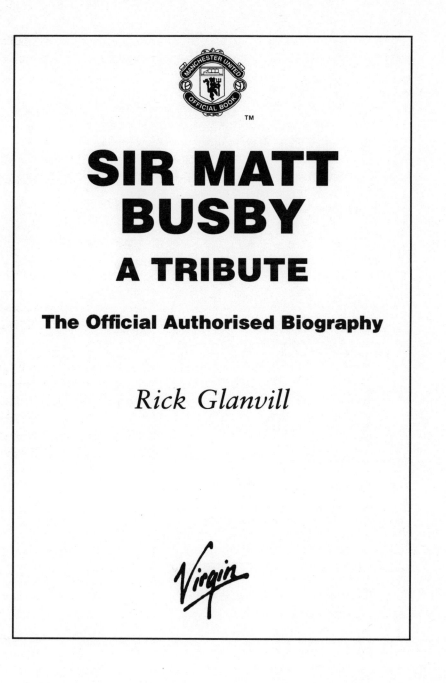

TM

SIR MATT BUSBY

A TRIBUTE

The Official Authorised Biography

Rick Glanvill

Virgin

What matters above all things is that the game should be played in the right spirit with the utmost courage, with fair play and no favour, with every man playing as a member of his team without bitterness and conceit.

Sir Matt Busby

First published in Great Britain in 1994 by
Manchester United Football Club plc
Old Trafford
Manchester
M16 0RA
in association with
Virgin Publishing Ltd.
332 Ladbroke Grove
London
W10 5AH

A catalogue record for this book is available from the British Library.

ISBN 1 85227 464 6

Produced by **Zone Publishing**

Phototypeset by **Intype, London**
Printed in Great Britain by **Butler & Tanner Ltd.**

Contents

List Of Illustrations

Foreword By George Best

Sir Matt Busby was one of those people who, if he's been in your life, it's been a privilege. When people talk about him as a legend, 'this great, great man', they inevitably look for skeletons – 'Surely nobody can be that perfect?' But he really was. In all areas.

The little things were important to him. I remember when my dad first travelled to Manchester, even though he returned a couple of months later, Sir Matt remembered his name, my mum's name and the names of the kids. He even remembered what whisky dad drank. Sir Matt had a wonderful way with people. I've never heard anybody say a bad word about him. And that's because there are no bad words to say.

When Sir Matt walked in a room the whole place lit up. He had the ability to shine in any company, from the day I met him, until the day he died. He was always relaxed. It's a wonderful and rare quality to be as much at ease with the Queen or the Pope, as he was down the pub with the rest of us.

In any list of the footballing greats you'll find Bill Shankly, Jock Stein, and Cloughie. They've all been called 'the boss', but there was only ever one spelt with capitals, and that was 'the Boss' – that's what they all called Sir Matt. When you've got Jock Stein and Bill Shankly saying that, it's some compliment. He really was the Boss of all bosses.

As anyone lucky enough to have sat in on one would tell you, his team talks were wonderful. Ten minutes before we went out he used to throw the ball to whoever was captain for the day, whether it was Denis, Bobby or myself. And as he threw it, he'd say, 'Just go out and enjoy yourself'. It's a great philosophy when you're under pressure and the spotlight is on, and Sir Matt's whole reason for living was to enjoy it.

Sir Matt Busby

There was a lovely shot of him last year after United won the Championship; I've only seen his face look like that twice. At the end of the 1993–94 season, and when he came on to the pitch after we'd won the European Cup. Put those two faces together side by side, and it looked like the same photograph. I always judge people by their eyes. Look into Matt's and they were brilliant. He was brilliant.

In later years he paid me a lovely compliment. We were recording a video to mark the 25th anniversary of our European Cup victory. The whole team went to Wembley, and stayed in a hotel down there for a lovely weekend. But around 6 a.m. on the Sunday, I got a phone call from the night porter, apologising, saying, 'Mr Best, the Boss is downstairs and he's asking for you.' I thought: 'All the team are here and he's asking for me!'

I got Sir Matt on the phone, and asked him what the problem was. He said he wanted to go back to Manchester. I jumped out of bed and ran down as fast as I could, but by the time I got there, he'd gone back to bed! Yet to me, that was a great compliment. All the boys were there – Bobby, Denis, Bill – but he said, 'Get hold of George'.

You have to be very lucky in your life to meet someone like him. And I was. Sir Matt Busby looked after me, he protected me. He gave me a few bollockings in my time as a player, but rightly so. I've said many times that he became my father. And my own father takes that as a compliment, because he thought the world of him as well.

The effect he had on my life was immeasurable. It's difficult for me to talk about him even now. I still go to games, and make a point of seeing the family. And I still expect him to walk in. The seat is still there with his name on it. No one sits there, and nobody ever will sit there. If anyone tried, there would be a riot. I like to imagine the old fella sitting up there somewhere, getting drunk and watching us and laughing with us. His spirit will always live on at Old Trafford. His spirit will always live on for me.

Acknowledgements

The author wishes to express his gratitude to Chris Maume for setting the ball rolling, to his agent Cat Ledger for kicking it into my half of the field, and to James Freedman at Zone and Mal Peachey at Virgin for refereeing so well. Also many thanks to Adam Porter and Joanne Parker, for their research assistance. He would also like to express his appreciation of the United staff, players and other interviewees who were kind enough to contribute to this project, especially Paddy Crerand (keep the faith!) and Alex Ferguson. Finally, the author's heartfelt thanks to Sandy Busby for his kindness and openness at a time when the loss of his father was still terribly heartbreaking. Hopefully the result has done the great man some justice.

Introduction – The Legacy

By any standard in football management, Sir Matt Busby was a colossus. He was more than a proud figurehead at Manchester United. He remains, as Ray Wilkins puts it, 'The figurehead of all figureheads – he *is* Manchester United.'

Football has a long memory, riddled with romantic, historic, traditional entanglements. It makes a major contribution to the game's richness; the manner in which football's grounds, teams and players swirl up out of the miasma to provide a constant challenge. It is rich in rivalry, spite and ignorance. But Matt Busby rose above all that. He loved the arbitrary nature of football, the infinite variety, the gloomy winter training session and the glorious Cup final bathed in sunshine. In fact Matt's story is much like that. His was a hard life leavened by moments of great joy and by the people he surrounded himself with – his wife Jean, his family, close friends and his beloved players.

His story belongs to all supporters, no matter what their tribal affiliation on a Saturday. For his is also that of English football itself. Its conquering lions, unfulfilled promise, its muscular prowess, rare genius, its knee-jerk bureaucracy and brilliant, baffling glamour and frustrations. But it is also the blueprint for success in the game. He was a man of immense, intense ambition, and the authority, will and occasional ruthlessness to achieve them. He carved the monolith that is the internationally renowned United from a rough hewn rock without a face. He became that face. He invested his life in and controlled every aspect of the club. Sculpted its atmosphere, its character and its self-image with a calculated and visionary design. Matt never allowed the club to spend more than it could afford to lose on the ground or the players who graced it. He embodied the dignity of the club. He built his relationship with those players on mutual respect and belief tinged with awe – a trick few of today's managers could perform, just as only a handful could then. Matt was aware of fallibility; he had a few demons of his own and recognised that footballers were, sadly, only human. So he allowed his team to express themselves not only in a mission to honour the beautiful game, but also in recognition that a head full of tactical tosh is not required in such a simple game.

There are always those who attempt to ameliorate the present game by impoverishing its qualities in the past. And it is true that there was some good fortune surrounding Matt's time at United – not least his arrival at a big club down on its luck and ripe for the picking. But, as former Liverpool and Scottish international footballer, now TV broadcaster, Ian St John avers, 'The game is still a brain game.' Matt's intelligent approach and personal qualities would prove successful in any era. Alex Ferguson, current United manager, fervent admirer and conscientious friend of Sir Matt in his later years, believes he would have triumphed in any era.

Alex Ferguson

(Manager of United since 1986, the man who resurrected the glory days at Old Trafford, bringing home the first Championship trophy in 26 years. In the 1993/94 season completed the double – a feat not even Matt could achieve.)

He was a gentle and humble man, but make no mistake: he could be tough when he needed to be. He was also very shrewd and a great handler of players. I have no doubt whatsoever that he would have done a great job in the modern game – great managers are great in any age.

Arsenal's Herbert Chapman might be the finest manager ever, Bob Paisleys all-conquering Liverpool might have won more silverware, but Matt is football's greatest legend and its conscience. There is much for everyone in football to glean from his blueprint for success. Every club needs a Matt Busby at some time in its history if it wishes to be greater than the bland syllables that make up its name. Sir Matt's son Sandy has an eloquent metaphor.

Sandy Busby

(Only son of Matt and Jean to survive. One time footballer at Blackburn. Brother to Sheena, ran Matt's souvenir shop at Old Trafford for some time.)

This man came and planted a seed in a bombed-out ground, and he watched the seed grow, he loved it and nurtured it, till the branches started growing outwards and upwards. Then the tree was struck by lightning. He started all over again, loving it and nurturing it, and the branches grew and grew to the ends of the world.

But there is much more to this biography than Matt's relationship with Manchester United. That his life story is also endowed with the classic ebb and flow, zenith and nadir of a Hollywood epic has often been overlooked. Hopefully that state will not persist after the publication of this book; if it does, the whole exercise will be something of a failure. His occupation of the centre-stage predated the tabloid press's invasion of privacy; at the time of many of his achievements television was a lantern flickering in the homes of the relatively well-off, and the game has a self-obsession that frequently denies life beyond its own parameters. But Matt's is an incredible tale by any measure, one that might make the reader ask 'Who wrote his script?' Matt was an intensely private man whose greatest moments of personal joy and despair were compellingly public. They are episodes around which legend naturally weaves its misty charm, and ones worthy almost of the Bible: the portentous birth in humble surroundings; the early 'miracles' against all odds; the glory of success; the descent into hell; the clashes with turbulent magicians; and the ultimate anointing as a hero amongst mortals.

Matt was born into the harsh world of Orbiston, near Bellshill, Lanarkshire, where football, drinking and the music hall were the great escapes from the pit or the steelworks. His father was shot during the Great War and he avoided emigration to America with his mother and adopted father in peacetime partly by heading down a mine and convincing Nellie Busby that there was a future for Catholics in a Scotland riven by sectarianism and poverty. He discovered the love of his life, Jean Menzies, soon after. Ironically, she was from a fervent Protestant family. But football took Matt to Manchester and Jean followed: the then-mighty City club at first, then on to a nascent Liverpool. The Busbys put down strong roots in Manchester. Two children outlived their beloved parents; tragically, four more sons perished in the cradle. War took Matt away from his young family, nurtured his concept of football and made him captain of a stellar British Army team on tour. The peace dividend was big for Matt: he was demobbed as the Boss at bombed-out Old Trafford and set about creating a club in his own image: popular, respected, successful, congenial.

He outmanoeuvred UK soccer authorities in the fifties and forced them to rethink their insular mindset on European competition, paving the way for all British clubs to enter the lucrative new competitions. And, having built a team still ranked as one of the greatest ever, bursting with brilliant talents like Duncan Edwards, it was in pursuit of the ultimate European goal that perhaps his worst moment in life, his nadir, was reached: the 1958 Munich air disaster. His team decimated, his own life so nearly lost, Matt rebuilt his dream, prophesied a decade of renewal, and – ten years later – finally lifted the European Cup. Those who survived Munich – Bobby Charlton,

Harry Gregg, Bill Foulkes especially – recognised the significance to Matt. He had been wracked with guilt over the air disaster, came close to quitting football, puzzled over why he had survived, and ultimately sought to reaffirm his life's work in the continued pursuit of his last, outstanding ambition. Such energy was expended in that pursuit. When the now beknighted Matt (and papally honoured Catholic) steered his team to become the first English winners of the European Cup, there was nothing more for him to achieve. The ghosts of Munich were laid to rest.

The period immediately after Sir Matt's abdication of the United throne was not a happy one. It was hard for him to see others allowing his boys, his club, to fall apart. In some ways the argument about whether, as a result of that, he meddled with his successors' duties is a side issue. His awesome managerial presence haunted the Old Trafford corridors. That, as much as anything else, hastened the dark days of relegation and turmoil of the seventies. And Matt can hardly be blamed for setting standards others couldn't fulfil. As Harry Gregg, the Big Fella, one of United's longest-serving players suggests, things were far from smooth. Sir Matt felt stuck between a rock and a hard place, not wanting to intervene, unhappy to let go of the reins completely.

Harry Gregg

(Goalkeeper in 'Busby Babes' team and survivor/hero of Munich air disaster, eventually replaced by Alex Stepney.)

I went back to Old Trafford as a coach when Dave Sexton was the manager, and Matt put his arm round me and said, 'There's something you're going to have to do. Go and put your arm round Dave's shoulder and help him.' A month later I said to Matt, 'You're going to have to do something, Boss' – and don't get me wrong, Dave Sexton's a smashing fella. But Matt said, 'I can't do anything, I can't. If I do something they'll blame me, and if I don't do something they'll blame me.' He was in a terrible position.

But Matt wasn't a saint, and it is wrong, unfair and unrealistic to paint him as such. He could be too principled, too stubborn for his own good. His enduring friendships were often partnerships formed to achieve his goals on and off the pitch. A craving for conquest was matched by a passion for the good things in life. He loved the buoyant company of 'rogues' as much as the guidance of men of God. Here was a man who would enjoy sharing a tipple of whisky cap with a visiting manager on match day, who would revel into the small hours with a coterie of his players and old friends like Paddy McGrath in a Manchester club; who was occasionally alarmed at the bill from the bookie; and who frequently sought sanctuary from his corked-up troubles on the golf course. Above all, Sir Matt remained true to his roots and his background. And it was perhaps the commercialisation of the game he loved, the inflated transfer fees he always feared, and a recognition that his era had passed, that finally loosed his hands from the reins at Old Trafford. United Chairman Martin Edwards certainly sees it something like that.

Martin Edwards

(Son of chairman Louis Edwards, entrepreneur-butcher and Matt's long-time friend and ally in the boardroom, now himself chairman.)

The day I became chairman in 1980 he was made president, a non-executive position. He never interfered, but he was always supportive. I was coming in with my own ideas, so he would never come to me and say, 'Do this or do that.' I knew he was always there, but I think times had changed in the game. Don't forget he retired in 1969, 11 years after Munich, and I became chairman 11 years

*after that. You didn't have things like club sponsors then,
for instance. It has become much more of a business than
in Matt's day. In his day the manager and the secretary
virtually ran the club. So he wouldn't have come to advise
me on the business side anyway – it was more likely that
a manager would go to Matt. He resigned from the Board
in 1981, when we bought Bryan Robson and Remi Moses.
As a director I think he felt £2m was too high a price to
pay – I think he felt the numbers were too big for him
to cope with. Which I can understand. In his day £115,000
for Denis Law was a huge sum to pay. Within 20 years
you're paying £2m. I think the game was a different animal
to what he'd known.*

Picture a happier, more recent scene. A free-kick from a 19-
year-old prodigy, wind in his tousled hair, loops into the top
corner like a bird in flight. In the directors' box, an 84-year-
old man watches the consummation of another dream, long
deferred. When Ryan Giggs helped Manchester United beat
Blackburn 3–1 in the last game of the 1992–93 season, they
played out the final act of a season which saw the end of an
agonising 26-year wait. They were champions again, and not
a single person in the new family of Old Trafford could have
been happier than Sir Matt Busby, CBE, KCSG, Freeman of
Manchester. Like no other United manager since Sir Matt, Alex
Ferguson had recaptured the burnished spirit that had infused
four great teams over two and a half decades that had witnessed
glory, despair and decimation.

Within nine months, as United continued their imperious
progress to a second successive title, Matt Busby had passed
away. And when, on a wet spring afternoon, Ferguson's men
beat Chelsea 4–0 to secure the double that not even Sir Matt
achieved, the only sadness of the day was that he was not at
Wembley to see it happen; all agreed they'd done it 'for Sir
Matt' in his absence. Matt's life was like that. It inspired celebration, not regret. He served the club for nearly half a century.

He arrived in the shadow of war and built from the ruins of Old Trafford a magnificent institution; the echoes of his triumphs and tragedies reverberated round the world. And they were shared among everyone at the club, from the manager himself to his devoted 'laundry lassies'.

Irene Ramsden

(Long-serving laundrystaff member – joined the club around the same time as Matt. Son Ken now maintains Ramsden family presence at Old Trafford.)

> *I used to say to Sir Matt, 'We've had the worst possible time in football with Munich, but we had the most glorious possible times in Europe.' And he'd say, 'True, lassie, true.'*

There is more to it than that, of course. When Giggs receives the ball, deftly secures it, shimmies coquettishly to wrong-foot his opponent and looks up to view the options available, he's acting in the long tradition of a United style, handed down over four decades from Cockburn to Colman, Best to Coppell. That is the tangible side of the Busby legacy.

One of the marks of an eminent man is his consistency. Matt was a model of that great asset. He treated each person the same, no matter what their perceived status. He made himself familiar with the commonplace, with details other less conscientious and thoughtful individuals would not have bothered with, and it is one of his most commonly repeated traits.

Whether there was an element of contrivance in this, as some people have lately suggested, is not the point. Even if, in later life, he would ask someone nearby to remind him of the name of a player's wife before he spoke to her, it is the fact that he bothered that is most telling; he recognised the importance of belonging, of being simply acknowledged. Matt was a 'people person'. He was a bigger man for his attention to the little things, and it was symptomatic that some of those men who succeeded him only had eyes for the big prizes. Such detachment ushered in the decline of United's extended family.

One of the time-honoured routines in the biographer's repertoire is that of colleagues and friends recalling the saloon-stopping impact the subject made simply by the act of walking into a room. In Matt's case, however, there is such overwhelming testimony and palpable proof of his immense presence, even as an octogenarian, that his charisma has never been disputed. The atmosphere of aloofness, reverence and transcendent affection was something he and his close colleagues had encouraged, though Matt's physical bearing, his quiet, natural charm and unquestionable authority in reality needed little assistance.

Matt's relationship with his beloved Jean – his crutch, his 'strength' – was the most important in his life, but he readily and easily made friends. Loyal, devoted friends. Some, like, Sir Bobby Charlton, were too in awe of him to consider themselves such until they felt they had earned it. Unlike many players over the years, the young Charlton didn't dare ask his manager out for a meal. (Even this year, on the receipt of his knighthood, the revered English football hero felt moved to suggest, 'I shouldn't be put in the same class as Sir Matt Busby.')

Testament to Matt's reputation also lies in the breadth of the friendships he nurtured, in all walks of life, through his modest sociability. Actors, comedians, film stars (Marlene Dietrich insisted they be introduced while performing in Manchester), singers, sports personalities all counted him as a good friend. Scouse comedian and football fanatic Jimmy Tarbuck was introduced to Matt in the mid-sixties, became a regular golf partner and close associate of the United manager.

Jimmy Tarbuck

(Liverpudlian comedian and football fan, golf partner and friend of Sir Matt.)

He liked a joke. Could he tell a joke? Could he bloody

*hell! No! He'd get the punchline half right – and I'd say
what it should have been. And he'd say, 'That's what I
meant'. And I'd roar. Then I'd have a dram and then he
might have a nice glass of cold champagne. He was very
generous. And especially with his admiration of other football teams. He was never in blinkers about Manchester
United. He would discuss other players and say 'He's a
great player' and all that. He had affection for Liverpool.
And he was much loved on Merseyside. Never mind the
rivalry. He was much loved because he played there.*

Millions of less celebrated people around the world admired
Sir Matt. Thousands felt compelled to contact him throughout
his life. When he retired from management, his stated intention
was to take things a little easier, but the steady flow of letters
from fans worldwide into his small office put paid to that. They
had grieved with him over Munich, shared the joy of his club's
Phoenix-like ascent from the ashes, the glory of European success, and now they mourn his loss early this year.

Ironically, it was perhaps Munich that clinched the worldwide fame he so sought for his United team. As it snuffed out
lives, so it opened hearts and doors to the Manchester club.

Even his great rivals were friends. The pages of this book are
peppered with tributes from the great footballing adversaries of
his day like Bill Shankly, Malcolm Allison, Jock Stein and Don
Revie. All numbered themselves among the ranks of Busby
devotees. (Which makes the revolting actions of some Leeds
fans, chanting Revie's name during a minute's silence in honour
of Sir Matt, all the more tasteless.) Only those rare bodies who
sampled the looser end of Matt's behaviour – most notably
Frank O'Farrell – retained a residual bitterness towards him.
'I've never heard anybody say a bad thing about him,' suggests
that flawed wizard of the ball, George Best, 'because there's no
bad words to say.' Steve Coppell, former United star, now chair
of the Premiership managers' organisation, tells a story that

shows the Sir Matt that most recognise: the humilty and uncommon decency of the man.

Steve Coppell

(Former United player, former Crystal Palace manager, now head of the Premiership managers' association.)

> *The first time I met Sir Matt I was very much in awe of the man. I was halfway through my second year at university when I was signed. Man United went on a world tour but I couldn't go because it clashed with my exams, so I flew out to Hong Kong later on. One good thing was that I knew I was supposed to fly out with Sir Matt. I got on the aircraft and was expecting to meet him so I trotted up to 'first class' to find him. But I couldn't see him, so I asked them to check the 'first class' list. He wasn't on it. I was disappointed but I went back to my seat and sat down. A little bit later on I was going down to the back of the plane. It was chaos. There were lots of families going back to Bangkok and there were loads of kids running around causing mayhem. And there he was – in the very last row of the plane in 'economy', down as plain Matt Busby, as calm as you like. I spent the rest of the flight talking to him and he was just so gentle and courteous. He knew who I was and was so gentle and polite to all the people around him. It was great for me because I had fourteen hours left of the flight to ask all the questions I wanted about Manchester United, and he answered them all. He was a lovely, contented man.*

Sit in Sandy Busby's comfortably affluent back room, its patio doors opening on to a round lawn and a spruce garden bowed with flowers, and you sense the aura of his father. Hear the deep, reassuring thoughtful Scots brogue still. Feel his presence in a favourite armchair in the corner, the silent void enhanced by the ticking of a clock. For Sandy, that silence is at times still too deafening. He breaks down often at the thought of the man he admired, loved and worshipped. 'You've no idea how much I miss him still,' he says. But I think we have. And I hope this book makes it clear just why.

As to the club he built, it's perhaps in the words of Martin Edwards, current United Chairman and son of Matt's great boardroom ally, Louis, that you'll find the keenest expression of what their longest-serving manager, director and president meant to Manchester United and many football fans the world over, and the enormous debt of gratitude that can never be settled.

Martin Edwards

It's a bit like losing your grandfather. He'll always be there. Or it's like Laurence Olivier in the theatre. If you were to ask other actors what they thought of Laurence Olivier they would all say that he was the one they all looked up to, the inspiration. I followed Matt from being a young boy. I saw him at his peak as a manager, the tremendous recovery from Munich to build the side of the sixties. Before Munich, very rarely did he buy. After Munich he had to change his philosophy, and he had to go out and buy. Beyond the tremendous respect I had for him as a football manager, I admired him as a man. He received every single honour that was going, really – he was a knight, a CBE, he got a Papal honour, the freedom of Manchester, but it never changed him. He was never one to insist that people call him Sir Matt, he was a very genial man, but most of all he was a man of humility, despite having won everything, despite the accolades wherever he went, despite all the bowing and scraping to him. It didn't matter to him, it didn't affect his personality. He was never big-headed, he never insisted on being at the top of the table, he just took what came to him. So apart from his tremendous ability, I admired the fact that he never changed – he was still aware of his roots, he was still Matt Busby the ex-miner, the ex-footballer, even though he'd achieved all these great things. We're all benefiting now from the foundations that Matt Busby laid. The only comparison I can think of is Bill Shankly at Liverpool. Bob Paisley won more trophies and had more success, but it would never have happened if Shankly hadn't picked them up from the Second Division and created a side that others benefited from later. If you think of the worldwide reputation Manchester United has, and the style we're known for, that is all really down to one man. If you think of the 24 years he was manager, we were champions five times and seven times runners-up; so for twelve of those seasons we were in the top two. It does tell you something, doesn't it?

The Early Years

Sandy Busby

He rarely spoke about his childhood, and I'm sorry he didn't. I'd love to have known, because people ask me where this greatness, whatever it was, came from, and I always think it must have come from his childhood.

That Matt Busby, a Scotsman, should spend two-thirds of his life in the north-west of England, as player, manager, director and president, was perhaps in the genes, perhaps a quirk of history. For the Busbys were from the home of the Strathclyde Britons, who had held sway from the south bank of the Clyde down to Lancashire from AD 400 to 900 when they were overrun by the Irish Gaels, the Angles and the Picts. The great teams Matt created would be a similarly heady mixture of races trawled from the four corners of the British Isles. Matt Busby was born on 26 May 1909, in one of 32 hundred-year-old cottages in the mining village of Orbiston, near the town of Bellshill, a satellite town north-east of Glasgow. In the speech he delivered when he was given the freedom of Manchester, Matt recalled: 'I was born in a pitman's cottage, and the doctor who delivered me said, "A footballer has come to this house this day." He may have said the same about most of the boys he brought into this world, but in my case it was very nearly proved wrong.' Indeed, young Matt might have emigrated to North America; we have the strength of his will to thank for the fact that instead he moved to England and brought glory to a smitten city.

His mother, Nellie, was the daughter of an Irishman, Jimmy Greer, who worked down the pit in Orbiston with Matt's father, Alexander. Matt was followed by three girls, Delia, Kathy and Margaret, in the years leading up to the Great War. Privacy was a luxury; baths were taken in a tub in the living room.

Bellshill is a town still riven with the enmity that character-ises sectarianism in west central Scotland. Matt's parents were a hard-grafting couple who refused to share the religious bigot-ries of so many of their neighbours – Catholic and Protestant in uneasy adjacency. Religion for the Busbys was a private matter. Socially, it was important to coexist, for life in this troubled coal and steel area was hard enough. With this in mind, perhaps, in 1914 Matt was sent to school at St Bride's in Bothwell (since demolished – the present school was built in 1973). It's a short trip from Orbiston but a world apart in atmosphere. Bothwell today is better known as the charming, adopted home of successful soccer stars, ex-pat English among them, and even in Matt's day it had a quieter façade than Orbiston and Bellshill. Not that the young 'Mattha' had many carefree years in which to enjoy it.

His family sought refuge from the toughness of life in an unforgiving area, but the catalyst for change was the war, which snatched the lives of Alex Busby, claimed by a sniper's bullet at Arras in France in 1916, and three of Matt's uncles. Of the Busby menfolk, only Jimmy Greer and Matt were left when the war ended. Already an intelligent and well-behaved boy, Matt was compelled by circumstances to grow old before his time. Maturity was a hat he was forced to wear at a young age, and like the trilby for which he was renowned in the fifties, it looked good on him.

Matt had always seemed wise beyond his years and eager to acquire knowledge; the death of his father, and his assump-tion of the role of man of the house now induced in the amiable youth a certain paternalism. It was a trait for which many a young man whose life was touched by Matt would come to be grateful.

When Matt was twelve, his school principal recommended that he should go to Motherwell Higher Grade (now a Ladies' College), five miles away. Despite the sacrifices necessary, with books and uniforms to buy, Nellie was determined to see her family better itself and saw to it that for the next three years he walked there and back every day. His headmaster noticed his unusual composure and serenity: already there was something different about him. It was regularly suggested that Matt would have made a first-class schoolteacher, and a measured, almost professorial tone was always discernible in Matt's stately voice.

Through these troubled years of wonder, Matt was already hooked on football. In later years, he would say, 'There were only two ways for boys to go in those days: down, working in the pits, or up, if you happened to be good at football.'

Ian St John

(Liverpool forward and Scots international under Matt in 1958, playing alongside Denis Law. Close friend of Paddy Crerand, George Best and Mike Summerbee, now an ITV sports presenter.)

I'm from the same background as Matt. My wife's from Bellshill and my mother-in-law worked at the same pit-head as Matt's wife, so we have a lot in common. When I first met Matt he would say,'How's your mother-in-law?' There was a link there, a bond that we were from the same background. People who have come away – like I've come away and Matt came away – they've done well. Football was the only thing we did down there. I remember when I was a kid we would play on a Sunday all day, and as young fellows we were quite privileged because we could have a game with the big boys. A lot of them were pros, junior players and ex-pros or whatever. That was how we spent Sunday. It was the game. There were no diversions, no golf, nothing. And also from there the one thing you learned very early is you can't be a poser. You've got to be a straight guy to get respect from people. That's the way the people are and they don't stand for any nonsense. People were poor in these mining villages – my mother couldn't afford to buy me football boots – but what they had was a lot of respect for themselves and their families and high moral standards.

The war had left millions of families ravaged, and life was difficult. Nellie went to work at the colliery (and latterly the steel works when that opportunity closed) while her father Jimmy looked after the girls. Young Matt would come home from school and, before he went out to play football in the streets of Orbiston, he would help Jimmy with the chores, perhaps in his own mind filling the void left by his father's death.

Matt and Jimmy developed a formative closeness. 'His grandfather was a very intelligent fellow, a great socialiser, a big theatre-goer, and he and my dad had this great relationship.' says Sandy, Matt's son. 'My dad would be playing football in the street, and along would come his grandfather and shout, "Bryn Boru, Bryn Boru, come on, we're going to the Glasgow Theatre to see the greatest of them all!," meaning Harry Lauder. My dad used to love it, and I think he picked things up from him.' The nickname had a certain resonance: Bryn Boru means 'leader of men'.

Jimmy was a marvellous man and inspiring company, but he liked a drink too much – and that was something of which Matt's mother never approved. Soon after Matt joined Manchester United, Nellie was staying with her son in Manchester when he brought a few footballing cronies back. They were in good spirits and poured themselves a couple of Scotches. Nellie blanched when she saw Matt. 'What's that in your hand?' she inquired sternly. 'Whisky, maw,' replied Matt. His mother retorted that he shouldn't be drinking 'that stuff'. 'Maw,' protested Matt, 'I'm 36 years old.' It was the first time she'd ever seen him taking alcohol.

Despite a weakness for the demon drink, Jimmy often displayed the leadership qualities later prevalent in his young grandson. Once, during a miners' strike, the great music-hall star Harry Lauder was reported in the local press as saying the pitmen should return to work – a tactless sentiment in this fervently socialist area. When he was next scheduled to play at the nearby concert hall, Jimmy stood in the stalls amongst a group of resentful miners, all with rotten fruit and vegetables at the ready. As the theatre erupted and missiles flew the moment Lauder appeared, Jimmy stood up and hollered: 'You don't recognise greatness when you see it. Let him perform!' As the Busby family history has it, Jimmy won the crowd over with a rousing rendition of 'I Belong to Glasgow', which was Lauder's favourite song. Understandably it was always one of Matt's favourites whenever he stood by the piano.

Cliff Butler

(United's club historian.)

I've been working on the match programme for nineteen years, and in the mid-eighties I was Matt's ghost-writer for a while, for programmes and books, and on a part-work about his life. He talked quite a bit about his childhood, and I think losing his father in a way became a good grounding for him; he became a leader of men early on, looking after his mother and taking on responsibility for the family. But I think he did enjoy his childhood, and he never lost his principles, never forgot his roots. He enjoyed the responsibility – he didn't look upon it as a burden.

He was wonderful to deal with. He made everybody feel important. Everybody felt the same, whether you were the chairman or the lads who swept the terraces. He always

*put you at your ease, always made you feel comfortable.
It was like talking to your dad. But I was still always in
awe of the man. He was a hero when I was a kid, and to
actually get to know him . . . it was like a* Jim'll Fix It, *I
suppose: to meet and speak with your hero, and actually
work with him.*

*He was the most humble of people. If anybody could
be excused for thinking they were special, he was the
person, but that was never a feeling you got from him.
Even people he never met he had an effect on – they felt
they knew him. I'm just so sorry I only got to know him
in his later years. I always joke that there have been only
four men in my life that I've loved: my late father and my
brother, and Denis Law and Sir Matt.*

Matt was frequently asked where his humanity and his fortitude
came from, and a reference to his early life in Orbiston was
the usual answer. 'Perhaps it came from my upbringing in a
mining village,' he would say. 'The family, the people there,
they would never lie down.' That upbringing established simple
principles that would be formative and would shine throughout
Matt's life. He learned about the respect that should be
accorded to all people, not just the privileged; about the prevailing goodness of the human spirit; and about the spiritual comfort of his faith.

Yet he also saw the other side of religion and it had a telling
impact on his character. Sectarian gang fights around Bellshill
were commonplace, especially when the hot-headed lads of
both sides were bevvied up of an evening. Everyone knew who
was Orange, or Protestant, and who was Green, or Catholic.
An innocent enough question to strangers – 'What school did
you go to?' – was enough to ascertain status if there was any
doubt. Matt grew to despise any kind of bigotry and proved it
by his actions. He was a great believer that football could bring
nations and people closer together, and the seeds of that belief
were sown on the 'playing fields' or streets of Orbiston.

Matt was a devout Catholic throughout his life, and Manchester United under his tutelage was renowned as a 'Fenian' team, although there was no religious bar as far as Matt was concerned: 'The only person who has to hold a cross in my team is the keeper,' he would say.

If Matt's later life was marked out by an ability to surround himself with people of loyalty, amiability and ability, it showed itself even at this young age and under those conditions. He gravitated towards another local youngster, Frank Rogers, a strapping lad and a notorious roughneck. Frank was a useful sort of pal to have around, whose immense power was startlingly demonstrated on one occasion when he punched the nose of a horse outside his house and knocked the poor beast to its knees.

Quite rightly, much is made of Matt's gentle nature, his 'niceness', which is an impressively consistent aspect of his character, but as anyone who worked with him or under him will tell you, he could draw on a hard, ruthless streak when necessary. As a youth he was never a thug or a troublemaker, and he'd try to convince his burly friend there was another way, a better way, beyond the violence and bullying. Even so, Matt must have known how to look after himself, for you don't survive regular confrontations with violent gangs by reciting Wordsworth. In fact, Frank and Mattha's relationship was based on the other abiding passion in Orbiston: soccer – the way up, and the way out.

His family had other ideas though. In 1919 Nellie had married Harry Matthie, whom she had met at work. Matt never really saw eye to eye with Harry, the half-sister and half-brother who followed, but he was affectionate and doting to Ellen and Jimmy the half-sister and half-brother who followed. Nellie and Harry wanted a better future than the one presented to them in a hard mining village in the mid-twenties, and considered emigrating to Canada, or Pittsburgh in America, where some of the Busby women had gone after the Great War had killed their husbands. Reports back were impressive. Matt was quietly appalled, but visas were applied for. A stay of execution was forced by the emigration office, however, for there was a six-month backlog. It was all the time young Mattha needed. First, though, there was the pit to contend with. Continuing at school was out of the question: Nellie wanted him to emigrate with her and the family, and they could not wait three years for him to finish at the grammar school in Motherwell. From Matt's point of view, if money was a problem he would go down the pit and emigrating would be unnecessary. The last thing Nellie wanted for him was mining, but he had his way. Even after so few years, he was already master of his own life, as he demonstrated with little fuss or conflict. On his sixteenth birthday Matt forsook education and went down the pit.

'From what I can gather he was quite a brainy lad,' Sandy says. When his headmaster heard he had to go down the pits because he had to bring some money into the house, he came to grandmother's and pleaded with her to let him stay on, as he had the brains to make a schoolteacher.'

Hugh McIlvanney

(One of the most respected and eloquent of British sports writers, the *Observer* scribe was one of Matt's great friends and confidantes in the media – the only reporter allowed into United's dressing-room immediately after the European Cup Final.)

It was utterly extraordinary that three great managers, Matt Busby, Jock Stein and Bill Shankly, came from the same area of Scotland, and it was, I think, very significant. These people absorbed the best of the true ethos of that working-class environment. There was a richness of spirit bred into people from mining areas. I'm likely to see it that way because my father worked in the pits for a while, but there is no question that there was a camaraderie. Stein said that he would never work with better men than he did when he was a miner, that the guys who got carried away with football were never going to impress him much, and although Shankly was completely potty about the game and was the great warrior/poet of football, he nevertheless retained that sense of what real men should do, the sense of dignity, the sense of pride. All of that was present in Matt.

What Matt really wanted to do, what was really keeping him there, was his football. He had learned the game playing in the streets with the men of the village for the so-called Orbiston Cannibals, feared as much for their footballing prowess as the ferocity of the tackles which lent them their name. In such a mining community football was all a young man could do for leisure – and Matt and Frank went on to play for the best youth side in the area, Alpine Villa. Success came early to them when Villa lifted the Under-18 Scottish Cup, and it was at post-match celebrations at Bellshill Miners' Club that he met Jean Menzies.

There can be little doubt that, like the besotted protagonists in *West Side Story* or *Romeo and Juliet*, Jean and Matt had an empathy beyond teenage romance. Jean was a pretty lass, as well-mannered and courteous as the handsome Matt. Through their traumatic experiences they shared a common sense of loss, separation and feeling for the sanctity of family life – a private and intense harmony that would remain undimmed over 60 years of joy and pain. 'There was no greater love,' says their son, Sandy. And no one ever knew Matt like Jean knew Matt.

As far as Matt was concerned, Jean's Protestant background was no problem, but he wasn't sure how his mother might react. Throughout his time as a manager, Matt's associates would marvel at how calm he always appeared, no matter how big the game. This was not the case in 1927. He was physically trembling the evening Jean first came round for tea, but not for the last time, Jean wasn't about to let Matt down. The tea was a grand success and Jean pronounced a 'right decent' lassie.

During this time, Bellshill produced three great sons of Scottish football – Alex James, Hughie Gallacher and Jimmy McMullan, who established themselves in the Scots teams of the twenties. It was Alex James who was Matt's first hero, Alex James of the flapping shorts and slicked-back hair with the centre parting, hero-worshipped in Scotland and London, where he became the mainstay of Herbert Chapman's great Arsenal team that won the League Championship four times in six seasons. Before that, though, Matt had had the opportunity of observing him at close quarters, for young Matt looked after the kit when James had played for Old Orbiston Celtic as a teenager, and one day he had the pleasure of lending James his boots. He marvelled at James's trickery and inventiveness, his charisma and flair and touch of arrogance. There was a muscular kind of beauty in such skill, a beauty that transcended the harsh reality of life in Orbiston. Matt's footballing life was inspired by players of James's ilk: Puskas, di Stefano, Charlton, Best, Law . . . and his United teams exuded precisely the qualities for which James is remembered to this day.

Whether by accident or design, Matt's decision to work down the pits gave him power. He joined the General Strike in 1926 – another lesson in unity and dedication – and remained a Socialist all his life. Now that he was earning, his voice had to be heard when the subject of emigration came up again. However, as he recalled in his 1967 Freeman's speech: 'My application for a visa was delayed at that time, and that delay changed the whole course of my life. Instead of emigrating to Canada, I emigrated to Manchester.'

Several years later, Matt paid for Nellie to visit her relatives in Pittsburgh. When she returned, he was anxious for the low-down on the land that might have been home. 'It's a mad, crazy place,' she declared. 'I'm glad we never went there.' That was music to Matt's ears, for privately, he always felt guilty that he might have deprived his mother of a dream fulfilled.

After the Scottish Under-18 Cup win, with his friend from St Bride's, Frank Rogers, he was invited to play for the non-league side, Denny Hibs, treading the same path as James and McMullan. The two pals shone there, and scouts were alerted. 'Rangers and Celtic were both interested,' says Sandy, 'and he went to Rangers for a trial. Then they found out he was a Catholic, and Celtic found out he'd had a trial with Rangers. But it was a blessing in disguise because he ended up in Manchester.' After no more than a few weeks Matt and Frank were off to join McMullan at Maine Road. In the Bank Restaurant in Glasgow, owned by Willy Maley, a former Celtic manager, Matt Busby signed for Manchester City. Jean pledged she'd wait for him in Scotland. And so began two love affairs that would last the rest of his life.

The Professional

I F THERE IS 'ART' in football, it's the sort that is best appreciated from a discreet distance; too close up, the blemishes
and blunders of the beautiful game and its heroes are all
too apparent. When the dapper Matt Busby arrived in Manchester in February 1928 as a professional footballer, his concept of the game was wrapped in the elegance, the beauty, the
escapism of his youthful experience. But at City he was to
experience the professional game in sharp relief, close up, warts
and all.

The decision to accept the offer had been a tricky one
anyway. It took some guts for an eighteen-year-old to leave his
family for an uncertain future in a profession – as he discovered
– of dubious gentlemen and impecunious players. When he
faced his mother with his decision, he remembered there was
'all hell to pay'. But Nellie succumbed and over the years grew
proud to read about and share her son's success as player and
manager.

Jean Menzies, three years later to be Matt's bride, initially
didn't believe you could actually earn money from playing
soccer. She had a point. The maximum wage, pegging players'
wages to a level acceptable to the clubs' boards, would last
another 33 years. A weekly wage of £5 a week during the
season and £4 in the summer wasn't going to buy the private
jets some of today's players have, and injury was a constant
threat.

At the end of the following month, Scotland's Wembley

Wizards trounced England 5–1 on their own turf. James played brilliantly and scored one of the goals. Then still with nearby Preston, he looked in to wish Matt well after his debut for City, in a Central League game at Deepdale. Unfortunately his magic didn't rub off, and Matt struggled to make a name for himself at inside-forward. From being a local hero in Orbiston, he was now on the lowest rung of City's 40 or 50 professionals striving to get themselves noticed, and the pros made sure he knew it.

At first the pace of the game was beyond him. Raw power was never Matt's game; he needed more time to think than he was being allowed. His confidence drooped and self-doubt haunted him. City were Second Division champions in his first season at Maine Road, but Matt couldn't share the joy. He slipped back to Bellshill for the summer to regain his confidence.

'At home I was on top of the world,' Matt recalled some time later, 'but in Manchester my confidence deserted me the moment I returned to duty in July. I actually dreaded the approach of each football season.' How dreadful must things have become for this soccer-mad lad to consider going down the pit again?

The next season saw him break into the first team, although he was still far from first choice. Peter Hodge, City's manager, tried him out in other forward positions, but consistency eluded Matt and he agonised that season over whether to go home to Scotland and Jean. 'I feel I am out of my sphere in football,' he wrote to her. How those words would ring hollow throughout the decades that followed.

Matt even had his bags packed on one occasion, before his Scots colleague and room-mate Phil McCloy talked him out of it in a conversation that burned the midnight oil – one of Matt's rare heart-to-hearts with a fellow player.

Things had to get worse before they got better: Matt contracted pneumonia. Jimmy McMullan, by then Scotland's captain, asked Matt to live with him and his wife and became a big influence on Matt's thinking. However, when the next season,

1930–31, came around, things had not improved and Matt half expected to be released by City. Yet his career was about to be revitalised, salvaged even, by a series of happy accidents.

Autumn's gloom prevented Matt from seeing the auspicious portents gathering. He was not even making the reserve team, and Manchester United's chief scout, Louis Rocca – who later intervened in a crucial stage of his life – came in for him. I'mpoverished United, however, could not afford the nominal sum of £150. ('We can't even afford 150 shillings,' said Rocca).

Then came the turning-point. As a manager, Matt tapped new sources of talent and ability in many a player by simple positional switches, a lesson he learned by accident in Manchester City's third team. 'Dr Johnson said one time that there was much to be made of a Scotsman if he was caught young,' he once said. 'I had decided that if much was to be made of me, then it would appear I would have to try some career other than football. Then suddenly in an emergency I was called upon to play right half-back in a Northern Midweek League game, and in that position and from that moment, success came to me.'

He had found his rightful place by dint of a triallist not turning up. He began to enjoy life again; for the first time since coming to England he actually enjoyed a game of football and the relief was palpable. Confidence surged through him. The next week he played for the reserves at right-half, and the week after that for the first team at Huddersfield, when, again fortunately for Matt, Barrass was injured.

The position was Busby's thereafter. As a wing-half he could orchestrate the play with his smooth possession, gliding runs, subtlety of control and pinpoint passing. He was a master of the disguised pass, and eschewed the obvious manoeuvre. City still failed to catch fire in the First Division – Herbert Chapman's Arsenal, Alex James at the helm, were the dominant force – but two FA Cup finals followed. In 1933 City met Everton and the formidable Dixie Dean. They lost 3–0, hopelessly outplayed, outfought and out-thought by a display from

Everton 'that has never been excelled in the final ties played at the Stadium', as the *Manchester Guardian* put it. Even the rated half-back line could not rise above the shambles, 'too often . . . immobilised between attack and defence'.

Lessons had been learned, though, and Matt's ascendancy continued.

Jimmy Heale

(Player for Manchester City in the 1930's.)

It's well known that Matt played at right-half for City, but really his strongest foot was his left. His top move was to get past a few players moving towards the centre of the field, then switch it by hitting a ball over to the corner flag where Ernie Toseland would already be into his stride. That created lots of goal chances. Matt was, I suppose, what you call a 'schemer' these days. He was such a good player and yet he only earned himself one cap before war-time. We often used to joke about how good that other fellow must have been to keep him out of the Scottish team. Matt was a great example to the younger lads. But like one or two other of the lads, he'd sneak off to the toilets for a Woodbine on occasion. Having said that I can rarely recall him swearing and he was a clean-living chap on and off the field. He was a great example to the younger players.

The 1933–34 season was probably Matt's best as a player. In October he won what should have been only his first cap for Scotland, in the 3–2 defeat by Wales. Remarkably, he was never selected again in peacetime. According to Paddy Crerand, the Glaswegian of Irish descent, there can have been only one reason for this: 'He only got one cap because there was a great deal of religious bigotry in Scotland, and still is to this day. I'm a Catholic, I played for Celtic, and it was much more difficult to get a cap for Scotland than it was if you played for Rangers, and you can ask anybody that, it's not a bigoted point of view.'

Crerand was capped only sixteen times himself. 'We were coming back once from playing Ireland in a World Cup match, and I got the man of the match award, and guys were around the plane shouting, "You Fenian bastard". It makes you understand what it's like to be black or Jewish.' What was probably as important a factor in limiting the international careers of these two was their 'Anglo' status. To varying degrees over the years, players who migrated to enemy territory have been overlooked in favour of those who stayed north of the border.

Hugh McIlvanney

It has been suggested that Matt was a natural subversive because he was a Catholic, one of an oppressed minority. But if that's the case, why were the other two great representatives of that tradition, Jock Stein and Bill Shankly, Protestants? What is more significant about Matt is that he was a working-class man from the west of Scotland, of a mining family. I'm not saying his Catholicism was anything other than relevant, because he was very devout, but to read into it as much as some people have, to trace his strengths to some kind of reaction to oppression, is, I think, simplistic in a way that is of help to nobody. We all know the horrors of sectarianism, and specifically the damage it has done in the west of Scotland, but to portray Matt as a great subversive who drew all his strength from that source is reasoning that suits the reasoner rather than the facts.

By this time Matt had established himself as a formidable force in the English game, outstanding enough to warrant an appreciation in the *Manchester Guardian* on the eve of the biggest day in the English football calendar: 'At his best he has no superior as an attacking half-back. To that extent, no doubt, his forward experience, chequered though it was, had been useful. At one time, having scored a goal worthy almost of the Baron von Munchausen, Busby became obsessed with attack, but today it is the rarity of his thrusts that give them greater menace.

'It is Busby's bewildering footcraft that most delights the crowds. His crouching style may not be pretty . . . but the control is perfect, the effect akin to conjuring. His dribble is a thing of swerves, feints and deceptions; few opponents are not hoodwinked by his phantom pass. Even the real one is nearly always masked: it skids off to the right when one could swear it was destined for the centre, and often when the right wing is the obvious way to attack, off goes the ball like a rocket to the left. Busby scorns the obvious.'

Matt wasn't perfect, though, as his right-back Sid Cann has attested. 'He wasn't too sound a defensive player, and his recovery when beaten was a bit slow, as I knew from playing behind him. But he was a fine player to watch in possession, and he would have revelled in a modern midfield role with freedom to move about and plenty of cover behind him.' Like the best in his craft, Matt balanced his lack of pace with sound positional play. Another weakness in some people's eyes, perhaps, was 'the spirit of adventure that will not be repressed even in front of his own goal. Sometimes he does things that make the directors feel old before their time. But who would have him different? He laughs equally at his blunders and his triumphs, which, of course, is the privilege as well as the proof of a great player. He would be a certain choice for that Select XI of Footballers Who Obviously Love Football – and that is the highest praise of all.'

Matt was beginning to shine in other areas, too, and was enjoying the respect accorded him. An early identifier of the value of good PR, as well as a man who had time for everyone, Matt was one of the few City players who always made allowances for autograph hunters. He would stop, smile with some humility, and sign.

Manchester was beginning to cast its spell on him. It was

brash, cosmopolitan, full of itself and full of thrills. Matt had married Jean in 1931, and they were happy together in the old cotton town, the hub of the Industrial Revolution. It was a city you could dip in and out of; throw yourself into its myriad pleasures or stand on the sidelines watching the others enjoying the rides. Matt and Jean were public and private as the mood suited. They shared things that were theirs alone to know, but they liked nothing better than to take in a show, share a raucous laugh in good company, have a singsong and burn the midnight oil. They were good company and, as throughout his life, Matt took pleasure in sharing the fun, if not necessarily instituting it.

Matt was also at the centre of bringing the good times back to Manchester: City beat Portsmouth 2–1 in the 1934 FA Cup final. It was the 'most exciting, if not the greatest final played at Wembley Stadium', the *Manchester Guardian* said. 'Manchester City, finding orthodoxy unavailing, became almost outrageously original in their attacking methods.' Matt stood out, 'the best of the half-backs: there were flaws in his defence, but his attacking thrusts were among the finest in the game.' The *Telegraph* considered Matt Busby 'the finest right-half ever seen at Wembley . . . [he] inspired the whole side'. Injuries meant that the unknown nineteen-year-old, Frank Swift, played in goal for City, having the year before occupied a half-crown space on the Wembley terraces. At the end, the young lad 'fell flat on his face in a dead faint', and had to be helped up to collect his medal. The same afternoon, Manchester United, still the poor relations, were drawing 1–1 with Swansea to avoid relegation from the Second Division.

Joe Mercer (dec.)

(One of the great post-war English managers (Manchester City 1965–71, Coventry 1972–75, England), and played under Sir Matt's managership as Everton player for the British Army touring team in the Second World War.)

> *What made Matt noticeable was the silkiness in possession,*
> *the way he drifted inside from the wing and then*
> *switched the ball back over the head of the full-back for*
> *his winger. He was a player's player, like Ball or Bell 30*
> *years later. He had this calm influence on events around*
> *him. I think Matt and Archie Macauley were two of the*
> *most delicate strikers of the ball there have been.*

The next season City finished fourth in the First Division. It was the highest position they reached in Matt's time there, and his fortunes deteriorated from then on. A torn hamstring refused to heal, and the ministrations of a Southport quack – whose methodology involved blocks of ice, a lot of wishful thinking and little else – were useless. Like many an injured player in those days, he was left by the club to make his own arrangements, and, eventually, he did. In March 1936, he was transferred to Liverpool for £8,000. 'There will be many a City spectator shaking his head over the transfer of Busby to Liverpool,' the *Manchester Evening News* reported. 'He had lost his form recently, but even then he looked better than the average half-back. Mr R. Smith, the City chairman, made it plain to me that City parted with Busby with regret, but that the club had been forced to a large extent by Busby's desire to leave. His wife has been seriously ill; he desires a change largely for her sake.' The following season Manchester City won the League. In 1938 they were relegated.

After the tribulations of City, Liverpool FC was a revelation to Matt. The tall, dapper young man who caught the tram each morning from east of the Mersey Tunnel had found a club which was not bedevilled by the internal snobbery and the acrid team spirit of the day. It was a club run in a way that would make a deep impression on Matt. While others encouraged a hierarchical structure where callow youths were the whipping-boys of old hands, Liverpool's atmosphere was comradely, almost like a family. Matt, deprived of a father at the age of six, treated like dirt as a junior by the pros at City, understood the need for a supportive atmosphere and, as an older player now, enjoyed playing the paternal role. He appreciated the generous attitude that pervaded Liverpool. Staff were well treated. Players at Anfield weren't treated like so many racehorses – packed off to the knacker's yard when serious injuries arose and lingered, as they did in those days.

At City, Matt had been left to fend for himself when his livelihood was threatened; at Liverpool he was gratified to see the more sensitive handling of his injured team-mate Jimmy McDougall, who was retained on full pay when not of any perceived use to the club. Matt was always someone who took lessons to heart – particularly those of a humanitarian nature – and he appreciated the Liverpool club's actions.

Yet this was also a time of tragedy on a personal level for Matt and Jean. They were to be blessed with two fine children in Sandy and Sheena, but Jean gave birth four times before those two. All four – boys every one – died within a few days of delivery. Understandably, it's not something the couple cared to discuss. Just once Jean, tears welling in her eyes, recalled the cot deaths to writer Donald Gomery in 1959. 'We could have had a forward line,' she joked, feebly.

On one occasion, as a child, Sandy was rummaging through some things in the house and happened upon a tiny funeral service memento. Jean was horrified, angry. There were some things only she and Matt could share, and some things it was best not to remember.

On the football front, things were looking up. The new manager at Anfield, George Kay, was a man Matt came to admire – one of the finest men he had met in the game. They were kindred spirits, sharing common views and goals. Although Liverpool won no trophies during Matt's three years there, he rediscovered the simple joy of playing the game, and the experience clearly honed his instincts about how a club should be run.

Installed as Liverpool captain, Matt blossomed into the figure that was to become so familiar: avuncular, dignified, graceful, dapper, looking more like a bank manager in his trilby and fawn Crombie overcoat, smoking a pipe.

In his first season, he and Kay marshalled resources and avoided the relegation that had seemed inevitable before they had arrived. As Liverpool rose up the division, the pair achieved their objectives by the application of principles that Matt would carry with him all his life: on the field, commitment to the ideal of football as a thing of beauty; off it, a determination to treat all who came into his orbit with simple human decency.

Liverpool finished the season, as the storm clouds of war gathered, on a roll; had Hitler not intervened, Matt believed, honours would have come to Anfield. Liverpool went on to win the title in the first season after the war. In August 1939, however, greater considerations than football were at stake – or so it seemed. Munich, a city later to be inscribed on Matt's heart for different, tragic reasons, was the talk of the country.

In their wisdom, at the outbreak of hostilities the Football Association suspended all players' professional contracts, virtually making every player redundant. Other measures from the War Office meant that crowd assemblies were reduced to 8,000 in evacuation areas, 15,000 in safe areas. Liverpool's professionals volunteered *en bloc* for the Territorial Army, and within weeks they were professional soldiers.

There's a story that when Matt enlisted, the official asked his occupation. 'Footballer,' replied Matt. For whatever reason, but most likely his deep, Orbiston brogue, Matt was registered as a 'food boiler'. Like so many aspects of the great man's life however, this has probably been mythologised – it's also been told of Hughie Gallacher and Bill Shankly.

Soon afterwards, the War Office decided that, wherever possible, footballers – food boilers even – should continue to play the game, representing whichever club was nearest to where they were stationed. Many were made physical education instructors to promote fitness and morale.

Matt's name was put forward as officer material by the FA secretary, Stanley Rous, who had refereed the 1934 Cup final.

Matt was sent to Aldershot, where he became a Non-Commissioned Officer. Company Sergeant-Major Instructor Busby would go on to play for Reading, Chelsea, Aldershot and Hibernian throughout the war. He even 'managed' Hibs for a while when stationed in Scotland. After the war the Edinburgh club was the most successful in Scotland, largely on the back of players recommended by Matt while he was there. Matt also won seven more Scotland caps, most of them as skipper.

In February 1940, those selected for the British Army side were asked to assemble in London from where they would travel to play a French Army side. The team included a tantalising glimpse of how a UK side would have shaped up. It included Matt, Tommy Lawton, Denis Compton, Joe Mercer, Maurice Edelston and Stan Cullis. A wartime friend, Cullis was to become Matt's first real managerial rival in the post-war years. At Wolves he proved himself a progressive thinker along the same lines as Matt, pursuing the policies of nurturing youth and entering European competition.

Exciting though the prospect was, Matt, with a poor stomach for marine travel, had his misgivings. He wasn't alone.

Tommy Lawton

(Great English international centre-forward, who played for Everton and Chelsea, and served under Matt's management of the British Army touring team in 1945.)

We were to sail from Dover and, on the same train going down from Victoria, Stan Cullis came up to where Matt Busby and I were sitting and said that as all three of us were notoriously bad sailors he had obtained a sea-sickness remedy which 'positively could not fail'. Cost of the three pills was a guinea [£1.05], but both Matt and I agreed that if they did all that was claimed for them we wouldn't mind paying a guinea each! We three waited until we had got aboard before swallowing the pills and then settled down

*below to a game of cards. With the passing of time our
apprehension decreased and our spirits correspondingly
rose. We acclaimed Stan a life-saver, we joked and went
into fits of laughter at the thought of some of the other
weak-stomached members of the party suffering at the
hands of King Neptune. Then after about an hour, Stan
said, 'We ought to be there by now. Let's go and look at
France.' In the distance we could see shaded lights of a
blacked-out harbour. 'Calais,' I exclaimed gaily. 'No,' said
a voice from the darkness. 'Dover. We are still in harbour.'
I'll draw a veil over the rest. We hadn't moved from our
berth. When we did, Matt, Stan and I dead-heated for the
ship's side. (Football is My Business)*

The match in Paris had a wider significance of course – it was
the last big game before Dunkirk. Other benchmarks in the
history of the conflict were echoed by Matt's football experiences. An England–Scotland game attracted 133,000 to
Hampden Park (crowd restrictions having been relaxed) in
April 1944 just months before D-Day. Matt played against Stan
Cullis and his former City team-mate, Swift, was in nets. Only
injury prevented Bill Shankly, on the outskirts of the team and
latterly such a great friend, rival and admirer of Matt's, from
playing in the return match at Wembley in October 1944.

As the war drew to an end in April 1945, Matt captained
his national side against the auld enemy at Hampden. Before
the game, the now veteran right-half was among those who
addressed inmates at Barlinnie Gaol concerning the benefits of
physical exertion and sport. Those benefits weren't quite so
clear to Matt the next day, when England ran out winners in
an ignominious 6–1 defeat.

But it might have been different. England's Joe Mercer gave
away a penalty at 3–1. 'I felt sorry for skipper Matt Busby,'
Tommy Lawton recalled shortly afterwards. 'While the penalty
area was being cleared of English players, Matt asked two Scots
to take the kick. One walked away without answering and the

other refused, neither wanting the responsibility. So Matt had to take it himself. Remember he taught Swift how to stop penalties in Frank's early days at Maine Road and you'll realise why there was no score . . .'

There was more to that incident than first appears. When Frank Swift joined Manchester City as a youth, Matt spotted his potential and made it almost his personal mission to look after Swift's welfare. He told him what to eat and when, how to train and look after himself physically and – not least – how to guard between the posts. Matt would practise with the young Swift for hours on end, flinging penalties at him until the young keeper could virtually read his mind as Matt hovered on the 18-yard area. It's said that Swift was praying Matt would end up taking the penalty that day at Hampden; it's certain that Matt didn't fancy his chances. As captain, he'd *have* to take the penalty if he couldn't persuade anyone else to. Even then, it seemed, the buck-passing stopped at the feet of Matt Busby.

Events were now moving fast and Matt had little time to console himself. Rumours circulated during the weekend of that last wartime Hampden international that a British Army soccer tour of Italy and the Middle East was planned, following recent army advances. Sure enough, on 5 May CSMI M. Busby, APTC, along with Swift, Mercer and Lawton, assembled at the Great Western Railway Hotel in Paddington for a tour scheduled until 2 June. Then, out of the blue, news broke of the German surrender in Europe. Official VE Day was still three days away, but Matt's hotel that night was the first to eradicate the blackout in a floodlit victory celebration. Frank Swift and Matt added to the general mood of joviality and relief with some homespun entertainment – Swift reciting Lancashire monologues and acting out comical mimes; Matt indulging his passion for the music-hall fare he had loved in his Lanarkshire youth. It's fair to guess Matt 'Belonged to Glasgow' that night, and probably took most of his fellow army tourists back there with him as he sang his heart out.

A few days later, the soccer soldiers flew to Italy. Matt was manager, with 'team attendant' or trainer Arthur Rowe, later the architect of the 'push and run' style that took Tottenham to the title in 1951, as his assistant. Amid the morale-boosting games with army teams, there were trips to Pompeii, the pilgrimage Church of the Madonna, the Naples Opera House, and the splendour of Rome, Florence and Rimini. There was time to chat with other pros, hear their grievances and hone his vision of the beautiful game.

There were terrible moments, too, as team manager Matt and the rest witnessed the wholesale devastation after the decisive battles at Cassino and Valmontone. The three cemeteries of war dead – with white crosses for Allies and black for Germans, left a lasting impression. However, in Rome a tour of the Vatican and an audience with the Pope would have buoyed Matt's spirits.

The gruelling, mosquito-ridden road trip to Ancona was memorable for the dust and white chalk churned up by the convoy of trucks. One of the vans was driven by Vic Wright, who in peacetime was a decent singer with the Joe Loss Orchestra – later house-band to virtually every post-match honours party, including that after the 1968 European Cup. Now, as he drove the dry roads of Italy, everyone and everything was coated with a film of chalk and dust, transforming the cream of British footballers into a gaggle of dusty millers. They stopped by a stream in the Apennines, homesick, filthy and fed up, and skinny-dipped, gambolling in the chill water and resuming the sparky banter. Someone chirruped that Matt 'was looking his age these days'.

In Florence, the lads encountered a South American army wide boy called Brazil Joe, a flashy, skilful footballer who was sufficiently impressed by the British contingent to suggest that some of them might return home with him and earn as much as £200 a game in Argentina. For this party of soccer Tommies, set to return to a maximum wage of £1.50 per game, it was a first encounter with the lure of big money abroad. They were soon brought down to earth; however, when a section of the British Army crowd barracked the soccer exhibitionists during a game against a Fifth Army side, featuring several Brazilians with taunts of 'Come on the D-Day dodgers!'

This was perhaps understandable but desperately unfair. Matt, along with many other footballers, had signed up to fight Hitler as soon as hostilities were announced. In a tacit and telling response to the incivility, Matt brought the house down in one stunning moment, dribbling past player after player on a mazy 50-yard run to leave Archie Macauley with an open goal.

In all, Matt and the others travelled 2,000 miles by truck on the Italian tour. It was a curiously emotional experience for all the team, as devastation, heartbreak and tedium at the endless round of official engagements and ENSA shows vied with boisterous fun, camaraderie and wonder at many of the sights.

Matt, the team manager and senior player at 35, was a model of fortititude and strength for the younger players when morale was flagging or homesickness gripped. Always the compassionate man, he worked hard to help everyone along, typically never mentioning his own undoubted stress at missing Jean and his young family. By now Matt had broad, supportive shoulders.

There were compensations. For Matt, not far behind the meeting with the great pontiff was the impression made on all the touring party by the magnificent stadium in Florence, a cathedral for soccer as impressive as Wembley. It was a huge concrete bowl capable of seating 40,000 in considerable comfort, with a 100-foot-high press tower in concrete and glass at one end; seeds of a theatre of dreams must have been sown in Matt's mind here. And he was already due to assume the managership of United as soon as he was demobbed.

Tommy Lawton

Matt Busby would have made just as good a schoolmaster as a footballer, and has the invaluable touch of genius in passing on the craft he poured into the game. Matt was one of the hardest-to-pass half-backs I ever played against. A master of positional play, with the natural ability of a top-class Scot to change the course of a game with a quick, shrewd pass, and with the energy which is never shown to better advantage than when on a losing side. I have never known Matt lose his temper or be other than his grand, sportsmanlike self. Perhaps my greatest memory of him was at Hampden last April, when he literally worked himself to a standstill in the lost Scottish cause. At the end, Matt just had enough strength to walk slowly over to Joe Mercer, the England captain, and offer his congratulations to our team. I shudder to think how I would have felt if I had covered the ground Matt did that day.

The war was an important stage in the making of Matt Busby. The qualities of leadership that George Kay had seen and nurtured at Anfield were able to flourish. For the first time, Matt had control of his own team, and his embryonic style, to some extent dictated by wartime conditions, would later become familar – there was no heavy emphasis on discipline, the atmosphere co-operative rather than hierarchical. Matt, though, was indisputably the Boss. And so it stayed.

Sandy Busby

People ask what made him so great. You're either a nice fellow or you're not, a villain or you're not. My father had principles, dignity, honesty, and the qualities of leadership. Wherever he went, whatever he did, he was made captain or leader. When the army team was formed in the war, he was made Sergeant-Major Instructor, and when they got a team together to play behind the lines to entertain the soldiers, they had players like Frank Swift, Tom Finney, Stanley Matthews, Tommy Lawton, Joe Mercer. But my dad was put in charge.

The Boss

Matt Busby

It was not an easy assignment. The ground had been blitzed, they had an overdraft at the bank, and what is more I had, no experience, as a manager, and I felt they were taking a great risk in appointing me. All I had, apart from playing experience, was ideas about what a manager should do, faith in those ideas and faith in the future of the club. (Freeman's speech, 1967)

Louis Rocca was Manchester United to the marrow – the sort of mover and shaker every club needs. 'I only knew him in the later part of his life,' says Les Olive, director and former club secretary, 'but he was very astute. He was a diabetic, but he would always offer me part of his lunch. He was always very interested in everybody, and he took an interest in me when I was a young boy starting out.' Rocca had served United for more than 40 years; he had suggested the name change from Newton Heath; In 1930 he had even tried to sign an unhappy wing-half from City called Matt Busby. But perhaps he saved his most important act until near the end of his time with the club. On 15 December 1944, Matt Busby received a letter:

Dear Matt,
   No doubt you will be surprised to get this letter from your old pal Louis. Well Matt I have been trying for the

past month to find you and not having your Reg. address I could not trust a letter going to Liverpool, as what I have to say is so important. I don't know if you have considered what you are going to do when war is over, but I have a great job for you if you are willing to take it on. Will you get into touch with me at the above address and when you do I can explain things to you better, when I know there will be no danger of interception. Now Matt I hope this is plain to you. You see I have not forgotten my old friend either in my prayers or in your future welfare. I hope your good wife and family are all well and please God you will soon be home to join their happy circle.

> Wishing you a very Happy Xmas and a lucky New Year.
> With all God's Blessings in you and yours
> Your Old Pal
> Louis Rocca

Matt met United's chairman, J. W. Gibson, and by the time the interview was over he had committed himself to the club. It was 15 February 1945. James Gibson informed the Board of Directors he was impressed by 'Mr Busby's ideas and honesty of purpose'. Four days later Matt was confirmed as a manager. He had been offered a three-year contract at £750 a year, but with the prescience and quiet persuasiveness that was to become his trademark, Matt managed to bring the directors round to his way of thinking: it's a big job, there are too many old players, there's not even a stadium or anywhere to train – if you want it done properly it's going to take at least five years. And so five years it was. Senior Sergeant-Major Busby, hailed as 'one of the greatest half-backs of modern times' by the *Manchester Evening News*, signed in his uniform.

On 22 October, Matt was demobbed and took over as manager. As he strolled up Warwick Road – now Sir Matt Busby Way – towards Old Trafford, he must have pondered whether this was the right move. Indeed, Liverpool still claimed he was under a player's contract with them. Throughout his managerial career, Matt was fond of reminding people: 'Money in the bank is no use to a football team. You have to put your money on the field where the public can see it.' But in 1945 the club was deep in debt and with no ground of their own where a crowd could watch them. The club had temporary office premises at the Cornbrook Cold Air Stores in Hadfield Street, Old Trafford, a company owned by James Gibson. It was Budget day, which was ironic for a club with a £15,000 overdraft. This was a Manchester United starved of success, having to live down the music-hall jokes of the thirties when they had flirted with the top two Divisions, being too good for the Second, yet not good enough for the First – the 'yo-yo years'.

The ground presented a huge problem. It had been the innocent victim of a German blitzkrieg in 1941, with firebombs deviating from the target and the inviting dynamo works, cable works and engine sheds of Trafford Park nestling nearby. The 'popular terrace' and main stand were decimated; the pitch was scorched to a cinder. Four years later, little had changed. When Matt took his first stroll round the pitch – a happy tour he was to perform regularly, well into his eighties – the damp stench of embers must have forestalled any grand visions of future glory.

Yet Busby inherited several assets at the club, not least of which was Walter Crickmer. Crickmer had become secretary of United in 1926. 'He was small man, a bundle of energy, always quick about the place,' remembers Les Olive. 'Nowadays you'd call him a general manager, looking after the executive side and administration.' He was an expansive fellow, known, with good reason, as Mr Man United. Crickmer it was who took the Old Trafford side into the First Division in 1938. But there was a far more vital development that year, when Gibson and Crickmer set up a vigorous youth policy through the MUJAC, the Manchester United Junior Athletic Club. The gains were immediate: although the first team finished only

43

fourteenth in the First Division in the 1938–39 season, the reserves won the Central League, the A team, with an average age of seventeen, won the open-aged Manchester League and the MUJAC their division of the Chorlton League.

While they waited for these seeds to bear first-team fruits, Louis Rocca had been busy signing players like Johnny Carey, Jack Rowley, Stan Pearson and Allenby Chilton. By the end of the war, United was a team considered old or mature, according to your view, but Rocca, Gibson and Crickmer had laid the foundations upon which Matt Busby could build a team, and a club, that would bring glory to the city of Manchester.

John Roberts

(Former player.)

> *What made him a great manager was that first of all he was an experienced footballer. Then there was his early life – he'd grown up for most of his life without a father, he'd worked in the coalmine. Then he'd come down to Manchester City at a time when, because of the maximum wage, clubs could afford to have 40-odd professionals. Then the Liverpool captaincy gave him experience as a leader, and he had to handle the war. So by the time he came to United he'd been rounded by life. And he was determined to be the manager. Although he had this avuncular image, which was justified, he was also a very hard man, and he made it clear from the start that he was going to be the boss, without boardroom interference.*

Matt was to be a new type of boss, sovereign of his club. Harold Hardman, Gibson's successor in 1951, understood this more than anyone. 'Matt will seek the board's advice, ponder over it,' he would smile, 'and then go away and do precisely as he wants.' However, Matt appreciated secretary Crickmer's work and much of what he wanted to achieve required the old hand's touch. 'I was a new boy in administration,' recalled Matt years later. 'Walter Crickmer's advice and guidance were of great value in those early years.'

Matt set about surrounding himself with skilled men of strong character – the sort of tough, reliable and talented folk he'd come to know as a youth in Bellshill and in the years since. His first recruit was Jimmy Murphy, who had played for Swansea, West Bromwich Albion and Wales. Apart from the few occasions they had faced each other as players, their first meeting had been towards the end of the war, while Matt was manager on the army soccer tour of May 1945. Murphy was a regular soldier, appropriately, as it turned out, a drill sergeant. He had taken over from Stan Cullis, organising troop entertainments in Italy, and one day got the chance to lecture about football at the forces' leave centre there. Matt listened intently at the back and liked what he heard. He offered him a job there and then.

Les Olive

(Long-serving United staffer who was the club secretary's assistant when Matt first arrived in 1945. Went on to become club secretary himself, before moving on to Oldham.)

I was seventeen years old when Sir Matt joined the club, working in the office at the ground while he operated from James Gibson's offices with Walter Crickmer. I left to join the RAF and didn't see much of him until I was demobbed in 1948. By this time the team had already set English football alight. I resumed my job at the ticket office, and on Tuesday mornings I was able to slip out on to the terraces to watch the weekly practice matches. Matt used to love these games, and he'd demonstrate how he wanted the game to be played. I saw at first hand how he handled the players, and later on, when I became secretary to the directors. He would always listen to what people had to say, he was always courteous, but if he thought he was right he'd be firm and determined. He wasn't just an inspiration to the players at Manchester United; he brought everybody into the picture. When I first came back after being demobbed, he would come into the office on Monday mornings, ask how things were, say hello, and then he would go to the laundry ladies and the groundstaff. We were much smaller then, of course – three cleaning the ground, two in the ticket office, with volunteers or part-time people when it was busier. On the coaching side there was Jimmy, Bert Whalley looking after the A team, and Bert acting as chief scout, or organising the scouting. Tom Curry was the first-team trainer and Bill Inglis the second-team trainer, and other places were filled voluntarily. There were quite a few people who came in that capacity, say helping out on Saturdays, and Matt made them feel part of the foundation in their own way. Everybody wanted to do it for Sir Matt – he seemed to bring the best out of everybody. He wanted it to be a family club and he played his part in making it that way by showing an interest in people, so that everybody was important. He used to say that we don't have first-team players and second-, third- and fourth-team players – they're all Manchester United players. In the end everybody wanted to be successful for him, or because of him.

Matt had found his perfect partner. 'Jimmy Murphy and Matt Busby together could have climbed Everest,' says Harry Gregg. 'Jimmy had an unbelievable bearing on what happened at the club. He was the practical guy out on the pitch. He would laugh with you, cry with you, physically cry with you; he would fight with you, physically fight with you; he would swear at you; he would drink with you. He was the complete opposite of Matt; he was fiery – half-Welsh and half-Irish, what do you expect? Matt made Jimmy and Jimmy made Matt. They needed each other.' Like many successful coaches, Murphy was a player with a strong physical presence who had made up for limited skill with judicious deployment of heart and mind. He had himself been coached by the celebrated Jimmy Hogan, an adventurous soul who had worked abroad before 1914, and he soon saw Matt as someone special. 'Patience was his greatest asset,' he noted. 'Our partnership was built on friendship, mutual trust and respect.'

For Harry Gregg, the other members of Matt's team were vital, too: 'Bert Whalley was a very, very, very nice person. I didn't know Bert as well as I knew the rest of them because I was a first-team player and Bert spent all his time with the young players. Tom Curry, the trainer, was a terrific fellow, he was a wonderful old fellow. Matt had a wonderful staff. He set ridiculous standards, him and Jimmy Murphy and Bert Whalley.'

Sandy Busby

I know I'm biased, but I call him a genius, because it wasn't just football he was great at. He had this canny way of knowing characters. If I'd done something wrong, the same as with his players, he'd just say something in a simple, nice way, give you a hint. It was a shame he couldn't spend more time with us, really – we could have done with seeing a lot more of him. In a way he had two families. Don't get me wrong, he adored my mother, he loved her to death, he admired her, she was his adviser in lots of things. But his other family was Manchester United Football Club, and that took up lots of time, because in those days there was only my dad, Jimmy Murphy and Bert Whalley running the coaching side. He came in with his idea of building from the boys upwards, so it became a family in itself. I suppose he was putting his own experiences into football.

After the travels and travails of wartime, Matt was happy to return with his family to Manchester. 'He loved the warmth, the people,' says Sandy. 'All the people who came from pit villages will tell you how depressing they were – all there was to do was hang about on street corners, go to the pub, and play football. There was no light. Then he came to Manchester and it was dazzling.' The Busby family moved into a three-bedroomed semi-detached house in Kings Road, Chorlton. 'We thought it was Buckingham Palace,' says Sandy. He remembers being homesick for his wartime home though: 'I loved Scotland. When my father was made manager of the Great Britain Olympic team in 1948, I could have gone down to London to watch the Games, but I said I wanted to go back to Scotland.' He also remembers his father acquiring some of the trappings of a comfortable lifestyle, but without a trace of ostentation. 'My dad wasn't a good driver, in fact he wasn't technical in any way – he wouldn't know how turn the water supply off. But he had a car, a Morris Rowley 10, his pride and joy. In 1968, after the European Cup, the club gave him a Jensen, but he went back to them after a while and said, 'I can't stand this car, it's too big for me.'

There were great years around the corner for the Busby family, though the young Sandy would have liked to have seen his father more often. But he understood that this was how the business of football was if you wanted to do it properly. He loved rubbing shoulders with his dad and the players when they all reported at the ground on Sunday morning for treatment. If he was lucky he might catch his dad having a cup of tea with his mum when he came home from school at lunchtime. 'How are you son, everything all right?' And then Matt would be off again, back to pursue his life's work, constructing a club in his own image, driving off around the country to check up a lead from one of eight scouts around the British Isles, or, more frequently as United's reputation grew, a tip-off from a well-meaning headmaster.

To begin with, rebuilding was desperately needed. United were playing at Maine Road, paying City £5,000 a year in rent, plus a percentage of the takings. In November Matt dipped into the transfer market for the first time, snapping up Edward Buckle from Leeds United. In February the balding Jimmy 'Brittle Bones' Delaney followed, for £4,000 from Celtic. He'd played for the Scottish national team under Matt's captaincy. It was a lot of money for a club that had none, especially for a player the wrong side of 30, but it was a master-stroke, and a bargain – Celtic had valued him at £10,000 and had turned down an offer from Sunderland of £20,000 for Delaney and Crum. Matt could be very persuasive when he needed to be.

Delaney provided the ammunition for Jack Rowley and Stan Pearson, one of the best striking partnerships the club ever had. Rowley had signed for United in 1937 for £3,000 from Walsall; in the war he played for Wolves, with whom he won a War Cup-winner's medal, as well as Spurs and the Irish side, Distillery. His proficient goalscoring – he scored eight in one game for Wolves and seven in a game for Spurs – was built on fine heading and a lethal left foot.

Les Olive

Matt never lost his temper, but nobody took advantage of him because they knew who was the Boss – if he looked at somebody in a certain way, they knew they'd gone far enough. He was always gracious in defeat. If we lost a Cup final, he would always go next door to the opposition dressing-room and congratulate them, and when we won he was quite modest. His attitude was that if you couldn't say a good word about anyone it was better not to say anything. There's no doubt he was responsible for laying the foundations upon which the present strength of the club has been built. In my time as secretary, no major decisions were taken without his approval, and the development of the stadium, which began in 1964, wouldn't have gone ahead if he had said the money was needed to strengthen the team.

A couple of weeks after Delaney arrived, Matt showed his willingness to wipe the blackboard clean and try something new. United played Bury in the war-relic Football League North. Matt sent the team out with three balls for the pre-match kick-in, and executed moves he had appropriated from recent UK tourists Moscow Dynamo and elsewhere. There was a new, open playing style. A fortnight later they beat Blackburn 6–2, with a hat-trick in nine minutes from Jack Rowley. They were irresistible. Later that month they played the British Army Overseas Rhine team. The plane made a forced landing coming into Hamburg. United lost the match 2–1 in front of 28,000, some Germans defying orders not to attend by shinning up trees to watch.

United finished fourth that season in the Football League North, playing some delightful attacking football. For the fans, United were an attraction again. Autograph hunters, who had left them undisturbed for years, were back in force; the city was waking up to the marvel in their midst, and United were readying themselves to assume the mantle of their city's premier team.

Before the Football League proper resumed, Matt began spring-cleaning: seven players were transfer-listed. He had reason to be hopeful, for other products of the MUJACs were still to be demobbed. There was Stan Pearson, there was Charlie Mitten, there was Johnny Carey. Mitten had been an office boy at Old Trafford before joining the RAF and had first come across Matt during the war. Johnny Carey was perhaps Busby's most important player in his first few years. A Republic of Ireland international who had come from St James Gate in 1936, he played in every position for the club except goalkeeper.

'Immense,' Matt was to say of him.

David Wicks

(Joined United in 1946 and became programme editor, a position he held for many years.)

*I met Matt first in 1946. I had just come out of the army,
having been delayed because I was a pro soldier. My dad
was a friend of J. W. Gibson, the chairman, and through
them I met the club secretary, Walter Crickmer, and he
said one day, 'Come and meet the new manager called
Matt Busby. He's a lad who used to play for City.' To my
astonishment, Matt was wearing a track suit and I said,
'What have you been doing?' To which he replied, 'Playing
a wee bit o' football with the lads.' I suddenly realised he
was the start of a new style of management from touchline
to track suit.*

At pre-season training on the University ground at Fallowfield,
before the beginning of the 1946–47 campaign, Matt could be
seen every morning stripped for training, clearly deriving as
much pleasure as the youngsters. His predecessor, Scott
Duncan, had never been seen without his spats and buttonhole;
Matt was one of the first of the track-suit managers, doing his
work in the training-ground mud, mucking in with the lads.

If this was part of the post-war revolution, it was just a
sideshow to the main event. Matt Busby's vision, honed by his
experiences as an idealistic young footballer at City and cultured wing-half at Liverpool, as sympathetic team manager of
the wartime British Army tour of Italy, fortified by his Bellshill
upbringing and nourished by a love of his adopted Manchester,
was now played out in real life. It was the biggest challenge of
his life so far.

In his 1958 biography, Matt revealed the underlying scheme:
'I did not set out to build a team; the task ahead was much
bigger than that. What I really embarked upon was the building
of a system which would produce not one but four or five
teams, each occupying a vital rung in the ladder, the summit of
which was the first XI.'

Sir Matt Busby

Bryon Butler

(Veteran football writer for *Daily Telegraph* and broadcaster on *Radio 5 Live*.)

> *One of Matt's strengths – and he had so many – was that he recognised quality in a player, just as easily as he recognised quality in a man. Players, if they play together long enough, acquire an understanding of each other and acquire a format and a method which develops. You can impose a format on lesser players who will never rise above a certain level. But Matt always actually put his money on talent, and for my money that would always be the right way. You not only get successful teams but you get attractive teams. And Matt never sent out a dull team in his life. He wasn't a dull man and he didn't have much time for dull football. He didn't contain games, he took over games.*

Matt's vision required a blank slate, a club to build from scratch. Just as catching them young was the answer to moulding players to play your way, with a strong team spirit, fierce loyalty and innate understanding, so it was with the non-playing side of the club. Attracting the best fledglings saved money – and hassle, as their attitudes were shaped by Matt. United had to be a club Manchester, and the world, would respect from top to bottom as a symbol of the best in football. He needed to build the spirit of a close-knit family with himself at the head: the Boss.

Respect for and loyalty to Matt himself was absolutely critical to achieving this goal. Both were carefully nurtured by Jimmy and the others. Jimmy would announce to his team that 'The Boss is gonna be watching tomorrow, so show him what you're made of,' or he'd take a player aside after training and tell him, 'You're doing well, lad, The Boss is happy with the way you're shaping up,' elevating Matt in young minds to the status of an immensely warm and yet somehow detatched overlord, all-seeing, all-knowing, In truth, though Matt needed little building up. He was always a man with a special aura, a presence, a quiet charisma that subtly made itself felt whenever he entered a room. Murphy's contribution was the icing on the cake.

The chief problem Matt faced as the first post-war Football League season began was who to leave out: Mitten, Delaney, Pearson and Rowley were being pushed for places in the forward line by the likes of Johnny Hanlon and Johnny Aston. They were off to a flyer, winning the first five games and following in the tradition established by the MUJACs: when they played Chelsea six matches into the season, seven of the team were Manchester lads: Crompton, Whalley, Cockburn, Aston, Hanlon, Pearson and Mitten.

Jack Crompton, one of those so loyal to Matt that he cropped up again and again, had joined during the war from the United's nursery club, Goslings. He was to come back after Munich to help Jimmy Murphy on the training side, and again in the 1970s to work with Tommy Docherty. Bert Whalley, the wing-half, who had come from Stalybridge Celtic in 1934 would retire at the end of the season and join the coaching staff, becoming instrumental in the rearing of the Busby Babes – before dying at Munich.

Others made an early impact. Henry Cockburn, from Ashton, was another Goslings recruit and another Louis Rocca discovery. He was only 5ft 4in but he could outjump men who towered over him. Some likened him to Matt's hero, Alex James, with his huge skill and good distribution – assets not lost on his shrewd manager. Cockburn was instrumental in United's bold start to the season. Johnny Aston, making his debut, would be converted to full-back later that season, and later formed with Johnny Carey the pre-eminent full-back pairing in the post-war years.

Both were shining examples of Matt applying lessons from his own experience. At City, fate had dictated that he switch from inside-forward to right-half, teaching Matt to persevere with players of promise and to experiment with positions. Carey was the first, starting out as an inside forward, before finding his vocation at right-back. Such conversions were to stand Matt in good stead throughout his reign at United: Roger Byrne, Jackie Blanchflower, Eddie Colman, Shay Brennan, David Sadler and even Bobby Charlton, to some extent, benefited from his patience and astuteness.

Perhaps that's why Aston stuck around. His playing career was curtailed by illness, but he joined the coaching staff, becoming chief scout in 1970 and eventually leaving with the sacking of Frank O'Farrell. John junior would be the man of the match in a European Cup final.

Salford-born Stan Pearson, he of the deceptive body swerve, was another whose talent Matt had the good fortune to inherit from before the war. He made his debut in 1937 at the age of eighteen in a 7–1 win at Chesterfield and played nearly 350 games for United. Charlie Mitten, born in Rangoon and raised in Manchester, joined straight from school and worked as an office boy. Mitten had first come up against Matt when he'd been playing for Chelsea in the wartime southern league and Matt was playing for Reading. Mitten's side won 1–0. The next time he met him was after he'd been demobbed from the Azores and a new era was beginning at Old Trafford. His grandson, Paul, is now on YTS forms with United.

Charlie Mitten

(One of the stars of Matt's FAC Cup-winning 1948 team. Although he made his full league debut after being demobbed in 1946 at the age of 25, he had been at United since 1936.)

Matt was always quietly persuasive, though I don't think he knew he was doing it at the time. He was probably the best man-manager in the football world, right up to today. He knew all the players' ins and outs, all their idiosyncrasies. We had very few team chats – he just said, 'Boys, you're at Manchester United, you're all good players, just go out and express yourselves, and most important of all, enjoy a game of football'. He knew the need for discipline, but you could come and talk to him about anything. He'd come and have a joke and a drink after the game. I always got on with him great, smashing. Because he knew I always used to deliver on the field, that's why. Sometimes I could do with a kick up the backside. I used to come in half an hour before the kick-off – I'd have been up to White City to have a look at the dogs, and he'd let me do that. I'd walk down with the crowd, chatting away, and I'd get in and be the first ready to get on the field.

There were other players for Busby to build on from before the war. Allenby Chilton had signed from Seaham Colliery in the north-east and made his United debut on 2 September 1939, the day before war broke out (the two are not connected). During the war he had kept himself fit as a cruiserweight boxer when he was stationed in Iceland.

Allenby Chilton

(Loyal servant of United, a born wing-half converted to centre, joined United just before the war and proved a great asset after it as Matt built his team around such quality players to take the Championship in 1952.)

He was cool, calm, didn't like bad language. He never seemed to lose his way. He was a gentleman. He never told you how to play – well you've got to play your own way. He'd praise someone who'd been outstanding, and say, 'If it wasn't for this man we'd have been beaten.' But he was a sensible bloke. I said to him once, 'We laid down the foundations for a great club.' He just smiled.

They finished second to Liverpool in the League in 1946–47

and had reached the fourth round of the Cup. It had been an uplifting first season for Matt. As it came to a close a young lad called Denis Viollet was scoring twice for Manchester Boys as they beat Farnworth Boys 8–0. There was much to look forward to.

Matt Busby, Manchester City's right-half in 1928.

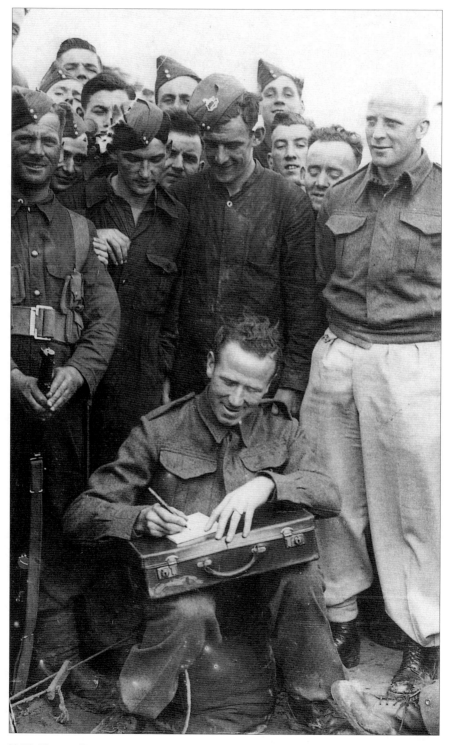

Matt in his army days.

The British Army dressing room at the Parc des Princes in 1940.

1939 - three international footballers, now army sergeants:
Joe Mercer, Matt Busby and D Welsh.

Captain Busby leads out his team.

April 1957: Matt Busby with his 'babes'.

February 1958: for some this was their last briefing.
Matt Busby talking to the players before the game against Red Star.

Leading out the Busby Babes for the 1957 FA Cup Final at Wembley.

Feburary 7th 1958: Matt with Club Secretary Walter Crickmer
shortly before the fateful trip to Belgrade.

The Cup

THE FA CUP HAS has always had a habit of conjuring draws in each round that seem to have an importance beyond the obvious. In 1947–48, the trophy trail for United brought high-quality First Division opponents at every stage, as if to provide the strongest test of Matt's nascent plan – Aston Villa, Liverpool, Charlton, Preston, Derby and Blackpool, with no replays and every match won by at least two goals. The game at Aston Villa in the third round brought out the best in Busby's boys. 'Jack won the toss and decided to kick downhill,' recalls Charlie Mitten. 'They kicked off and scored in the first minute. We thought,"We'd better pull our socks up here", and by half-time we were 5–1 up – Johnny Morris got two and Stan, Jack and Jimmy one each. We cruised a bit and they got to 5–4 with about ten minutes left, then Stan Pearson nipped in for the sixth.' In the semi-final United beat Derby County 3–1, thanks to a Stan Pearson hat-trick.

Before the final, as the team prepared at a hotel in Weybridge, Tom Jackson wrote in the *Manchester Evening News*: 'Matt Busby, the quietly-spoken Scot who at 38 is in such good physical shape that he gets through a hard practice game with the enthusiasm of a youngster, is undoubtedly one of soccer's greatest manager-discoveries. The Busby touch has become famous.' Jackson rated the team's worth at £100,000. On Cup final morning, Matt came down to breakfast. Most of the players were already down. They'd read the day's papers and were not looking forward to Matt seeing the back pages. He

57

sat back, picked up his paper and saw the headline: 'United manager accuses his players of being swell-headed'. He turned ashen grey, let the paper fall in front of him, and picked it up again as if he couldn't believe it. Cool, pipe-smoking skipper Johnny Carey, more usually noted for his dry humour, strolled over to Matt and said, 'Don't worry about it, Boss. We just don't believe such a story.' A full retraction soon followed.

The final has been called the greatest of all time. Like most of United's finals it certainly wasn't short of incident. United began slowly, lacking rhythm. Then Stan Mortensen was tripped by Allenby Chilton in what Chilton swears to this day was in the 'D' of the penalty area – 'He went down about five or six yards after I tripped him,' he says – but the referee gave a penalty: 1–0. Jack Rowley walked the ball into the net for the equaliser. As Blackpool overcame their Wembley nerves, Mortensen slipped in to make it 2–1, but, fuelled by the will to attack that had brought them 95 goals already that season, United set about Blackpool. Johnny Morris picked out Jack Rowley with a free-kick and 'the Gunner' headed home another equaliser. United took over. A clearance from Jack Crompton found Stan Pearson, whose 25-yarder went in off the post to make it 3–2, then Johnny Anderson scored from 35 yards in the dying moments. 'Actually, it was one of the easiest games I ever played,' says Charlie Mitten. 'We had a little chat before – we were a bit worried about Stan Matthews. The way to play him was for the full-back not to tackle him, but to jockey him, and the winger to come back and chase him and take the ball off him. That's all we did first half, and we were still losing 2–1, so we thought, "We're an attacking team," and we went off and attacked them.'

Raymond Glendenning, plummy doyen of radio commentators, saw United's triumph built on the fact that 'Chilton had the measure of Matthews'.

Soon afterwards, the *Manchester Evening News* had the prescience to publish an early tribute: 'M. Busby, the manager, has an uncannily brilliant eye for young local talent's possibilities, whether in their usual or other positions, a believer in the certainty of good football's eventual reward and a friendly, yet when necessary, firm father of his family of players. Between them they have built a club spirit which is too rare in these days, a spirit which enables men to bear cheerfully personal and team disappointments and to ignore personal opportunities to shine for the good of the whole. They have made it likely that this club spirit will persist.'

That summer Matt also had the honour of managing the Great Britain team in the Olympic Games in London the same year. Enlisting a team of true amateurs in the face of 'shamateur' opposition, such as Eastern bloc army teams, he nursed them to the semi-finals where they bowed out to Sweden.

Bill Shankly (dec.)

(Fellow Scot and rival manager at Liverpool [1959–74], the man who laid the ground for Liverpool's domination of English football in the seventies and eighties.)

'Matt Busby is without doubt the greatest manager that ever lived. I'm not saying that I think he's the greatest manager, I'm saying he is the greatest manager – facts can prove that. I happened to be stationed in Manchester when the blitz came to the city, and I saw Old Trafford a few days after it had been blitzed. When I looked at it I thought that's the end, there'll never be another football team again. Tommy Curry was trying to keep things going, and there was no water running through into the place even to have a wash so that the players could train. It's the most amazing thing that this club now and this ground have risen from that. This is a tribute to Matt Busby. The man was blessed with ability and of course he used that ability. After the war Matt Busby was lucky – I must say this – to have a team, most of whom could play, even though most were veterans. But many teams were in the same position and

they got rid of their's and Matt of course kept his and even added to them by signing fellas like Jimmy Delaney who was an invaluable asset. So until Matt got his young boys ready, giving them time to get ready, he used his old players. Then of course came the Busby Babes. And that's Matt's foresight, Matt's ability. Everything a man needs to become a football manager, Matt Busby has. There's no doubt. He's an inspiration to anyone; always willing to help you. And he would never guide you or tell you to do anything wrong. I think that he's an inspiration to everybody.' (The Busby Dynasty, BBC Radio Collection)

The next season started off badly. Before the first game, against Derby County, there was a dressing-room row over extra payments. Most clubs found illegal ways of augmenting the maximum wage, but Matt refused to countenance covert operations. Manchester United would act correctly at all times – this was as much a part of his vision as the style of play. A disgruntled side lost the game 2–1.

Popular, extrovert Johnny Morris had a dashing animal magic that the United crowd adored, but he and Matt never saw eye to eye. Matt's man-management skills were developing, and most players responded well to his steel fist in a velvet glove. Not Morris. 'I've tried every angle,' Matt was said to have confided at the time. 'I've bullied, I've used flattery, I've tried every way, but I just can't get through.' Morris was the sort of person who knew when he thought he was fit and would publicly state so. When the Boss heard him picking himself, he was furious at the challenge to his authority and Morris soon became the first in a select line of rejects punctuating Matt's managerial career. He was sold to Derby for a British record fee of £24,000.

Matt's good-mannered geniality often led observers into the trap of believing he was soft. But as Nobby Stiles ruefully observed, when the Boss was annoyed with you, he didn't 'hand round the toffees'. Matt Busby was not a soft man. He was tolerant, but had a steely resolve and determination not to be diverted from his own itinerary. Billy Whelan, who perished at Munich, once went into Busby's office and said he should be dropped. Busby looked at him with calculating graveness. 'No one tells me who to put into my team and who to drop,' he said, coolly. 'I manage this side. If I keep you in it is because you are playing the way I want you to. Keep playing that way and don't ever do this again.'

Bryon Butler

He got inside players. It was a natural thing. And probably one of the great arts of management is getting players to play for you because they want to play for you. That's to a great degree tied up with respect. People had respect for Matt. Some managers lead, some managers push, some managers whip, some managers demand. Matt managed to get the best out of people in another way. Not that he couldn't drive, not that he couldn't command; all these things he could do. But he drew the best out of players in the best possible way.

Matt always held that a happy player off the field was a good player on it. The United week forged a social routine too. Afternoons might be passed down at the golf club at Davyhulme, the Mere – Matt's cherished course, and scene of one of his holes-in-one. On Fridays Jean would take the wives and female staff at Old Trafford out for the evening. Saturdays – and footballers have always made the most of Saturdays – might find Matt till the early hours, with some of the players and their wives in one of a few favourite Manchester haunts, or with friends like Paddy McGrath and bookmaker Johnny Foy at a little restaurant in Cheshire. On Sundays the players reported to the ground. Monday reports were collated on all players in all teams at every level from first team. Occasionally the team would be taken off to Blackpool; such trips were good for team morale, and until 1954 Paddy McGrath, an enduring friend of Matt's for half a century, had business interests there.

Paddy McGrath

(Matt's oldest and dearest friend, a former boxer who forged his business out of wartime commercial concerns in Blackpool. Owned Cromford Club, a haunt and haven for United players and Matt and Jean.)

> *In Scotland you get Rangers and Celtic, and when Matt took over here someone – I won't mention his name, he's dead and gone now – said, 'It'll be another bloody Celtic here.' Matt was what people are asking for today. He wasn't pious, but he was a bloody good Christian.*

Paddy McGrath was Matt's closest friend. If the players were like the sons he and Jean were deprived of, Paddy was like a brother. A Collyhurst lad, he has watched United for 70 years. 'They used to be up and down like a yo-yo,' he recalls.

The bond with McGrath – a feisty former prize-fighter and always exuberant company – was one of the strongest and most enduring of Matt's life. The pair had met shortly after Matt had taken over at United. 'He came in the Savoy Café in Blackpool with the United team. He used to be chairman of the Catholic Sportmans Committee, and he invited me on the committee to bring in some punters from Blackpool. Later on, when I used to go out with Matt and his wife, I used to have a regular booking on Monday nights at the Ardwick Hippodrome, but if Matt had a football job on I'd take his wife. We'd to go on to the Princess pub on Princess Parkway, where they had a lounge with a Palm Beach orchestra and wicker chairs, and the four of us used to go in and have a few drinks and chat.'

Paddy McGrath

*He knew he was popular with people – he wasn't a fool.
But he never lost his humility. He'd always use the phrase
'in my opinion'. Jean was part of the Busby legend. I've
been out with Matt and he's promised someone two tickets
for the match on Saturday, but she was the one who had
to remind him. He had a tremendous memory for faces.
When I had the Cromford Club I used to get all the
sportswriters in. They always used to say they could get
all the stories they needed there on Saturdays. And I used
to get all the cricketers in, Gary Sobers, people like that.
We had the Australians in the day Jim Laker took his
wickets at Old Trafford. Matt was in, and Keith Miller
and the rest of them were all shaking hands with Matt,
making a fuss of him. Then a pal of mine called Jimmy
Clancey, a working lad who'd only met Matt once, about
ten years before, came walking into the bar, and Matt said,
'Jimmy, how are you son?' He shook hands with him and
brought him into the company.*

Louis Rocca, Paddy McGrath and Matt shared several things
in life, not least their Catholicism. All three knew about preju-
dice, still remnant in Manchester society and with a long
history.

In 1852, the *Manchester Guardian* reported an anti-Catholic
rampage in Stockport, near Manchester. 'We regret to have to
record one of those digraceful riots which exist only where the
lower-class Irish dwell in considerable numbers – arising out of
the perpetual feuds between the Irish Catholics and the lower
class of factory hands,' it snobbishly pronounced. 'The rioters
proved themselves zealous iconoclasts, for they destroyed every
cross and crucifix, picture, image, statue, candlestick . . . Fights
between small bodies of both factions continued for some hours
afterwards . . .' Such hue and cry tactics had become marginal-
ised by Matt's Manchester days, but discrimination was now

institutionalised, respectable. Matt thought he'd escaped such bigotry, and certainly the glory he helped bring to Manchester must have helped eradicate it.

Johnny Foy, another whose company Matt enjoyed, was a prominent bookie in the area. Like most people, Matt liked a little gamble here and there – the dogs at Belle Vue, the horses, but nothing heavy. He was too well aware of the pernicious effects on a sportsman's home life. On one occasion Jean saw the statement from the bookmakers and made her concerns known. After that, Matt generally tried to reach the post first when the statement was due, but it was only a minor hiccup in a harmonious marriage. Sandy doesn't recall his father placing a bet during the last 30 years of his life, although in the last few years Sandy would work out a few horses for his dad to watch on the TV at home.

At the dawn of the fifties, Matt was one of Manchester's most prominent citizens, yet he always retained the humility and concern for others. He made it his business to know every-thing about a player before and after they were on the United books. 'He'd say, "What do you think of so-and-so?" ' remem-bers Paddy Crerand. 'He'd ask about their private life too, because it was no good having the talent if you're going to waste it on wild nights all the time. And he'd ask maybe up to a hundred people. It was a smart way of going about it.'

It was also a shrewd, tangible way of making everyone feel they contributed towards United's success. Matt always went out of his way to show that everyone was valued at the club, no matter how lowly. He ran United from top to bottom, but he made sure it was a happy ship.

Irene Ramsden

I joined United in 1952. Matt was a smashing young man, very debonair. He was always a gentleman. He made a point of coming to talk to everyone. One time we had a bit of an argument with one of the directors. It was a

*night match and at the time we only had two sets of kit,
so we used to have to work all hours to get the kit ready.
This old director was at the dressing-room door and we'd
come in to go to work. Of course he didn't know us and
he shouted after us. We were only young and we felt shown
up, what with the supporters being there as well. We were
going to leave. Sir Matt got to know about it and he came
to us and he said, 'Whatever problem you have, if anybody
ever upsets you, you must come to me. Because this club
is just a wheel, and everybody is a cog turning that wheel.
If things aren't working for one, everyone's put out by it,
and it's no use to us, that. No one's bigger than the club.'
That's the sort of man he was.*

Matt made sure, wherever possible, that United staff were
always looked after socially and financially. He was to argue
fervently against the maximum wage – 'There are artists on the
stage,' he'd say, 'who earn £1,000 a night: why not footballers?'
– even though in practice United kept players' earnings pegged
to a workable minimum some time after the maximum wage
was abolished in 1961. But if the players were kept down by
the maximum wage, Matt was not. The month he sold Johnny
Morris in 1948, he signed a contract for a salary of £3,250 –
five times what he was able to pay his players, and more than
four times his starting salary in 1945. Refusing approaches
from Spurs (they offered him £50 a week) and Manchester City
cannot have been difficult.

In fact, United's finances had improved immeasurably. The
vast crowds, the pros' wage limit and the fact that a building
licence for Old Trafford took a few years to come through
meant that the coffers were swelling and the overdraft had
vanished. From 1946 to 1949 profits were just shy of £100,000.
(The first time United were to slip into the red again was when
they paid Torino £115,000 for Denis Law.) Matt could have
gone out and bought a team. Instead, in the summer of 1949
he had intensified the scouting, everywhere from Ireland to

local Water Board teams – better to grow your own in a carefully monitored nursery than pay over-the-top prices for the finished product reared by someone else. And it had paid off.

The nursery was planned with thoroughness and care. Landladies were hand-picked and vetted to look after the boys as well as providing accommodation. Matt would sit in on every interview. Curfew time was ten o'clock. If some errant lad was not in by then, the landlady had to ring in and report the fact. If a landlady had problems of her own, the boys would be removed from her care. Matt never took anything for granted. An eighteen year-old himself when he was thrown into the den at City, he recognised the value of a comforting home-from-home.

The charming, reassuring presence of chief scout Joe Armstrong was responsible for bringing the best to him. He was a retired GPO officer, whose diplomacy was crucial to Matt's plan to harness best young talent in the country. He was the first line of seduction, winning over the parents of gifted youngsters. Matt once suggested that Armstrong 'has probably discovered more stars in the raw than anyone'. Such was the success of the youth policy that United were accused of having scouts in every village, although in fact they only had eight. 'I believe in quality not quantity,' Matt would say.

Paul Doherty

(Former journalist on the *Manchester Evening Chronicle*, now Controller of Sport at Granada TV.)

> *My father managed the Northern Ireland international team. He was quite a famous player, actually. He was a contemporary of Matt Busby's, though Busby was older. They both played, not at the same time but within a year or two, for Manchester City. The old man was a manager of places like Doncaster Rovers, who were then in the Second Division. At Doncaster he had one or two quite*

promising and famous – to be famous – players. Harry Gregg was the goalkeeper before Busby signed him for United, and they had a protégé, a fifteen-year-old at the time, Alick Jeffrey. He would have been outstanding, he was the sort of Duncan Edwards of the future, and Busby tried to get him. Somebody from Old Trafford went to see Jeffrey and his parents and lined him up to go to Man United. There was never any doubt in my mind from what I had heard that Manchester United would be as quick and as sharp as anyone in obtaining a player. The problem was, my father heard about it. So the old man went over to see Busby whom he always considered an honourable man and, so I am told, said to Matt that if he went ahead with this signing which was against the spirit of the relationship which they had, then he would not want to be involved with Matt Busby again in the future. I vividly recall Busby tore up the forms there and then. And Jeffrey stayed at Doncaster.

Matt could be ruthless when he wanted to be, or needed to be. That's how United managed virtually to own the FA Youth Cup when it was introduced, capturing the 'future stars' trophy for the first five years of its existence, from 1952 to 1957. The first two finals were against Wolves, and there are people in the Midlands – mostly supporters of Wolverhampton Wanderers – who have never forgiven Matt and United for snatching the pride of Dudley, the Midlands and England schoolboy, Duncan Edwards, in 1952.

Once Jimmy, Bert and Matt had witnessed his prodigious talent, after a fortuitous tip-off from his old friend Joe Mercer, there was only one team that was going to win his coveted signature. Matt had been talking to Mercer, then captain of Arsenal and currently taking the England schoolboys for training in Blackpool. It was a group bulging with talent – David Pegg, Roy Perry, Alec Farrall, Mark Jones, but one thirteen-year-old lad stood out. Matt had come to check on Farrall, but

Mercer marked his card. 'He's Manchester United-mad,' he told his wartime pal, referring to Edwards. By the time Joe Armstrong had worked on Edwards' parents and the management team had proved that United was a genuine family club, Matt's task was easy. He recalls the time in his autobiography: 'There was no need to "sell" United to big Duncan. As soon as I introduced myself, he said: "I think Manchester United is the greatest team in the world. I'd give anything to play for you." Edwards, one of the greatest footballers Britain ever produced, was stolen from under the nose of Matt's Wolves rival, Stan Cullis. United proved, time and again, that they were prepared to do that little bit extra, make that dive for the tape, to land the best.

Not that Matt was given to overblown promises or flattery. Another England schoolboy's parents could attest to that. David Pegg was spotted by northern scout Norman Scholes at the same time as Duncan Edwards. His father was a miner and, determined that his son wasn't to be taken for a ride, he met all the clubs interested in his young lad. Always the same question: 'What do you think of my son's prospects?' It would have been easy to promise the earth. Matt wasn't like that. With typical understatement, the United manager told him, 'With reasonable luck, your son will be successful as a professional footballer.' Pegg became a Red.

A measure of the operation's success is the fact that only four of the Busby Babes, were already on the books when the call went out to capture the cream of the nation's footballing youth. After Tommy Taylor had been bought in March 1953, not a penny would be expended in transfer fees until Harry Gregg was signed in 1957.

Charlie Mitten

We were local heroes – the people of Manchester loved us, and Matt. People used to give us presents, bales of cloth for suits, that kind of thing. It was like walking on air.

But it wasn't just jolliment all the time. We took our football really seriously. I've played with really good players round the world, I've played with di Stefano, but I never played with so many good players in one team.

There was no easy ride to a position of respect. the 1949–50 season, when they came fourth, had been disappointing in relation to the high standards United had set themselves by finishing second three seasons in a row. Such times in football are when a manager is under the most intense pressure (apart from when relegation looms), and when players' feet become itchy.

Charlie Mitten was an outstanding player, scoring fluently from the wing, but by 1950 the iniquities of the maximum wage were too great to bear, and when United toured the United States that summer, Mitten took the opportunity to extract from the game what he saw as a fair price for his bootwork. Soon after they arrived in New York, Mitten received a phone call from Neil Franklin. Stoke City and England's flying centre-half had been approached by FC Santa Fe de Bogotá in Colombia, offering terms far in excess of the £750 a year, including bonuses, that Mitten was making at United. 'I'd done all I could for Manchester United, we'd won everything we could, my contract had expired, so I thought, "The one thing we've not got is money." Ten pounds a week wasn't enough, not for a professional, anyway. So I went out and got a five grand signing-on fee and five grand salary. I said to the Boss at the end of the tour, "I'm going to have a look, Boss, and I'll come back and see you before I do anything." I liked it out there. It was palatial compared to what I was living in; a beautiful house, chauffeur, car. They hadn't joined FIFA then, that's why they could get the best players in the world without paying any transfer fees. The standard of football was good – Uruguay had just won the World Cup and we played them in Bogotá three weeks after in a friendly and beat them 3–1. We had great players like di Stefano and Hector Rial.'

For Matt, who perhaps recalled the wartime offer from 'Brazil Joe', it was an understandable temptation, although the loss of an outside-left he rated as one of United's greatest ever players was grievous indeed, and his authority had once again been undermined. 'He wasn't very pleased,' says Mitten, 'but he said jokingly to me, "Would they like a manager?" '

Matt had a quaint view of financial security sometimes. He thought players deserved bigger rewards for their talent, but disliked it if they acted to better themselves. David Miller's *Father of Football* biography cites an example. In 1956 Wilf McGuinness complained that two players of the same age were earning more than him. 'Son,' said Matt. 'Don't go chasing money. If you're good enough, you'll get it; same with publicity, anything.' It says a lot about Matt's approach to life.

When Mitten returned he was fined £250 by the FA and suspended for six months. Matt put him on the transfer list. 'He told me it was because of discipline,' Mitten says, 'but I think he'd have liked to have kept me. I said to him, "What if I don't want to be transferred?" and he said, "Well, you'll be in limbo then." ' Once again, Matt – and United – lost out for the 'sin' of remaining true to his principles.

Martin Edwards

Everybody had the idea that he was – not quite a soft touch – but almost. But inside the velvet glove was an iron fist. You don't get anywhere in life, particularly managing football clubs, without being hard at times, but he was always gentlemanly, and the players who worked for him always felt he was fair. If you're hard and fair, then that's acceptable. He was canny but with a soft exterior, and he had this aura about him. When players went in, to confront him they were almost lost before they went in, because they knew that here was this seemingly benign character who everyone respected. So it was very difficult to deal with him, and I think he knew how to play that as well,

*in the nicest possible way. The players never lost faith that
he would do his best for them.*

During the 1950–51 season, as United's form was still mediocre,
Matt felt it necessary to issue a statement, which in the light
of what followed now seems ridiculous. 'I am not resigning,'
he told the magazine *All Football*. 'I am not being sacked and
there is neither trouble nor panic in our camp. These rumours
seem to have started because we are not the glamour team we
used to be. Maybe we are not. You cannot stay on top all the
time and we had a longer run than usual . . . There is nothing
to panic about. Before long you will see Manchester United
back on top, beating the best.' He was right. United drew one
and won two more league games before the end of the season,
finishing second to Tottenham Hotspur.

But Matt knew his side was an aging one, however, and the
following November he gave debuts to two of the young lads
he'd been nurturing – the 21-year-old left-back, Roger Byrne,
and an eighteen-year-old half-back, Jackie Blanchflower, whose
footballing talent, unusually, came from his mother, who played
for a women's team. His brother, Danny, of course, who was
seven years older, would go on to win the double with Tottenham.

Jackie Blanchflower

(Belfast native who joined United in 1949 at sixteen and was
a genuine 'Busby Babe'. Retired after Munich disaster.)

*The first time I met Matt was at Victoria Station in Man-
chester in April 1949, when I was sixteen. I'd just come
on the boat train from Belfast. He took me to his house
and his wife made me breakfast, then he took me to look
at the ground, and fixed up digs for me. He had to sign as
my legal guardian in those days, and he was like a father,
a very kind, quiet man, who looked after us like we were*

his own. We remained friends after I gave up. That's what he was most of all, really, a friend you could go to and ask a favour. And you always knew that he would do what you wanted him to do for you.

The boys' debut was a goalless draw against Liverpool, after which the *Sunday Chronicle* reported that they were 'among the successes of the game . . . Blanchflower was always in the picture with telling passes and first-time tackling that did much to upset the smooth harmony between Payne and Liddell.'

On 26 April 1952 they played Arsenal in what was, arithmetically speaking, a title decider. Arsenal needed to beat United 7–0; and indeed, there were seven goals, but six of them came from United. Jack Rowley scored a hat-trick, Stan Pearson got a couple and Byrne scored what the *Dispatch* called 'one of the most brilliant goals of the season', latching on to a square ball at the end of a mesmerising Rowley dribble. United were champions. It was Matt's second taste of major success as a manager, but the nursery still hadn't been harvested. Later that year, Matt was to tell astonished shareholders, concerned about the antiquity of the team, 'No need to worry, we have £200,000 worth of players in youth and reserve teams.'

A return to the States that summer confirmed for Matt that although United had won the title, the best of his team had been seen. The transatlantic voyage on the *Queen Elizabeth* had another long-term significance, for it was there that the players first became aware of Louis Edwards. At dinner in the first-class restaurant one night, a bottle of champagne was sent to their table by the silver-haired businessman they'd affectionately come to dub 'Champagne Charlie'. He raised his glass in a toast.

Louis, who owned the butchers, Louis C. Edwards and Sons, with his brother Douglas, had been introduced to Matt a couple of years before by Tommy Appleby, a mutual friend who ran the Manchester Opera House. They quickly became firm friends, Louis becoming another bewitched by Matt's charming personality and warmth.

Martin Edwards

Matt and my father were great pals. They used to go out every Saturday night for a meal at the Bridge in Prestbury – they did that for many years. Being pals, with Father being chairman and Matt being manager, things would evolve – they chewed things over and they began to think alike. They were both very ambitious for the club, and father would bend over backwards to try to make United successful, and that suited Matt down to the ground, because he wanted the best players and the best team. So it was a very good relationship for Manchester United.

Berry and Byrne were playing at the start of the 1952–53 season, when United beat Newcastle 4–2 in the Charity Shield, and in December David Pegg made his debut, not long after his seventeenth birthday. An outside-left for England school-boys, like many of the fledglings, he was self-confident and assured. His debut, against Middlesbrough, was the start of a run of nineteen League games on the trot; up till then, the left-wing duties had been shared that season between Jack Rowley, Roger Byrne and Harry McShane (the father of *Lovejoy* star Ian McShane, he would later work as scout and announcer for the club). Although the transitional team finished a disappointing eighth that season, the most important activity at the club was the triumph in the inaugural FA Youth Cup against Stan Cullis's Wolves. In the side were Eddie Colman, Duncan Edwards, Billy Whelan, David Pegg and Albert Scanlon.

Wilf McGuinness

(Busby Babe, groomed by Matt as a coach and potential successor. Served as United manager in 1969–70 and was later appointed Youth Team coach.)

When I captained Manchester, Lancashire and England schoolboys, a lot of clubs were chasing me. With me in the England team were Jimmy Melia, who went to Liverpool, and Bobby Charlton. A lot of offers came in, but I saw United beat Wolves 7–1, with people like Eddie Colman, Duncan Edwards and David Pegg. Little Eddie had played for Salford Boys but he hadn't played for England Boys, and the way he was playing I thought, 'If they can improve him and make him play like that, what can they do for me, a schoolboy international?' Watching that team play, more than anything, made me want to join Matt Busby and Manchester United. My first impression of him was the lovely way he spoke, how gentle his voice was, the soft brogue. I met him first with my parents, and the way we were looked after was great; he seemed to know my family background, and whenever he was chatting with me after that he always mentioned my parents and my brother, Laurence.

There was a process of fairly rapid evolution going on, so that when the seniors bowed out of the Cup, only Rowley and Chilton were left from the 1948 Cup winners.

In March 1953 Matt demonstrated that although he preferred to develop his own youngsters, he was not afraid to splash out. On the day Stalin died he went to Barnsley and paid £29,999 for Tommy Taylor. More than a dozen clubs had been trying to secure his services, though he wasn't keen on leaving his home town. It was a record fee for United, the odd price coming about because Matt was reluctant to burden the 21-year-old with a £30,000 tag. The extra pound was passed over the desk. He was robust and immensely skilful, inclined to clumsiness on his off-days, but the sort of joker in the dressing-room that Matt always had a fondness for.

In another of his celebrated positional switches, Matt was to convert the goalscoring inside-left into an out-and-out centre-forward of dash and panache, who would go on to score 128 times for United in 189 games and hit the net sixteen times in nineteen outings for England. A statistical measure of his quality was his record in Europe for United: eleven goals in fourteen games.

The circumstances of Taylor's move also indicated Matt's sensitivity. Not just about the '£30,000 tag', but also in the fact that he deputed Johnny Carey to go and look at the Barnsley player at Leicester when his long-serving skipper's playing days were clearly over. 'Would you like to do a job for me?' Matt asked. Carey saw Taylor play and enthused wildly about him. 'Yes,' said Matt, supping on his pipe, 'that's the ninth good report I've heard about him.' Typical of Matt's management psychology: valuing your contribution, making you feel special, but gently reminding you that you're just part of a team, a cog that turns the wheel.

Paddy McGrath

Matt told me he'd sometimes go in at half-time and hear a carry-on in the dressing-room. He'd knock on the door before he went in, and he'd say 'OK, all right, let's forget that now, there's another half'. And at the end of the game he'd do the same – he'd stand outside the door and hear them fighting, and he'd go in and say, 'Right, finished now, go home, take your wives out, we'll discuss this on Monday'. He said that if you go steaming in it's useless – they know they've made a mistake, they know they've played badly. If you leave it till Monday, they've thought about it, they've talked to their wives, talked to their friends, they don't come in under the same pressure.

Sir Matt Busby

The next month, with Henry Cockburn injured, Duncan Edwards made his debut. At sixteen, he was 5ft 10in, and a hefty 12 st 6lb, with legs like tree trunks. At the end of the season Johnny Carey announced his retirement, at the age of 34. 'I don't feel capable of playing the brand of soccer for another season,' he said. Dignified and calm, he had been Matt's representative on the field in the nine different positions he filled at United. Roger Byrne stepped up to fill the captain's boots. Matt's second great team was taking shape.

Golden Apples

Bryon Butler

The time I remember Matt most vividly was when the game seemed to be dominated by two people: himself at Manchester United and Stan Cullis at Wolves. Matt, with his belief in 'the beautiful game', although it wasn't a phrase that was coined then, he was the artist, whereas Stan was the champion of the long ball and the technician to some extent. We had Matt with his lovely measured tones – his voice got deeper and deeper as the years went by – and Stan, who used to spit out his words. Players used to say that when he had a go at somebody he used to strip paint off a wall. They were such contrasts. Two different men and in a way they represented the two different faces of English football. I'm not saying that one is right and one is wrong. They were two rights in a way. That was proven by the success they had. But English football then really began and ended with Matt and Stan Cullis, two great men.

Especially in peacetime, a nation regards itself in terms of its performance on the world stage. Every four years we are reminded of the fact at the World Cup, and standing in the world league table is a source of shame or rapture depending on how representative teams acquit themselves against foreign opposition. The early 1950s were a dispiriting time for English

77

football, at least as far as their standing in the world game was concerned. The humiliation of a World Cup defeat at the hands of soccer novices United States in 1950 might have just been one of those things. However, the depth to which English football had slipped was demonstrated in 1953 and 1954 by the 6–3 and 7–1 demolitions at the hands of the Hungarians. While Prime Minister Macmillan was hailing a new age of prosperity, a wind of change was sweeping football. It was time of self-doubt for England: 'Outplayed, outpaced and outshot.' Colonials were pushing John Bull around on the world stage, and Magyars were teasing the bulldog on the pitch.

For Matt, though, the football played by the likes of Kovacs, Kocsis, Czibor, Puskas and Bozsik – 'his favourite, a cultured wing-half like himself', remembers Sandy Busby – was an inspiration. Lessons from eastern Europe weren't lost on him – not least the fact that Hungary were World Youth Champions in 1952. The *News Chronicle* had it about right: 'It's back to school for England . . . They taught us two lessons . . . 1. The value of positioning. 2 Accurate distribution of the ball.'

Floodlit friendlies against foreign competition became the fashion of the early fifties. In 1954, Moscow Spartak, Honved, Red Banner and Inter Milan were among those visiting Britain. Stan Cullis's League champions, Wolves, skippered by Billy Wright, defeated Racing Club of Buenos Aires, Maccabi of Tel Aviv and Spartak Moscow. Yet it was the defeat of Honved – Puskas, Bozsik et al. – that inspired Cullis. 'From a prestige point of view we have struck a great goal blow for English football,' he barked, played 'the good old British way'. The *Daily Mirror* crowed, 'Wolves . . . can rightly claim themselves club champions of the world.'

But not yet. The European Cup was still a year away, even if Matt Busby and Stan Cullis had realised its importance. For Matt, the dream had to begin at home. It was the right time for a risk. In October 1953 United were in Scotland for a friendly against Kilmarnock. Matt played a round of golf at Troon, turning the question over in his mind, and by the nineteenth he had decided to blood some youngsters. In the floodlit friendly, Henry Cockburn broke his jaw. This opened the way for Duncan Edwards, and in the next two League games, against Huddersfield and Arsenal, Edwards, Jackie Blanch-flower, Bill Foulkes, and Denis Viollet established themselves in the first team. These two games are often thought of as being the birth of the Busby Babes, but in fact Roger Byrne had been virtually ever-present since his debut two years before and Johnny Berry had established himself in the title season, while Tommy Taylor was already well into his stride. David Pegg had had a run in the first team, although he didn't establish himself until the autumn of 1955; the likes of Colman, Bent, Whelan, Charlton and McGuinness were yet to come.

Bill Foulkes

(Long-term member of United's team from 1957 to 1968. Big central defender who played in 1968 European Cup final.)

It was inevitable that when I became a coach myself I was strongly influenced by his ideas, his thinking. You had to win under Matt, but you also had to play well – that was what was most important. He'd say, 'If you play well, it'll all come together, but you must play, you must entertain.' He was a fatherly figure, always somebody I could go and talk to. He'd always listen to what you had to say, and if he could help you he would. He'd always give you good advice. I remember him mostly for how he handled the problems, how he dealt with the people. He could be a little authoritarian if you can call it that, but I think you have to be a great manager, and to me he's got to be the greatest manager ever. He wasn't a ruthless man at all, but he was very strong, and being strong he could also afford to be nice. But he was very, very determined; if he said something had to be done, he meant it and everybody had to do it. Otherwise you were out, and that's the way he

*had to work. But he was a wonderful human being. When
my mother died he was very helpful to me – he and Jean
really cared and helped. After the crash he must have felt
some responsibility, but I still believe it was a great
decision. He stood up against these bureaucrats. He had a
great vision of football – he was a very forward-thinking
man, always thinking ahead. He thought about Europe
long before anybody else in the country did. He was a real
leader, taking the responsibility. And his vision is now
reality.*

For the next two seasons Matt harvested all Jimmy's 'golden
apples', as he called them. The 'Busby Babes' moniker had
begun to stick, but Matt disliked it intensely – his task was to
turn boys into men, not 'babes'. As he had set out to do, Matt
had surrounded himself with a team full of character that had
grown up together and lived and breathed United. They were,
to all intents, his children. But babes they weren't.

The cornerstone of the team was Roger Byrne, who had
matured into a leader and a great full-back. Matt once said he
had never seen Stan Matthews or Tom Finney have a good
game against Roger. He read the game brilliantly and took the
whole field of play into his perspective, always knowing where
he should be. He would find the most telling pass and generally
found the target. Matt placed the biggest premium on good
midfielders, for with a couple of schemers in the centre, you
could control the game. 'Roger was more like a cricket captain,'
says Wilf McGuinness. 'He had a lot of authority and you did
what you were told. You used to have to knock at the dressing-
room door – you couldn't just walk in the first-team dressing-
room.'

The attrition rate in a team of perfectionists was high, as
McGuinness recalls. 'Matt once said to my wife, "I've got a
terrible job tomorrow. I've got to tell a lot of young lads they're
not going to make it for United, and I won't sleep tonight. I
hate it. But I always tell them that because they're not making

it with us, it doesn't mean they won't be professional footballers." '

For Sandy Busby, who often trained with the players, Roger's talents extended beyond his consummate skills on the pitch: 'I think he'd have been the next manager. At first he was a wild lad, a bit uncontrolled. He and my dad had one or two head-to-heads early on, and my dad would tell him, "You're on your way," but when he matured he appreciated what my dad was doing. During the last couple of years you could see my dad and him getting closer together, talking about the game, situations. Little Eddie Colman wasn't the greatest of trainers – he just wanted the ball. He was stationed at Catterick for his National Service, and if you were a footballer you were made a PTI instructor straight away. Now Eddie was just telling the lads to get on with it themselves, and he was getting a bit unfit, plus he liked his jar. One Sunday morning I was running round the pitch with him, and out comes Roger. He said, "Sandy d'you mind if I have a few words with Eddie?" So I dropped back and saw this tête-à-tête going on, then Roger ran back up the tunnel. Eddie's face was as red as a beetroot. I could see he was a bit upset, so I said, "What's up with you?" "He just had a right go at me," Eddie said. "If I don't buck my ideas up I'll be out of the team." I think my dad must have passed the message on and let Roger deal with it.'

Eddie, they said, could send the stand the wrong way with his shimmy. 'I've met a lot of people,' says Wilf McGuinness, 'but I've never met anyone with such a lovely personality as Eddie Colman. He was bubbling. When the Teddy Boy outfits came in, Eddie had one, drainpipe trousers, suede shoes with the crêpe soles, and he was a jiver. I never saw him lose his temper. On the pitch he was quick without looking it. He had a lovely body-swerve and jink, great control. He used to sell people amazing dummies.'

David Pegg was likened to Tom Finney on the left wing, while Albert Scanlon, his rival for the position, had a brasher style about him. Scanlon, Charlie Mitten's nephew, would survive Munich. Denis Viollet would go on to beat Jack Rowley's club scoring record, with 32 goals in 1959–60. He made his debut in April 1953, securing a regular place the following season. With his subtle touch and superb body-swerve, he and Tommy made the perfect pair.

Augmenting the attack was 'Billy' Whelan, who arrived from the Home Farm club in Dublin. 'What a great player Billy Whelan was,' says Wilf. 'He was slow, but he kept the ball brilliantly, and his goalscoring record for an inside forward was magnificent. He could dribble, keep the ball all day, score great goals. When we played in the Blue Stars youth tournament in Zurich for the first time, in 1954, when the World Cup was played in Switzerland, the Brazilians saw us play and wanted to take Billy back to Brazil. That's how talented he was. He was like a European Brazilian.'

Then there was Duncan Edwards. Matt once said of him, 'He is the greatest player of his age I have ever seen. Yet although he has soared up among the stars, his feet are still on the ground.' He'd been looking for a weakness, he told Jimmy, but he gave up. Murphy concurred. 'Duncan Edwards was head and shoulders above everyone else,' said Bobby Charlton. 'Jimmy Murphy told me, I've got a player called Duncan Edwards. He's got a great right foot, a great left foot, strong in the air, magnificent in the tackle, reads the game brilliantly, has a tremendous shot, and when I knock the rough edges off I'm gonna make him a decent player'.

Duncan could play as a deep-lying centre-half, or in midfield, and sometimes up front, play it short or zip off pinpoint 60–70 yard balls. One day Stan Pearson saw a strapping youngster lapping the track about a dozen times. When he asked Jimmy Murphy who he was, Jimmy told him he was the best player he had ever seen.

'It's easy to get carried away,' says Bill Foulkes, 'but Duncan had everything. He was powerful, technically as good as anyone, and he could read the game as if he'd been in the game 30 years, even when he was seventeen. He was a freak to be honest, mature beyond his years. He always behaved in the correct way – everything he did was correct. He'd obviously been well tutored when he was young. He was one of the boys, but he was also a gentleman, the model professional. 'I was understudy to Duncan Edwards, when you look at it,' says Wilf, 'and trying to get a game in his position was like trying to climb Everest twice in a day.'

McGuinness and Charlton were the two standouts in the second of the five successive FA Youth Cups in April. Bobby had come from Ashington, Northumberland, the nephew of Jackie Milburn. He had first come across Wilf when Manchester Boys had played East Northumberland Boys, when they were both fifteen. He had introduced himself to Wilf after the game, as Joe Armstrong had already made contact with them both after a tip-off from Bobby's headmaster.

Soon Bobby was in Manchester, living in digs at Mrs Watson's. He started school at Stretford Grammar, but as they insisted that he play for them on Saturday mornings, within three weeks he had started an apprenticeship as an engineer. He did that for two years, but it wasn't really necessary, for he was already a star in the making: all it needed was the close attentions of Jimmy, Matt and Bert to transform him into one of the best-known, most popular footballers in the world.

When asked how he set about creating a football team, Matt was fond of recalling the apocryphal words of the sculptor when asked how he turned a slab of stone into an elephant: 'He said, "Easy. I just knock off all the bits that don't look like an elephant." ' So the United elephant was beginning to take shape. While the first team was ticking over, the reserves and youth sides were winning everything in sight. Crowds of 15,000 were commonplace for reserve matches. 'We had a great reserve team,' remembers Shay Brennan. 'Mark Pearson, Alex Dawson, Johnny Giles, me at left-half, Wilf at right-half – one of the best teams I ever played in at Old Trafford – we'd regularly win games five or six. And in the youth team, when we played Chelsea in a semi-final we got 30,000 there and 30,000 back at Old Trafford.' For three summers in the early fifties, Jimmy and Bert took the youngsters to the Blue Stars tournament in Zurich, which they won for the first two seasons. These tournaments were an enormously beneficial part of the youngsters' education, familarising them with different systems and footballing philosophies. The third year they went, they lost 1–0 to a Genoa side who came out of their own half once during the match. Frustrating, certainly, but another building block in the Babes' education.

Sir Bobby Charlton

(Graduate of United's youth policy, survivor of Munich and star of both England's 1966 World Cup success and United's 1968 European Cup triumph.)

It was a really really lovely place to be. Sir Matt Busby, Jimmy Murphy, Bert Whalley threw everything into the game, everything into their club. Nothing else mattered. Not only a terrrific place to be but they had terrific players. They won the FA Youth Cup the first five years of it's existence and they were producing young players that went straight from the junior team, straight through the Central League team, straight into the first team. They very rarely bought a player; they used to grow their own. (The Busby Years, BBC Radio Collection)

By late October in the 1955–56 season, United were top of the table. Losing just once after New Year's Day, they took the title in swashbuckling style by a haughty eleven points. The average age of the team was 22. How good would they be with a bit of experience under their belts?

With three games to go, another post-war record crowd of 62,277 saw them play Blackpool, their closest rivals for the title. For Matt, however, the week of the game was overshadowed by the death of his mother-in-law. He drove up to the colliery village of Bothwellhaugh in Lanarkshire for the funeral. At the time he called missing the game the 'toughest decision' he had had to make in football. Earlier in the week, he had been in a car crash near Huddersfield with Jimmy and Bert. The car was wrecked; Matt and Jimmy had knee injuries and Bert suffered shock.

Harder decisions were to arise, not least how to let his son down easy. A keen footballer, Sandy had left school and was training and hanging out with the Manchester lads. When he was seventeen, Blackburn wanted to sign him. He asked his dad what he should do. Matt wasn't keen. 'Finish your apprenticeship first, son,' he advised. Sandy was as keen on becoming an electrical engineer as Matt was a Formula 1 racing driver and he said so, but Matt wouldn't have it. 'Why don't you go into it part-time?' he finally proffered. In the end Sandy played professionally for Blackburn for three years.

Though some commentators admire Matt's sensitive handling of a willing son who wasn't quite good enough to follow in dad's footsteps, Sandy feels differently. 'I don't think it was because he thought I couldn't make the grade. I just feel he thought that being a footballer was too precarious a career at that time,' he says. Whatever, it was further evidence of Matt's great, enduring compassion. He always saw the wood for the trees, the detail and the larger picture.

Bryon Butler

There was a great degree of privacy about the man. I think the thing which struck me most of all about him was his humanity. He was a man of parts. He was also a man with a common touch. Nobody in football was busier, but he always seemed to have time for people, and when you spoke with him, he made you the focus of his attention. He actually made you feel that you mattered to him.

Before the vital Blackpool match, Roger Byrne, according to

his captain's column in the *Manchester Evening News*, had never known the Old Trafford dressing-room so quiet before a match: 'One wit said, "Somebody has dropped a pin," so quiet was the room.'

In retrospect, it's easy to read such events as portents of the tragedy that lay ahead. But United had no reason to fear for their future while Matt was in charge: in the League campaigns since the war, they had finished second, second, second, fourth, second, first, eighth, fourth and fifth – the last three in a time of transition. Now they were champions again.

Wonderful Wonderful Life

Wilf McGuinness

I spent almost eighteen years at United, and I'm happy to be back there now hosting the sponsors on match days. It's in the blood. Anyone whos been there will tell you there's a place inside your heart, or your brain, that's United. The main reason I love the club so much is the Busby Babes. I grew up with them. They were my true pals – we took our first pints together in the night clubs, the first time we stayed in a hotel abroad we were together, the first time we won big trophies was together, we were growing up together. It was a wonderful, wonderful life. Whatever happened afterwards, I still had half of me at United wherever I went.

In later years, Matt would spend less time coaching, but in the fifties he was still occasionally the track-suit manager, joining in the five-a-sides. 'Any time he took notice of you, you felt ten feet tall,' says Shay Brennan. He had the same effect on Wilf McGuinness: 'We used to have a Tuesday practice game, and he'd come and see us. We didn't see a lot of him – he was often in a suit by then, but he did put his track suit on and come and join us, and when he did there was a buzz about the place and you wanted to show him how good you were. All of a sudden it was really competitive, really special. His presence was enough to get us all going.'

Bobby Charlton

He wasn't really what you'd call a football coach; he didn't teach you anything technical, but he always got the best out of his players. If you lost, you felt for him as much as yourself.

The United way of coaching did not come just from Matt. 'Jimmy had a big hand, and Bert Whalley,' says Wilf. 'Then when we were ready, Matt would take us and do his stuff and rub his magic on you. Tom Curry and Bill Inglis, in their white coats, told us what to do. A lap and ten sides warming up, a few exercises and stretches – "Walk the bottom, when you walk, walk briskly" – they had us marching along because Tosher [Curry] was that sort of guy. Bert Whalley was a gentleman, a lay preacher, he was gentle, he'd have a little bit of fun, he was never nasty with you. Whereas Jimmy would rip you apart if you did the wrong thing, and you had to be tough to take it. If you were soft you went under. People used to say he would make you or break you. I think you would make it yourself, but if you didn't have it he'd expose the flaws. He was a gentleman but he was hard: he made me cry as a young player, but I made sure I could prove him wrong, and I wouldn't give in until I'd showed him that I could do it, which was what he wanted.'

Hugh McIlvanney

I knew Matt well, and whenever we met up we usually had quite a chat. He was a very strong presence, but a very benign presence, which is a very endearing quality, especially in very strong personalities. He didn't have the slightest professional mistrust of journalists. It didn't occur to Matt to be excessively wary, because he trusted his own instincts and he trusted his own capacity to deal with people. He would only tell you what he wanted to tell you

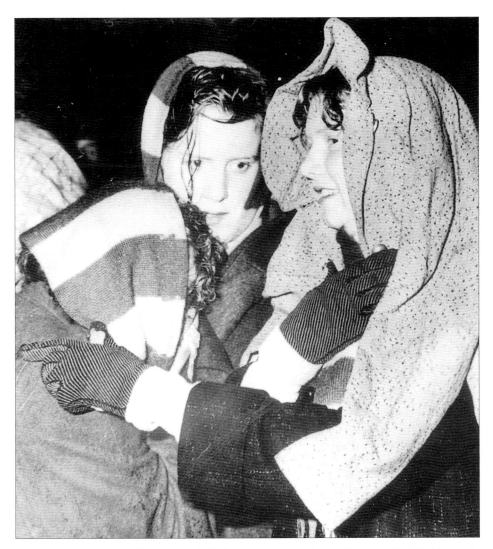

February 8th, 1959: Fans across the country hear the news of the Munich tragedy.

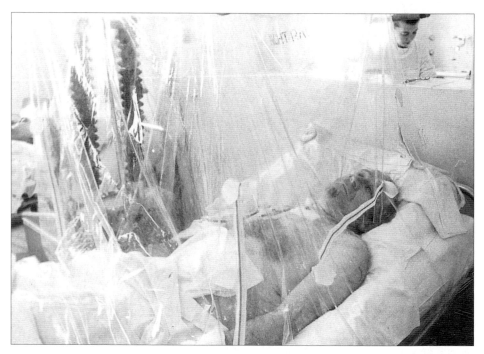

Sir Matt Busby lies seriously ill in a Munich hospital.

April 1958: A recovering Sir Matt enjoys some fresh air from a hospital window.

Matt leaves hospital on crutches.

Jean and Matt on the train home from Munich.

Matt on crutches makes his way home as young fans pay their respects.

Neighbours, photographers, and fans welcome Matt Busby home.

Sandy Busby leads his father to his seat as Matt attends his first match after Munich.

anyway. He was very contained when he wanted to be, but he was happier when he opened up and let the warmth of his nature come through. There was always a very tough man operating, not contrary to the benignity of his nature but in tandem with it. The warmth and kindness and genuine courtesy of the man, the fact that he had time for everybody, that he would go out of his way to do you a favour, all that had twice as much value in a sense, because you knew that this was not a fellow who was eternally soft. The way, when I was a young reporter, that he always used to come round the tea room and make sure I had a lift – that was entirely characteristic of him.

While Jimmy barked his exhortations and imprecations, Matt was the father-figure, embracing his family. 'Jimmy used to frighten me,' says Shay Brennan. 'Sometimes I suppose I looked scared, and he'd say, "The day I stop shouting is the day you start worrying." I got on great with him, though, and when I got in the first team we became drinking partners.' They made the perfect double act. 'Jimmy would never speak when the Boss was speaking, but he was the complete opposite,' says Harry Gregg. 'His team talk against AC Milan, in the European Cup semi-final, for example, when Matt wasn't there, was amazing: "The Italian bastards: I was here during the war, they shot your fathers and mothers!" I laugh when people say now how compatible they were, but if Matt hadn't come back from Munich, Jimmy would have started the Third World War. But he was a wonderfully gifted and intelligent football man, a very passionate man.'

Harry Gregg

To know a man properly, you have to cross that man, you've got to fall out, no matter who it is in life. I was a blue-eyed boy, so I saw that side of the Boss, when I was the 'Big Fella', and then I was the naughty boy, so I saw that side of him too. But I'm proud of the fact that he trusted me implicitly. When I managed, I took a lot of inspiration from him – I learned an awful lot from him. The finest thing I remember about Matt was this: I had qualified as a coach early on, and wanted to stay in the game, and I asked him one day, 'Boss, what do you think makes a good coach?' He took a couple of puffs from his pipe, and he said, 'A little bit of knowledge and a good personality.' Now I'm an old man myself, I know how true that is. I don't think he knew his qualities himself. He was really and truly, through all sorts of circumstances, always the same man, with the same face.

The team talks had the virtue of directness and simplicity. You play it simple – if you see a red shirt, give it to him; you don't carry the ball when you can pass. Time-honoured footballing virtues. 'And never once did he tell you to go out and kick a player,' says Shay Brennan. 'Sometimes you'd mistime a tackle and he'd have a go at you. And he'd talk to you individually. If I was playing, say, Cliffie Jones, he'd say, "You know what to do, play him inside," or "Keep him out on the touchline." His secret was that he brought in good players then let them get on with it.' The best players playing in their best positions – not a bad game-plan for someone who wasn't supposed to be a great tactician.

Wilf McGuinness

People say about Matt that all he used to tell you was to 'just go out and play'. He did tell you that, but we used to have a team talk on the Friday. He'd go through the opposition individually and we were always amazed how much he knew about them. He'd like tell us things like, 'The goalkeeper's left-handed, he kicks with his right foot,' or, 'He's better on his right side than his left, he doesn't like coming for crosses.' He'd go through the strengths

*and weaknesses of each player – strengths first, then weak-
nesses – then he'd go through our side individually and
tell us how he expected us to play. So on the Saturday he'd
come in and wouldn't have to say much, things like, 'We've
not been playing our football, we've been giving the ball
away, so let's play to feet,' or, 'It's going down one side all
the time, let's change the play,' simple things that everybody could understand. He might ask the centre-forward,
'How many attempts on goal have you had lately?' Or if
a defender was getting too clever he might say, 'It's not
like you to dribble with the ball. You know you're not a
dribbler, why don't you pass the ball? Your job is to stop
them and give it to someone who can dribble.' He was a
tactician. People say it was just things like man-management that made him a great manager. It was his football
brain that made him a great manager! He knew good
players, and how to get the best out of them. He did that
by keeping it simple. The hardest job in football is the
manager's job. Coaching is brilliant, you can have fun with
the players, you can have a whisky, but you can't do that
as a manager. There has to be that line. When I had my
twenty months, I could see what made him a great manager. He could handle the press, the media, players,
everybody.*

Matt was one of the first managers to recognise the importance
of the press to Manchester United's image, and therefore its
chances of attracting the best young players in the British Isles.

Paul Doherty

*My first encounter with Matt was a daunting thing. I came
to Manchester to work for the* Chronicle *as a cub sports
reporter and they told me to ghost Matt's weekly column.
The whole thing had a terror about it – writing articles for
the most famous manager in football. He was fatherly; he*

was also extremely kind and understanding with me. The vivid thing I remember about it is that very often Matt wasn't available. I used to sit down with some trepidation and concoct subjects around 'this is what he must think'. I'd to knock it together and put it in the post to him and more often than not we wouldn't hear back. But he never once said 'No, that's not right.' On the occasions I did go down and see him, he'd invite me into his office and would sit me down directly opposite him across his desk, where I would be in a chair which was obviously – whether intentional or not – a lower chair than his. You'd ask him loads of questions, he'd give you answers and you'd say, 'That would make a good story.' I would walk away from Old Trafford maybe an hour later, thinking that he had told me everything that was happening in the football world and that I knew the secrets of everybody and everything. Then I would get back to the office and analyse what he had told me, and in truth – and I'm not being unkind – he'd told me nothing. He was brilliant! He had the press of that day eating out of his hand. He manipulated us better than anybody I've ever seen.

'He used to say how good the press lads were when he was managing,' remembers Paddy McGrath. 'If they got on to something, he'd say to them, "Well, lads, you're on the right track, but don't come out with it yet, you might spoil what I'm doing. But I'll give you first bite." He wouldn't lie to them, and they never let him down.' It was only when Matt had no more bites to offer – on his relinquishing the management position – that the press turned to sharks. Until then, Matt and the press were a mutual appreciation society. Not that Matt was giving the press the whole story, for he was a professional, manipulating the papers in a way that few others of his day considered worthwhile. It was another aspect of the aura built about him, and he'd also use the press as an unknowing accomplice if necessary. When he was disciplining players, the final sentence would be a stern, 'Right, son, the fine is £200 and it's double if a word about this ever appears in a newspaper.' Denis Law was on the wrong end of Matt's ease with the press, as he recalled after Matt's death. 'Sir Matt did have a hard streak, and I was taught my lesson in some style. After a reasonably good season, I wasn't too happy with my wages at United, but being a coward, I couldn't bear the prospect of a face-to-face showdown with the Boss. I decided to write a letter demanding a pay rise or a transfer. I was holding the club to ransom and the Boss knew it. He didn't bat an eyelid but simply announced to the press that I was on the transfer list. He didn't even ask me to head back for talks. He called my bluff brilliantly. I had to back down, and when I returned to Old Trafford he invited me into his office and from his drawer pulled a written letter of apology from me to the club. I duly signed it. Sir Matt then let the press know I had climbed down, sent a letter of apology and that the matter was now closed.

'For public consumption his parting shot was that no individual was bigger than the club. The truth is that soon afterwards he pulled out of the same drawer another document: a new contract for me which included a pay rise. But the public never knew that he had given me a pay rise and I realised that the only way you could do business with Sir Matt was on his terms.'

Bryon Butler

He did mature over the years, becoming more of a humanitarian as the years went by. He was very focused early on. But when he was talking to reporters – I remember seeing this several times – if there was someone, perhaps a younger reporter or somebody on the fringe who he didn't recognise, he would always look over the top of everybody else and make a point of finding out who he was. I have seen young reporters grow five inches taller in about six minutes with Matt. Whether it was something he deliber-

93

ately acquired or whether it just came naturally to him, I don't know. It was a great knack. He was a great PR man – not only for himself but for the club and for football generally.

The lads on the groundstaff, like Shay Brennan, would train with the first team in the mornings, then perform their chores in the afternoon, cleaning the boots and the dressing-rooms. In the evenings, there was a city buzzing with life. 'We used to go to dances at the Plaza and Locarno, and the films – we had a free pass for the cinema, so we'd go two or three times a week,' says Shay. Occasionally they would get into trouble.

'Matt seemed to know everything that went on,' says Wilf. 'Sandy used to pal out with us, and he'd say, "My dad's found out where we were last night." He had us in many times saying, "I know where you were last night. The problem is, you might only have a couple of drinks, a lager and lime, but by the time it gets back to me it's five or six pints. So watch what you're doing." There were no fines or anything – it was just a quiet word, and with 99 per cent of us we'd make sure he wouldn't find out again. I'm not saying we didn't do it again, but we'd make sure it wasn't something that could be talked about or picked up on. So it did have an effect on us, and guided us in the right direction.'

Nobby Stiles suffered one or two of Matt's tellings-off: 'I was up in his office a few times when I was a kid, and he could be stern. You didn't mess about with him, but I think he liked a bit of devilment. He'd be telling you off, but he'd have a glint in his eye.'

Hugh McIlvanney

What the players feared was not his anger but his disapproval. In common with most of the great managers, Matt's way of exerting authority was mainly to persuade people that they wanted his approval. He'd embarrass you into behaving well, much like Jock Stein, whose first words to me used to be 'Have you phoned your mother?' and there was a lot of that in Matt. You felt you wanted to be shown in a very good light when you were with Matt. His wisdom came from an understanding of people, and there was no mistaking it. You could be standing beside Matt in a room where there was a film star, a cardinal or a king, and if Matt were there, you'd know who was special.

Jackie Blanchflower liked to head for the greyhound track: 'We weren't great gambling people, but we liked a game of cards, liked a drink or two, or three, but we were careful when we did it. Matt would always get to know where we'd been, and he would say, "I don't want you to go there," so we wouldn't. There were a couple of places that were a bit shady – when you've had a few drinks they all look the same.' One place that wasn't shady – it had Matt's imprimatur – was Paddy McGrath's Cromford Club. 'It was a respectable club,' says Jackie, whose wife sang there. 'The sort of place a man could go with his wife and not meet his girlfriend, if you know what I mean.'

For Matt, too, these were heady times. His friendship with Tommy Appleby, manager of the Manchester Opera House, brought him into contact with many of the celebrities who appeared in Manchester. As well as Marlene Dietrich, Tommy introduced him to Howard Keel (a lifelong friend), Maurice Chevalier, Laurence Olivier and Vivien Leigh, Max Bygraves, Leonard Bernstein, Peter Ustinov, Noel Coward. Tommy tells the story of how one young performer, who came to be a star in another field, almost joined Manchester United. It also serves to illustrate the kindness and consideration Matt extended to others as automatically as breathing,

'When *South Pacific* came to Manchester in 1950 for an eight-week season with a large male cast, one young man named Sean Connery raised a football team from the company. He asked if I could get some fixtures for them. I said I'd try and arrange games with Manchester Police, the Fire Brigade,

and the *Daily Herald*. I asked him where they intended playing, and what they were going to do for kit. It was obvious
they were going to buy their kit, which would have made a
large dent in their low wages, especially when they also had to
pay for their digs, so I told him to leave it with me, and went
to see Matt at Old Trafford. Without hesitation, he said they
could use the Cliff, with full use of all the facilities, and he lent
them a full set of United strip and boots. I saw their first game
and was so impressed with Sean's skill that I asked Matt to
come and take a peek at their next game, the upshot of which
saw him at Old Trafford in a try-out game with the United
players, culminating in Matt offering him a two-year contract.
Although he was flattered and honoured, Sean said he wanted
to proceed with his stage career. We all know of his success,
not on stage but on film, but he has never forgotten the kindness
and interest shown by a great man.'

Tommy Appleby MBE

(Close friend of Matt's and manager of the Manchester Opera
House, where he introduced Matt to Louis Edwards.)

*The football world rightly paid proud tribute to Sir Matt
for the greatness he brought to the game in every way. As
a friend of over 46 years' standing, I can pay homage to
his outlook on life away from football, all those fine qualities which showed him to be a good-living family man and
a credit to his church and faith. He liked a day at the
races, and he loved taking his family to the Opera House.
He took them to most of the opening nights, and I was
able to take them backstage and introduce them to the
artists and entertainers. I always knew that United were
well-known to many celebrities outside the UK, but one
day, when Marlene Dietrich was coming to the Opera
House for a week and I met her at Ringway, I was stag-
gered when she produced a photo of Matt and said in that*

inimitable voice of hers, 'Do you know this man?'. She explained that her daughter, who lived in Rome, was an ardent Man United fan, and had told her that she must meet Matt when she came to play the Opera House. It was a terrific first night, and I took Matt, together with Vi Carson, who played Ena Sharples in Coronation Street, *backstage to meet her. A lovely photo was taken of the three of them, Matt with one arm round Marlene and the other round Vi. I called them my half-back line, and the photo can be seen today in the Theatre Museum at Covent Garden. Matt, it was an honour and a pleasure to have your friendship for over 46 years, and the love and respect of your dear family. You will never be forgotten, not only in the worlds of football and the theatre, but by everybody who had the honour of knowing you.*

'Matt didn't like big occasions,' says Harry Gregg, 'and at big banquets and functions – of which there were many – he could be found in a room somewhere in the hotel with half a dozen of the players. I've seen him dance the conga, talking about the game. I remember him getting up to sing "Glasgow Belongs to Me" to a conga beat in Rotterdam. It was the first flight after Munich, at the end of the next season, and it was a wind-down job. As he was singing, we got up behind him, grabbed him round the waist and did the conga as he sang.'

Les Olive

Jean was a powerful presence at Old Trafford in her own right. It wasn't just a question of her support for Matt himself, as wife to husband. She also took a great interest in the young ones. In the early days, players were coming out of the forces, and in some cases hadn't lived in the Manchester area. Or you might get young players getting married, most of them living in houses owned by the club. Matt would want to make them feel welcome and at home, and Jean would do that, deal with any problems they had settling down. Like people with young families – she'd help them with everything, right down to where to get the best furniture or the best doctor to use. In the early days she was very much involved and if the wives had a request, say they wanted the house decorating, they would go to Jean and sow the seeds. At Munich she took charge of the wives and relatives who went out there. She had her own problems, of course – Matt wasn't expected to live after Munich – but she was still overseeing the rest of the party, sorting out hotel problems or money problems, smoothing the way and sorting things out. On match days she would be there to look after the visiting ladies. She was a very warm personality and she made them all very welcome. She liked to watch the game as well – I don't know if it was a case of if you can't beat them join them, but she was always here. She was a lovely hostess.

Jean played her part in making United a club to be part of, often taking the players' wives and girlfriends out, and on match days she lent the woman's touch, demonstrating that football need not be exclusively a man's world.

Charlie Mitten

If my mother was alive today she'd give Sir Matt and Lady Jean a good reference. On match days, Lady Jean always used to come and fetch my mam and bring her into the refreshment room for a cup of tea with all the wives, and my two lads would have a couple of apples, sandwiches and a flask of coffee, and they'd all sit there and have a chat like it was a picnic.

Into Europe

Bryon Butler

There is the story that comes up time and time again. The European Cup had started, and Chelsea said no – the Football League were frightened of the notion that it was cutting across their interests. Matt went down to the FA and saw Stan Rous and said 'Is there anything in the small print which actually precludes us from taking part?' And Stan said no. So Matt went ahead and made all the preparations and then presented it to the League as a fait accompli. *They couldn't do anything about it. In that sense it was his dream, his holy grail. Munich cut across the first; it was the second great team which managed it.*

The domestic title won, now was the time for Matt to test his footballing philosophy in the wider arena – Europe. In April 1955 the French sports paper, *L'Equipe*, had convened a meeting of sixteen leading European clubs, including the English champions, Chelsea, to discuss a Champions' Cup. Chelsea were keen to join up but were cowed into submission by the Football League, who saw such international relations as an unnecessary gimmick and intrusion into domestic fixtures. Matt, however, was having none of it. He persuaded the United board to accept the invitation: it would bring cash to pay for floodlights and the expanding wage bill, and it would provide extra competition to keep the huge number of first-team-calibre players happy. Most of all, it was a glorious challenge. There was nothing to discuss.

Anderlecht were the preliminary-round opponents. Matt went on a spying mission two days before the first leg, but a delayed flight meant that he saw only twenty minutes of their 5–1 conquest of Antwerp. The Belgian champions were unbeaten for nine months and had recently dispatched Arsenal in a friendly, so when Duncan Edwards pulled out on the eve of the game with an injured toe, there might have been reason for apprehension. But the 2–0 victory over a side containing six Belgian internationals was comprehensive enough, and Anderlecht's captain, Jeff Mermans, capped 57 times for his country, was impressed. 'I've never played against a team so adept at the best continental style of football. These United players have the craft of the Hungarians and the stamina of the Russians. It was an education to see the kind of football I never expected from an English side.'

The day after the game it was rumoured that the Football League would press United to withdraw if there was any danger of fixture congestion, but Matt was adamant: 'We intend to go on.' For the return leg at Maine Road a fortnight later (Old Trafford was still without floodlights), the Belgians made six changes, while Edwards reclaimed his place from Blanchflower. The *Manchester Evening News* greeted the Belgians on the day of the match: '*Soyez les bienvenus! – et que la meilleure équipe remporte la victoire!*' And victory did, indeed, go to the best team. At half-time United led 5–0, Tommy Taylor setting them off in the eighth minute. They had doubled the score by the end, Denis Viollet scoring four and Taylor a hat-trick. 'We have nothing to be ashamed of in being beaten by such a team,' Mermans said. 'They should pick this whole team for England.' In fact Billy Whelan was Irish, but his point was well made.

A 3–2 aggregate win over Borussia Dortmund saw them through to the quarter-finals, where they played Athletic Bilbao (whose hybrid name came about because the club was founded by ex-pat Britons). The flight to the Basque country was unsettling: rough weather following a refuelling stop in Bordeaux meant that the captain, Charles Riley, had to circle for twenty minutes in turbulent gale-force winds. Bilbao airport was actually closed, due to the weather, and United's plane was the only one to land that afternoon. Duncan Edwards was airsick. It had rained solidly for 48 hours, and United were 3–0 down at half-time. It ended 5–3, with Bilbao having secured their £200 win bonus. If United had prevailed, they would have received the statutory £3. The journey home began with players and officials helping to wipe snow off the wings, and on the way there was a hazardous landing and take-off at Jersey. United were becoming well versed in the perils of air travel.

By this stage, even the authorities were beginning to see that there might be a future in European club competition, and a few days before the second leg the League and FA announced talks to discuss a European Super League. They're still discussing it nearly 30 years later.

On the eve of the second leg, reporters and Old Trafford groundstaff stood mesmerised as the Spaniards went through a 45-minute ballet-style training session. This fancy continental stuff was truly foreign and reminiscent of the visit of Moscow Dynamo in 1945, when they had handed flowers to each of Chelsea's bemused players at Stamford Bridge. As Bilbao came off the pitch it was reported, dubiously, that 'a faint aroma of perfume lingered disconcertingly'. The next evening United treated the 70,000 crowd to a stunning display, dousing the fragrant Spaniards 3–0. Henry Rose, the *Daily Express* reporter who died at Munich a year and a day later, described it as 'the greatest victory in soccer history'.

England's Euro dreamers left the field to a massive ovation. 'They play with such passion we were overwhelmed,' Athletic's captain, Piru Gainza, said. Weeks before, Matt had applied to the Football League to pay special bonuses of £50 in recognition of his side's achievements. Unsuprisingly the vindictive League gave him short shrift. Always angling to keep his players happy, Matt made sure his boys did profit, however: the £3 bonus was augmented by a payment of £5 – because they were playing under floodlights.

The mighty Real Madrid were next, but before that there were domestic matters to attend to, as United were going for the treble of League, FA Cup and European Cup. In the League, United were four points clear by January and the title was never really in doubt. A 4–0 thrashing of Sunderland four games from the end of the season secured the first leg of the treble.

Altogether, United had scored 103 League goals, and would finish up with an astonishing 143 in the 57 games they played in all competitions. It bore testament to Matt's attacking style. Moreover, the 1955–58 team gives the lie to the idea that Matt was no tactician. Throughout this period United employed a 4-2-4 formation – wingers dropping back to help the midfield when necessary – before world champions Brazil made it fashionable. Matt also introduced the idea of playing defensively on the away stage of two-leg matches.

Irene Ramsden

He made that club. He had to fight to get into Europe. I don't think anybody at the club realised the enormity of playing in Europe or what it was like. I mean, they really enjoyed going on the trips. We used to have to shake the kit out on the laundry steps because it was caked in mud. It was awful. It had been in a heatwave and been in a bag all the way back. I think they've got more kit now than they know what to do with.

As the first leg of the European Cup semi-final approached, United reached the FA Cup final. But Madrid beckoned. There were 250,000 applications for tickets at the Bernabeu Stadium. Receipts were expected to be a world record £55,000 – only the 1950 World Cup final in front of 250,000 at the Maracana Stadium had come near to such colossal figures. Real had already won the inaugural Champions' Cup the year before, and the array of talent at their disposal was awe-inspiring. Matt had flown to Nice to see them win 3–2 in the quarters, so he knew what United had to contend with. When he was once asked which player he would most like to have signed for United, his reply was instantaneous: Alfredo di Stefano. He might have had trouble with the maximum wage, though, even if it was up to a princely £15 a week by then, for the Argentinian maestro was reputed to be on £300 or £350 a match for Real. A centre-forward hanging back, he had a uniquely strategical view of the game, combined with amazing stamina which allowed him to play flat out for 90 minutes. The combinations he worked with Gento (and Ferenc Puskas, when he joined the following year) were powerful weapons in Real's armoury. Add the skills of the little French winger, Raymond Kopa, plus the stubborn defence of Zarraga, Marquitos and Muñoz, and the Spaniards presented a formidable barrier to United's hopes of reaching the final.

In the week leading up to the tie, Granada bowed to a massive public outcry at their decision to show only highlights of the second leg, and announced that they would show the whole match live. A couple of days later it was announced that the Tatler News Theatre in Manchester would screen the FA Cup final live, too. Even 'little England' was catching European Cup fever.

A few days before the game in Madrid, a young wing-half shone for England Boys in a 2–0 win over Wales in front of 90,000 people at Wembley. His name was Nobby Stiles. He had been a United fanatic as a lad, his heroes had been the 1948 team, Johnny Carey, Stan Pearson, Jack Rowley, Henry Cockburn. When he joined, his idol would be Eddie Colman.

On the eve of the first leg in Madrid, Matt took the team to see Antonio and his Spanish Ballet. Playing in all red, 'Los Chicos' ('the lads') – as the Spanish press labelled them – lost the game despite Ray Wood's magnificent performance in goal. Real 'hacked, slashed, kicked and wrestled their way to a 3–1

103

victory', according to the *Daily Herald*. There was no disgrace in defeat. The referee, Leo Horn, said: 'The second goal of the Spanish side was the most beautiful moment I ever saw at a soccer ground', while a Madrid player said to Matt afterwards, 'If you came to manage us, we would win every trophy in the world.' Matt replied: 'If you gave me di Stefano and Rial, we could win every trophy in the world.'

A few days before the return leg, Matt made nine changes from the side that had beaten Sunderland to clinch the League title. United beat Burnley 2–0.

John Roberts

When Real Madrid came to play United for the first time, myself and some friends cycled from Stockport to Manchester Airport, which was a lot smaller than it is now of course, and we actually walked on to the tarmac, parked our bikes and waylaid di Stefano and got his autograph, which I framed. Matt Busby was there in his trademark trilby and his pipe, and I could see him waiting to greet the great Real. I'd go and stand on the Stretford End or the Warwick Road End. In those days the Stretford End wasn't the big deal it became – it was just another part of the ground. A few times I pretended to feel faint and I was passed over the heads and watched some of the great moments sitting with the St John Ambulance guys on the touchline. It was fascinating to watch 'the Tank', Duncan Edwards, run out with those massive thighs – whenever the team ran out you always saw Duncan Edwards' thighs first. And watching Real in their white uniforms, like snowflakes in the sun. It all seemed part of the rock 'n' roll era.

The second leg marked Old Trafford's first floodlit night in Europe, with 65,000 witnesses to another magnificent night for United. Profiting from a di Stefano backheel, Kopa slid the ball past Wood for the first goal, then Rial exploited an open goal to make it two. Behind 5–1 on aggregate, United came out fighting for the second half, and soon Billy Whelan snapped up a loose ball to give them hope. United attacked in waves and tempers flared. Near the end, when Torres fell to the ground, apparently pole-axed after colliding with David Pegg, red shirts pulled one way, towards the touchline, while white shirts tried to haul him back to his resting place on the pitch. United were rampant, and Alonso performed heroics to keep them out until Bobby Charlton, making his European debut in place of the injured Denis Viollet, equalised with five minutes to go. United were out of the Cup, but only at the hands of the greatest team in the world. United had departed the European Cup, but their appetite, and that of the British public, was whetted. Santiago Bernabeu recognising a team of kindred spirits, attempted to lure Matt to Spain. 'Their actual words were, "We'll make it heaven and earth for you", and I believed they would,' recalled Matt some years later. 'They were a tremendous club. I seriously thought about it for a week. But then I thought about Manchester. 'I came here as a seventeen–year-old boy. All my friends are here. I wrote back saying "Thank you, but for me heaven and earth are here." I've never regretted it. I shan't leave Manchester now.'

Later, Real also revealed an interest in Bobby Charlton. Their treasurer, Raimundo Saporta, asked him at Madrid airport, 'How would you like to play for Madrid, eh Bobby?'

Matt's view of Santiago Bernabeu's 'tremendous club' had been confirmed by United's experience during the first leg, when Real taught him the value of an unfailingly high standard of hospitality and courtesy to other clubs and managers. To Matt, Real Madrid was class personified.

The treble had gone, but there was still the first League and Cup double of the century to play for. On the morning of the Cup final, a beautiful spring day, Matt woke up never more sure of his side winning a match. But within minutes of the start, there was a mountain for United to climb in their 'unlucky' changed white strip. Ray Wood collected the ball and was preparing to kick it upfield, when Peter McParland charged into him, shattering his cheekbone. At first the collision appeared accidental, commentator Raymond Glendenning seeing it as 'just one of those things'. Substitutions were yet to be allowed.

'I now believe that Ray Wood was targeted, deliberately put out of the game,' says Bill Foulkes. 'It was the way it was done. I watched him, he went right for him, he head-butted him. It was too obvious because Ray had the ball in his hands for seconds before McParland came in. His head went straight into his face and he was out of the game. That cost us the Cup. Now I wasn't a dirty player – I'd go in hard, but I'd go for the ball. If that had been anywhere else but Wembley, I don't think MacParland would have lasted the game. My first reaction was "Right, you're going out of the game", but it was Wembley, so you had to restrain yourself. If it had been at Aston Villa he'd have got it. And what was worse, referees in those days were strict, but the ref didn't even speak to McParland.'

The *Daily Mirror*, always eager to praise, slow to chide Matt's team, asked afterwards, 'Why should a massed crowd, paying a rajah's ransom, be robbed of value for their tens of thousands of pounds?'

Jackie Blanchflower took over in goal, and United fought hard for a goalless first half, Ray Wood coming back on and playing on the right wing just to make up numbers. At half-time, Ted Dalton, the physiotherapist, took Wood to the back of the stadium and tested him with a few shots and throws, but could see no more than a couple of every six Ted sent down. He stayed on the wing after half-time, a concussed passenger. United had lost their balance and rhythm; McParland, ironically, scored twice. Tommy Taylor pulled one back, and in the dying minutes Wood went back in goal as United threw everything they had at the Villa goal. But it was not to be.

Tragedy

Matt Busby

I am a Catholic. I have always believed in an after-life, but what was an after-life to those lads? What power was it that could allow them to be destroyed? It had shaken my faith. I was very mixed up in the mind. I was absolutely certain that I would have no more to do with football. I didn't want to see anyone who had the remotest connection with the game. I was horrible to live with. (Talking to Ian Wooldridge, 1983)

Around Christmas the following season, United enjoyed a seven-game unbeaten run. They were back in the title race, playing well.

The Leicester game marked the debut of Harry Gregg, the 'Big Fella', as he would soon be known to Matt, who paid Doncaster Rovers £23,500 for him – then a record for a goalkeeper. Once again Matt demonstrated that when he did go into the transfer market he was prepared to be bold and resolute. The deal also exemplified the higher principles Matt applied compared to some other managers.

Harry Gregg

Sheffield Wednesday had come in for me, which was a great boost for a young player at a Second Division club.

They'd made an offer, which had been rejected, and then there were whispers that the great Manchester United wanted Harry Gregg, which was indeed an incredible boost. People say the crash made Manchester United famous, but that's not true; they were becoming known worldwide. Out of 40-odd players he'd only bought four, and I was one of the four. So the very fact that they were interested in me was unbelievable. I reported for training one morning and afterwards I was told to be back in the medical room for two o'clock, which I did – players in those days were more subservient than they are today. The physio, Jack Hudson, said to me, 'Go across to the far side of the ground, there'll be a turnstile open. Go through the turnstile and there'll be an estate car there. Get into the back and pull a rug over your head.' I did all that, then someone got into the car and I was driven to somewhere I'd never been before, the manager's house. I was taken inside and told, 'Manchester United want to sign you.' Peter Doherty said, 'We'd rather have you than the money, but you've got to have your chance,' and within five or ten minutes Matt and Jimmy arrived. Peter introduced me to them and said, 'The boy's ready to go, Matt.' And Matt said, 'No, I want to have a word with him. Do you want to join Manchester United?' he asked me. 'Yes,' I said, 'I do.' 'Well, before we go any further, young man, we don't pay any money,' meaning they didn't pay under the counter – it was quite clear, quite clean-cut. I said, 'Yes.' So the deal was struck, I travelled over the following morning by train, and was met at the station – in those days it was Piccadilly not London Road as they call it today by Jimmy Murphy, the Boss, Jackie Blanchflower and Jean, Jackie's wife. And so I joined the great and illustrious Busby Babes.

Gregg rapidly became aware of the resources at Matt's disposal: 'My first game was against Leicester City, and either that day or the following Saturday the reserves went to Barnsley and they had ten current internationals. For my debut he dropped Ray Wood, who'd played for England; he left out Jackie Blanchflower, Ireland's centre-half, and brought in Mark Jones; he left out Billy Whelan, the Republic of Ireland's inside-forward, and brought in a boy called Bobby Charlton; he left out "Digger" Berry and brought in Kenny Morgans; he dropped David Pegg, England's outside-left, and brought in Albert Scanlon.' Riches indeed.

Arthur Rowe

(Architect, as manager, of Tottenham's so-called push-and-rush team in 1949–55.)

I'm quite sure, knowing Matt Busby, that the style of play of Manchester is built on the knowledge that there are eleven players on each side and only one ball. That players without the ball have to get into the best positions they can to get the ball from the one that has it ... but I can't agree that Manchester play a more intricate way than Spurs. If you go through the 1957 team that won the League, you would have to work hard to find truly great players. Berry, Whelan, Tommy Taylor, Viollet and Pegg – they were very capable but they were playing to order and precision.

That month, Duncan Edwards was voted third greatest footballer in Europe by leading sportswriters. Only di Stefano and Billy Wright got more votes, with Tommy Taylor fifth.

In Europe, United had marched through the preliminary and first rounds, beating Shamrock Rovers 9–2 on aggregate and Dukla Prague 3–1 on aggregate. On 14 January 1958, they beat Red Star 2–1 at Old Trafford, with goals from Eddie and Bobby. Before the second leg in Belgrade, there followed two League games which underlined the fighting spirit and sheer inspiration of which they were capable. First, Bolton were dis-

posed of 7–2, and on 1 February they played Arsenal at Highbury in a match that drained the emotions of those who
witnessed it. Matt fielded the side that would play in Belgrade,
with Blanchflower, Pegg, Berry and Whelan all rested. Duncan
Edwards latched on to a Taylor pass and lashed the ball past
Jack Kelsey for United's first goal. Arsenal fought back, but
Scanlon ran the length of the field before crossing to Charlton,
who unleashed another unstoppable shot. Taylor made it 3–0,
and by half-time the game seemed won. With half an hour left,
however, David Herd, who was to join United three years later,
put one past Harry Gregg, and within two minutes Arsenal
were level, with goals from Jimmy Bloomfield and a magnificent
diving header from Gordon Nutt. A desperate, glorious battle
ensued, and though lesser teams might have pulled everyone
back in defence, United knew only one way. Scanlon and
Charlton combined for Denis Viollet to make it 4–3. They still
weren't finished, and Tommy Taylor scored his 112th goal for
United. It was his last. Still United attacked, and Derek Tapscott
penetrated their exhausted defence to make it 5–4. At the final
whistle players fell into each other's arms and spectators hugged
on the terraces. This was the last hurrah, on English soil at
least, for a team that lit up stadia wherever they went with
their joyous, uninhibited football.

Paddy McGrath

> *He used to say, 'There's only one way to play football, I
> don't care what the experts say, and that's four at the back,
> two in the midfield and four up front.' He said if you go
> one down there's great rejoicing, we've won the game.
> When you've got four forwards and the others joining in,
> you can easily pull a goal back. If they score two, you
> score three.*

Every catastrophe has its share of awful ironies and, in retrospect, ill portents. So stories of fate and fortune surround United's descent into the hell of Munich like a shroud.

In the last game before the trip, against Arsenal, it's said that Duncan Edwards crocked an opposition player. The injured Gunner was intent on wreaking revenge once he was up and running again, and as the game progressed chased Edwards with the clear intention of putting him out of the game. The Arsenal skipper, though, apparently stepped in and calmed his team-mate down. Had he not intervened, Edwards might have been on the treatment table on the Monday morning, rather than on the fateful aeroplane that afternoon.

Wilf McGuinness's name was actually on the team sheet to go. 'There was an injury doubt about Roger Byrne,' he recalls, 'but I twisted my knee on the Saturday in the reserve match against Wolves. I came off and my knee locked. I went in on the Sunday morning and they said, "it looks like a torn cartilage." '

When the United party left for Belgrade, an ominous pea-souper was there to see them off. Matt's stalwart pal, Paddy McGrath, might have been on the chartered flight. 'In those days a lot of the directors didn't bother going and Matt had some spare seats. He used to take me on the coach to matches sometimes, and he said to his wife, "I'm going to invite Big Paddy to Belgrade." My wife, Jean, was expecting at the time and Matt's Jean said, "You can't ask him to go, Jean's near her time, she won't like it." So he said, "All right, I'll not ask him."

Frank Swift, who was writing for the *News of the World*, was a big United supporter, or at least a big Busby supporter, the two having played together at Manchester City. When the *News of the World* wouldn't pay for him to go, Matt invited him to go with them.

So Frank Swift it was; Swifty, who'd been 'adopted' and coached by Matt as a youth at City; Swifty, who'd travelled 2,000 miles behind the lines in Italy with Matt's army team; Swifty, who'd saved Matt's penalty when the auld enemy triumphed at Hampden in 1945; Swifty, Matt's old friend.

Sir Matt Busby

Jimmy Murphy, Matt's lieutenant, was one who missed the flight. He was on duty at a Welsh international.

The party set off without a director amongst them. The night before the Arsenal game, one of the board George Whittaker, had died in his bed at the Russell Hotel, United's regular haunt in the capital. Louis Edwards, blocked from becoming a United director by Whittaker and a regular traveller with the team, stayed behind to attend the funeral. But Matt's friend, Willie Satinoff, whose family owned the Alligator clothing company in Manchester and who would almost certainly have become a United director in time, did make the trip. The week before, he had asked Matt to say a few words at the Liberal Jewish Synagogue, where Matt's subject was, ironically, 'Flying, football and the modern age'. He was in buoyant mood. Three days after the Belgrade game, Wolves were due to visit Old Trafford in a match that could land United the title for the third consecutive year – a post-war record.

The European Cup quarter-final second leg against Yugoslavian champions Red Star in grey, austere Belgrade was, with hindsight, a magnificent epitaph for the flamboyant 1958 team. Already 2–1 ahead from the home leg, the Reds went in at half-time 5–1 up. Bubbling Bobby Charlton's first of his brace was the pick of United's three. He picked up the ball 40 yards out, stole ten yards and unleashed the kind of thunderbolt that would become a familiar calling card wherever kids kick a ball around. (Twelve goals in eleven games since December now marked his introduction to the United team.) United were surely through to the next round. At half-time, Matt encouraged his lads, pointing out the Yugoslavs' frailties and rallying his troops around the United crest they wore on their jerseys. Perhaps he knew what was coming. In the second half, Red Star threw themselves forward stylishly and urgently, laying siege to Harry Gregg's goal and drawing level on the day with two minutes to go. But Gregg was magnificent, and United clung on to earn their place in the semis. It was another typically swashbuckling performance, mixing the gallant and the engaging, the gutsy and the glamorous. Tom Jackson, filing his report for the next day's *Manchester Evening News*, wrote: 'United will never have a tougher fight than this.' In a cruel twist, Jackson's prediction was printed in the same edition as the first reports of the crash that virtually obliterated the Manchester team.

'We felt we were good enough to win the European Cup, we really felt it,' says Bill Foulkes. It was a sentiment shared by Matt. The mood was ebullient, relaxed. The players, smart and generally well-behaved at the usual insistence of Matt – 'Youre not just representing Manchester United, but the city of Manchester as well' – endured a stone-faced ceremony and banquet, then happily unwound into the night. Matt reminded his players of the domestic challenge ahead on Saturday – his persuasive 'reminders' were generally more effective than strict curfews – then found a quiet room and enjoyed a few drinks with journalists and other non-combatants.

'Some of the boys went out to the British Embassy with the pilots, the stewardesses and the radio operator,' remembers Harry Gregg, 'and the rest of us played poker until about four or five in the morning. It was one of those nights when Mr Gregg was having a good time, skinning the school. Travelling to a "satellite" country in those days, as well as a suitcase of clothes, we were advised to take a suitcase with as much food as possible. So the landladies and wives had packed food for us, and halfway through the night we had a party with hard-boiled eggs, biscuits, and everything else they'd packed. It was a great evening. I went down the corridor and found [reporter] Henry Rose looking for the keyhole of his door, and I had to find it for him.'

The morning after the night before, the assembled company was muzzy-headed, keen to get home and prepare for the Wolves clash. But the return trip on 6 February began fitfully and remained so. 'We got to the airport and there was a very long delay,' recalls Harry Gregg. 'Digger Berry had lost his passport, and you didn't get out of there without it. So we went out of the hotel, turned out everybody's pockets – no luck. It was a huge, overbearing lady who handled the immigration, and eventually it was decided to unload the hold, were they found Johnny's passport in his suitcase. So we set off late.'

Captain James Thain was in command of the Elizabethan Class G-ALZU AS 57 'Lord Burghley' BEA charter flight. His friend, Captain Kenneth Rayment, was co-pilot. The plan was to make a refuelling stop at Munich and be back in Manchester early that evening. 'There were two card tables in the midships of the aircraft, a six-seater and a four-seater.' says Harry Gregg. 'The six-seater had five playing from the original school of six because I'd decided to take the Michael. I'd been getting a lot of pain and punishment – "Ah, Greggy, you miserable bastard, give us a chance to get our money back" – and I said, "No, I'm having a kip." So I sat two seats from the bulkhead on the four-seater side of the plane, looking diagonally across at the six-seater, one seat behind. I decided that when we landed at Munich and took off again I'd give them a chance to get their money back. I went down the plane, got a lot of pillows and cushions, stretched myself out in the two-seater, still getting pain and punishment from the lads. Bobby Charlton and David Pegg were across from me to start off with, and behind them was the wife of the diplomat from Yugoslavia, Mrs Lukic. They were tight against the bulkhead, and directly behind me was Peter Howard and Ted Hillyard. Everything went OK, we got away from Belgrade with no problems, though the visibility wasn't good. It was snowing over Munich, and we didn't realise where we were until we were nearly down on the ground.'

They were not due to disembark at Munich, as refuelling was going to take only twenty minutes, and by 2 p.m., with snow sheeting down in the bitter cold, they were ready to continue their journey, co-pilot Rayment taking over at the controls from Captain Thain. At 2.31, a message went to the control tower: '609 Zulu-Uniform is rolling', but as the 'Lord Burghley' attempted take-off, the engines sounded an uneven note and Captain Rayment abandoned the attempt. The problem was not unknown in Elizabethans. It was called 'boost surging', where a very rich mixture of fuel caused the engines to over-accelerate, especially at airports well above sea level, like Munich. The crew decided to have another try, letting the throttles out more slowly. At 2.34 permission was given for a second take-off attempt, but this, too, was aborted 40 seconds later. The 'Lord Burghley' taxied back to terminus.

Harry Gregg describes a scene typical of such occasions: a heady brew of trepidation, bravado, optimism and, most awfully, innocence. Little things would become dreadfully absurd and pointless in hindsight. 'We disembarked, went inside the airport, bought presents, cigarettes,' he remembers. 'I bought a packet of Players, gave one to Blanchflower, and the lads were saying we might go back overland via the Hook of Holland, having a good time with a few beers.'

Duncan Edwards sent a telegram to his landlady, Mrs Dorman, at Gorse Avenue in Stretford: 'ALL FLIGHTS CANCELLED – STOP – FLYING TOMORROW – STOP – DUNCAN.' Within five minutes, however, they were told to go back on the plane. 'Jackie Blanchflower knocked out his cigarette and put it behind his ear,' says Harry Gregg. 'The snow wasn't deep when we got on board, no more than footprint deep. We got back on. I got back in my place, and the lads started again – "Give us a chance you miserable swine" – and we set off down the runway. I knew there was something very wrong because the lad Cable, the steward who was killed, was strapped in the back seat. This time Bobby and David moved from where they'd been sitting opposite me, and Frank Taylor sat there, directly behind the school of five. Directly in front of me was Billy Foulkes, who wasn't as tall as I was, and I could see his head over the top of the seat. Kenny Morgans was playing with him at the same table – they were playing 'Find the Lady' or something – it wasn't a gambling school. I thought to myself, "If this thing belly-flops it'll jack his brains out," because above his head was the bulkhead, which held the wings on. So in my own simple Irish way, I decided I'd get down below the height of the back of the seat. I opened the front of my trousers and pulled my tie down. Again, there was no panic, but there was unease – more than unease from some people.'

Once more fate was to intervene in vicious fashion, as Harry Gregg recalls. 'I got down in my seat and we started off for the runway when there was a call to halt because someone was missing. It was Alf Clarke, of the *Manchester Evening Chronicle*, and he got a lot of stick from his colleagues as he got back on board. Roger Byrne was a very poor flier; Johnny Berry wasn't a great flier, and that was at the best of times. Looking across at the six-seater I saw poor Roger, his face was contorted with fear. I might have been a bit shaky – everyone was a bit shaky – but I laughed because I thought, "He's frightened," and sometimes you react strangely to other people's fear. Johnny Berry said, "We're all going to get f***ing killed here, what are you laughing at?" And Billy Whelan said, "Well, if anything happens, I'm ready to die." We set off again, and I watched snow coming off the wheels like a speedboat. This time we went past places I hadn't seen before, she started to lift, there was an unmerciful screech and bang, and everything went upside down, round and round, and it felt like something had cut the top of my head off.'

The 'Lord Burghley' careered and skidded off the runway, broke through a fence and went across a road. It was impossible to control: the left wing smashed into a house and along with part of the tail was wrenched off on impact; the cockpit struck a tree and the right side of the fuselage smashed a wooden hut containing a truck – by chance loaded with tyres and fuel, which exploded into a pungent fireball. It was a horrific scene as the mangled Elizabethan lay half buried in the icy sludge and mud. Harry Gregg's actions in the immediate aftermath are in the first order of heroism and humility.

'There was no screaming or shouting,' he says. 'It was pitch black, and it was daylight when we took off. I thought, "I'm dead, I'm in Hell." I'd been brought up on hellfire and brimstone and damnation. There was blood running down my face, and I was afraid to reach up in case the top of my head was gone. Then I saw bits of fire and daylight above me, and I thought, "I'm not dead." I reached out to unfasten my safety belt and found out I didn't have one – I found out later that my window was on its side, and I was partly on the ground.

'I crawled up a steep incline towards daylight, kicked the hole a bit bigger, looked down, and lying below me in the snow was Bert Whalley, who was dead but without a mark on him, lying just below me in the snow with his eyes wide open.

'I kicked my way out, got down on to the ground and realised that most of the plane was gone – no wings, no tail-end. It had broken off exactly at the wings. In the distance I could see five people running through the snow and Jim Thain came round the side of what was left of the cockpit. He had a little fire extinguisher, and he shouted out, "Run, you stupid bastard, run!"

'All I could hear was hissing, then I heard a child crying, and I shouted, "Come back, there's people alive in here!" but they carried on running and shouted back at me "Run!" and I screamed again, "Come back, you bastards, there's people alive in here!" I went back into the plane, stepped over one or two people who were badly knocked about, terrified of what I would find. I found the baby's carrycot that had been buried, and it was empty, then I scrambled towards the crying and found the child. I ran about 50 yards to the radio operator, Rogers, gave him the child, and turned and ran back, looked inside and found the child's mother. I physically kicked her through the hole. She had both legs broken and a fractured skull – it was incredible she lived. I tried to get Ray Wood out but I couldn't. Albert Scanlon's head was like a hard-boiled egg that had been cooked too long; he was bleeding from the ears, eyes, nose and he was starting to burn, but I couldn't get him. He made an excellent recovery later.

'I got out of the aircraft again and went round the back of what was left of the front section, and saw Bobby Charlton and Denis Viollet lying there. To me they were both dead – why I picked them up I don't know. I was a fairly strapping fellow, and I grabbed the two of them by their waistbands and trailed them through the snow a fair bit away. Bobby wasn't cut at all, but Denis had a very bad cut on his head and I left them for dead. The next person I found was the Boss. The part of the plane I came out of was about 30 or 40 yards away from where the rest of the plane had gone into the petrol dump. It was like a huge dart sticking into this house, and it kept exploding, exploding. Midway between the house and what was left of the nose, I got to the Boss. He was propped up on his elbows, with his feet straight out in front of him, one ankle turned completely the wrong way. He didn't look badly cut up – he had a small cut behind his right ear. He was moaning, "My chest, my legs." I straightened his foot, propped him up and talked to him, then made my way to two more people.

'Jackie Blanchflower was crying that he'd broken his back, but I don't think he realised that lying across his legs and midriff was Roger Byrne. Roger did not have a single mark on him, but he was dead. Jackie's right arm was hanging off, so I took my tie off and tied it round the top of his arm as a tourniquet. I tied it too tight and the tie broke. I looked up and saw one of the stewardesses had come back. She was standing there looking – she didn't know what day it was. I said, "Get me something to tie his arm with," and she just stood there looking at me. The plane kept exploding, and I said again, "For f***'s sake, will you get me something to tie his arm with?" I was able to stop the bleeding with half of my tie.

'Then people started to turn up with all sorts of things, coal wagons, Volkswagens, lorries. One guy turned up in a long tweed coat, with a medical bag and a hypodermic syringe. I was on my knees talking to Blanchie, and when there was another explosion, this guy fell on his backside. The biggest shock was seeing Bobby and Denis. I'd pulled them out for dead, and there they were standing looking at me. Billy Foulkes and myself were taken away with two bodies. One of them, I didn't know who it was, but found out later it was Johnny Berry, who also later recovered. We were taken to the Rechts der Isar hospital, where we met up with Peter Howard, Ted Hillyard, the crew, a Yugoslav journalist. Denis Viollet was taken to a ward, while the rest of us were put in a waiting room. Then I heard over the intercom that Frank Swift was dead. Now he was a real hero, everybody's hero, and the strange thing was that even though I'd seen death earlier on, touched it, to me Frank was the first one I knew was dead.

'We were kept there for a while, then those who were able to had to go and identify people in the corridor while they were working on them. They took me to a room to give me an injection, put me on the table and I got off. They gave me the first shot, and I said, "I'm not staying in here." Foulkesy was next, but I said, "You stay, I'm not." While we were walking down the corridor, the Yugoslav journalist, a huge man, suddenly collapsed. He'd been going about on a broken leg. They gave injections to Peter and Ted and Bobby, and when they gave Bobby his he fainted, so he was taken to the ward. Then we were taken to the Starhaus Hotel. The manager was more than kind – he gave me clothes, and put us on the top floor away from people. We spent the night there. I stood at the window watching the snow till it covered the cars below. Halfway through the night we had a call to say that the crew were going to eat. We decided to join them, and Jim Thain and I talked about what had happened. I said, "Jim, I saw the wheels lock and unlock twice." He said, "No you didn't," and I said, "Jim, I watched them lock and unlock." He told me about the final run, about V1 [Velocity One], the point of no return, when you have to lift the undercarriage and get off the ground. He said that point had been reached.'

Meanwhile, back home, news of the crash was coming in on the wire. Ironically, Manchester's evening papers, the *News* and *Chronicle*, were first to carry the story. The *Evening News* late final was chillingly splashed 'UNITED CUP XI: 28 DIE'. Although the eventual body count was less, it was only marginally so. Tomorrow the nation would be stunned; that first night, grief was a private affair for Mancunians.

Sir Matt Busby

Wilf McGuinness was enjoying a quiet day in the city centre on the day of the crash. 'I was with a friend of mine who worked on the distribution side for the *News Chronicle*, Joe Witherington. We'd had a bite to eat, it was late afternoon, and we were in Princess Street, going into Whitworth Street, and we saw a placard, "United in plane crash". I wasn't worried; I thought they'd had a bump on the runway or something. But we went to the *News Chronicle* offices and heard there were deaths. Nobody knew who, but I was in a state of shock. Then news of some survivors came through, but still no news of who'd died. My mother, a very religious woman, used to go to the Novena service, and I went with her when I got home, and all through the Novena I was crying and praying. I went down to Old Trafford the next day. Freddie Goodwin and Ian Greaves were there, but no other first-teamers. Nobody spoke. Then the week became a blur. We were told to come in on the Monday, and the weekend was just a fog.'

Jimmy Murphy had arrived back from Cardiff on the Thursday and took a taxi to Old Trafford. No one was around when he got to his office. He had a drink. When Matt's secretary, Alma George, broke the news to him, it didn't register at first, so she felt she had to tell him again. He started crying as it hit him; he went into his office and cried for twenty minutes.

Sandy spotted the placards on his way home from Blackburn Rovers, where he was a player. 'I thought it was just the papers building up a story, then it struck me that perhaps I'd better phone home. I went into the telephone box on the station and an aunt from Scotland, who happened to be staying with us, said, "Is that you Sandy? Get home straight away, get home son." So I jumped in a taxi and got home. My mother was in what I call a semi-coma. The house was getting more packed with friends and relations, then the news started coming though – there was no good news at first.

'The news about Frank Swift came through first, and who walks in the door but his wife, not knowing. All my mum was doing was staring into the fire. People were talking to her and

120

Sir Matt presented to the Lady Mayoress.

Sir Matt and Lady Jean at home.

Sir Matt Busby in 1961, watched by young United players.

A group of schoolboys meet Sir Matt, Derek Dougan and Bobby Charlton.

Bobby Charlton embraces Sir Matt with Jimmy Murphy and Jack Crompton after the '68 semi-final in Madrid.

Bobby Charlton and Sir Matt finally conquer Europe.

Matt encourages the team as extra-time approaches in the European Cup.

Time to celebrate: the European Cup is United's.

Sir Matt with his young fans.

A proud Busby family show off Sir Matt's knighthood.

Matt presenting the European Cup at the town hall.

Matt with the European Cup

she wasn't responding to anyone, not even Sheena and myself. Now I'm not the most religious fellow, but I was saying a prayer by the side of my bed when my uncle John came flying up the stairs, shouting "Sandy, Sandy, he's alive, he's alive!" '

What happened next is testament to Jean's indomitable spirit and incredible selflessness. She had faced the prospect of losing her greatest friend, the love of her life and the only man who completely understood her, but as soon as Matt was pronounced alive, she snapped out of her stupor and immediately sent her children, Sheena and Sandy, round to the houses of the ones who were known to have perished. Such generous acts were what the Busby dynasty was founded on, but never were they so vital as after the Munich disaster.

Paddy McGrath first heard about the accident at home the same afternoon. 'There was a lad who played for Manchester City called Roy Warhurst,' he recalls. 'He was a hard man, and he always used to give the United lads a rough time of it when he played against them, though he was a very nice lad off the field. My brother was at a reception at the Cromford, and he rang me about four or five o'clock and told me. He said, "Roy Warhurst's sat here, I've just had to get him a brandy, he's in such a state." So I phoned Monsignor Sewell, Matt's parish priest, and said, "What shall we do?" He said, "You pick me up and we'll go round to the house." Bill Ridding was there when we got to Kings Road. He'd played for United in the thirties, and for City, but by then he was managing Bolton. He was absolutely marvellous. He manned the phone as all the press lads were ringing from London to find out who'd been saved and who hadn't. Frank Swift's wife was there and his daughter and son-in-law, and Bill called me over and said, "Can you get Frank's wife away? He's been killed." Henry Rose was a pal of mine – he was the first man to christen me Paddy – he said Edward didn't go with McGrath. His girlfriend, Elise Nichols, was there, and although she didn't know he was dead yet, she kept saying, "I know my Henry's been killed." '

The next morning, the press reported 21 dead, including

seven players: Roger Byrne, who would have learned, had he returned, that his wife Joy was expecting a child and whose son would later be a ball-boy for United; Tommy Taylor, who had been planning to marry his fiancée, Carol; Geoff Bent, who left a young wife, Marion, and a baby, Karen; the dashing, handsome David Pegg; the devout Catholic Billy Whelan; the irrepressible 'little Napoleon' Eddie Colman; Mark Jones, who left a young wife, June, and young son, Gary. From the coaching staff, United lost the irreplaceable Bert Whalley and Tom Curry; club secretary Walter Crickmer, an old ally of Matt's also died; Willie Satinoff; and eight journalists, among them Alf Clarke of the *Manchester Evening Chronicle* (without whom the plane nearly took off), lovable rogue Henry Rose of the *Daily Express* – Matt's usual read – Don Davies of the *Manchester Guardian*, Frank Swift of the *News of the World* and Tom Jackson of the *Manchester Evening News*. One of the cabin crew and a supporter also died in the wreckage of the 'Lord Burghley'. Matt, Duncan Edwards, Johnny Berry and Captain Rayment were fighting for their lives. Like Duncan, Kenneth Rayment would succumb to his injuries, although Duncan clung on to precious life for fifteen days with the same superhuman strength that made him such a force on the field. Doctors said it was a simple lust for life that kept him alive so long. Admired even in dying, one of England's greatest footballers, the most brilliant of the 'Busby Babes', finally yielded to kidney failure.

Bryon Butler

I did several interviews with Matt, including a half-hour programme on Munich, and had long talks with him about it. Matt was asked the same questions so often. It became sadder and more poignant as the years went by. You would ask a question and he would pause and have a little 'mmm', as if he was thinking up new great thoughts about it. In fact, he'd done so many interviews with so many people about it, all the answers were pat. It was like pressing an internal start button and out it would come.

Johnny Berry and Jackie Blanchflower survived, but neither played again. Jackie wasn't able to leave the Rechts der Isar for three months: 'My pelvis was fractured and my kidneys had been squashed by the seat belt; every rib was broken, both arms and both legs. I tried training again, but I had a bad arm, which had metal gangrene in it, and I had a plaster on it for two years. I used to go to London and they'd sniff at it and say, "Come back in a couple of months." That eventually healed by it'self, but it's deformed. I had the option of having it locked at the elbow. Doing that restricts your movements, but you learn to live with these things – you start putting on ties with your left hand, and eating with your left hand, and holding glasses with your left hand.'

John Roberts

Some years after Munich, I wrote a book, The Team That Wouldn't Die, *and I interviewed Matt in detail. He was very co-operative and the club was very helpful. We sat in his office – he was then general manager – and he threw his mind back for me, remembering all the players, why he was attracted to signing them in the first place, their attributes, what they did for the team. The pain he felt came through. Inevitably, the full stop at the end of many sentences was that the person he was speaking about didn't exist any longer, that they'd been removed from life before they'd had a chance to come into their prime as footballers and human beings. Some people thought it was a mawkish idea, but I know from letters I received from some of the relatives that they were pleased that the memories were being preserved.*

As Matt lay under an oxygen tent on the fourth floor where

the most serious cases were, his chest smashed and lungs punctured, a priest administered the last rites – twice. The hospital issued a bland statement: 'We do not have much hope of saving him.' At least he was alive, and while he was, there was always the chance. Matt had always been a struggler, a tough man, no shirker of confrontation. Now, at 48, he faced the biggest challenge of his life.

Jimmy Murphy set aside his own grief and threw himself into action. United's League campaign was suspended and Wolves, originally United's next scheduled opponents, went on to win the title. Jimmy flew out to Munich the next day, along with wives and relatives. 'Jimmy asked Bill and me to stay another day,' says Harry Gregg. 'He wanted us to show our faces, to let the ones in hospital know there were people alive. I had to have some work done on my back, because I couldn't move it, I couldn't get out of bed. I went to the hospital to have an injection in it, and saw the survivors. Professor Maurer, Jimmy, Bill and myself went to every bed. Duncan said to Jimmy, "What time's kick-off?" Jimmy said, "Three o'clock son," and Duncan said, "Let's get stuck in." As the professor took us to Matt's bed, he said, "Strong man, 50–50; Duncan strong, 50–50; Frank Taylor, 50–50; Jackie Blanchflower, 50–50." Then he got to Johnny Berry, who was wired from every finger and toe, and said, "25–75, maybe better. But I'm not God." Matt was able to say a few words. "Take care of things for me, Jimmy."

Carrying On

AS JIMMY WAS FLYING out to Munich, the United board were meeting at a house in Cheshire. George Whittaker's death had left three directors: Alan Gibson, who hosted the gathering, Harold Hardman and William Petherbridge. Walter Crickmer's assistant, Les Olive, was appointed acting-secretary, a position that was soon made permanent, and the minutes recorded Louis Edwards' appointment as an additional director of 'the Company'. In his absence, Matt had gained another great ally at United, another strong man of character.

'It was Matt who'd introduced my father to Harold Hardman,' says Martin Edwards. 'He wanted to bring father on to the board because he was the right sort of material to be a director – he would bring new ideas to the club as a successful businessman.' Louis Edwards would, in time, become Matt's closest ally at United, encouraging him to spend as much money as was necessary to rebuild after Munich.

Les Olive

I was a very inexperienced club secretary, thrown into the job after the Munich accident, and Matt always found time to help me with advice and guidance. I could always rely on his wise counsel, which smoothed the way for me considerably, and I was proud to become part of his team off the field.

125

The weekend after the crash, sporting events worldwide bore silent, respectful witness to the team Matt had built and seen shattered. At football and rugby league grounds around the UK, crowds observed a minute's silence; at Bad Gastein, in Austria, 10,000 spectators at the European Ski Championships stood hushed while the floodlights were dimmed; a soccer crowd stood silent in Hyderabad; on the Sunday, football grounds all over Europe stood silent. Eintracht Frankfurt were due to play Arsenal in a friendly at Highbury; the team flew on two separate planes.

In the sort of dramatic and spontaneous public outpouring of grief that periodically grips football – Hillsborough, Bradford, Heysel – well-wishers came to terms in different ways with Munich and its repercussions. At the Plaza Ballroom in Manchester, managed by Jimmy Savile, people rained money on to the dance floor.

An appeal set up by the Lord Mayor of Manchester, Leslie Lever, swelled. At Stamford Boys' Secondary School in Ashton, two boys knocked on their headmaster's door and handed over £7 10s in pennies; the men and women of Strangeways Prison raised twelve guineas. As the city's mourning continued, the mood of atonement even reached industrial relations, two men who had been sacked for taking time off to attend Eddie Colman's funeral being reinstated by their bosses.

As well as a beloved black labrador retriever, crash victim Mark Jones possessed around 50 aviary birds. His wife, June, issued an appeal, and people rolled up in ones and twos at his house with cages to take them away. That wasn't all June Jones should be respected for. 'She made all the difference,' says Paddy McGrath. 'She said, "What about these girls, they've got no wages?" She saw that they got some money, and she took them all out to Munich.

Not everyone was so sensitive, though. In an odious incident that was to have a sickening echo at Matt's death – when a pallbearer took photos of Matt lying in state and was said to have removed locks of hair and name tags – Professor Maurer and the relatives of the hospitalised players complained bitterly of the intrusiveness of press photographers at the Rechts der Isar. Within hours of the crash, the 'gentlemen' of the British press were ratting round the wards snapping anyone they could find, no matter how poorly. 'On Saturday morning Mr Busby, who is seriously ill, asked me to save him from the photographers,' said Professor Maurer in a statement. 'He said, "The flashes are hurting my eyes." '

The hospital staff, under the direction of Professor Georg Maurer, were magnificent. The happenstance that Germans should be his salvation wasn't lost on Matt. 'Ironic, wasn't it, that until then Germans to me were Germans – the enemy, if you like. I'd joined up to fight them before the war began, I was called up the moment it started and was in it right through to 1945. And yet there they were saving my life and others; there was nothing they could have done that they didn't do. You learn as you grow older.' Matt was to maintain contact with Maurer and the German nurses for years after and, in a curious sort of homage to his lost family, observed every anniversary. The portly professor Maurer was present at Old Trafford for the Manchester Derby a year after the tragedy.

Jimmy eventually led Harry and Bill home from Munich. Air travel was never even mentioned. They journeyed by train, then a boat across the Channel. A Daimler took them from London to Manchester. 'It was a horrendous journey,' says Bill Foulkes. 'Every time the train braked I could feel it.'

Irene Ramsden

My sister and I polished all the coffins of those lovely boys when they came back. They were all put in the old gym before the parents came and we polished all of them so they looked as they should.

Throughout the weekend, ten bodies lay in state at Old Trafford. 'Jimmy took control,' says Wilf McGuinness. 'Gordon

Clayton and I were injured, so we stayed behind while Jimmy took the lads to Blackpool, and it was left to Gordon and I to go to all the funerals, to represent the playing side. Fortunately that's a fog now as well.'

It was to be a week lamentably filled with funerals: on Tuesday, Willie Satinoff and Henry Rose; on We'dnesday, Roger Byrne, Frank Swift, Eric Thompson, Archie Ledbrooke; on Thursday, Tommy Taylor, Geoff Bent, Bert Whalley, Tom Curry, Alf Clarke; on Friday, Eddie Colman, Walter Crickmer, Tom Jackson.

On 12 February, six days after the crash, Duncan's condition worsened. and an artificial kidney was rushed from Freiburg. In addition to severe shock, he had suffered chronic kidney damage, broken ribs, a pneumothorax, a broken pelvis, a smashed right thigh . . . As he underwent a six-hour operation, the players left in the hospital watched Milan play Borussia Dortmund in their quarter-final on television. The next day Duncan woke up, murmuring, 'Where am I?', and yelling, 'Goal, goal!' It was immensely distressing.

At least Matt was improving, though. He was well enough to have some scrambled egg and a glass of beer.

Matt Busby

To be honest, I suppose I wasn't sane. I was raving and creating hell with everyone. Why us? Was it some human error or had this been decreed from above? If so, why hadn't I died with them? What was so special about me that I'd survived?

At home, United asked local clubs to put forward the names of their most promising players to enable them to field the usual five teams. Ferenc Puskas and Zoltan Czibor were two of the more prestigious players who offered to play for United. It was a handsome gesture from Puskas, whom Matt had actually tried to buy in 1956 when the Hungarian uprising occurred, but the Football League still operated a ban on foreign players. For the most part, United would have to place their faith in untried, unproven players.

Reinforcements did arrive, however, like cavalry relieving a besieged fort. Jack Crompton returned from Luton as trainer/coach and 32-year-old Ernie Taylor arrived from Blackpool. Taylor might even have been on the 'Lord Burleigh'. 'I sometimes used to meet Ernie in a little pub in Blackpool and have a few jars and talk about football,' says Paddy McGrath. 'One day, just before Munich, he said to me, "I'm on the transfer list, and he'll let me go for £8,000." I asked where he was going and he said, "I'd like to go to United." I said I didn't think Matt needed anybody, but he said, "I'm not talking about the first team. I'll play in the reserves, bring those young lads on, and if he's got a vacancy in the first team I'll play, and if he puts me back in the reserves the week after I'll accept that. I think I could do the young lads a lot of good." So I had a word with Matt and he said, "That's marvellous – I'll have a word with Joe Swift tomorrow. How much are they asking?" "£8,000," I told him. As it happened, Joe Swift came on and offered him £12,000 for Colin Webster; Matt asked him about Ernie, and Joe offered him a straight swap, but Matt said, "You've offered him to someone else for £8,000." He said he'd deal with it when he got back from Belgrade. "You can tell Ernie it's on the cards." I told Ernie and he said, "I want to go now. I'd like to go Belgrade with them."'

Instead, Ernie was in the team thirteen days after the crash, a desolate We'dnesday night. Among the throng at the scoreboard end for that Sheffield Wednesday cup clash was Denis Law. He felt he had to be there as did nearly 60,000 others.

The match-day programme looked macabre: blank spaces were left where United's players should have been. The FA wasn't immune to sympathy and they had waived the Cup-tie rule, enabling players who had already turned out in the FA Cup that season to play for United. Thus Stan Crowther, was able to play, after dashing from Aston Villa to sign half an hour before kick-off. 'I didn't know some of the players I was playing with,' says Harry Gregg, along with Bill Foulkes the only Munich survivor to play that emotional first game. 'People talk about Shay, who became very well known, but I like to think of the ones who played in that first game, and the next, who didn't really make it at United after that – Bobby Harrop, Ian Greaves, little Mark Pearson. One of the sad things was that in football, and in journalism, there were people who were pushed into the footsteps of great people too soon, and it ruined them.'

Shay Brennan, making his debut at outside-left, was man of the match. 'I had no idea I was going to play,' he says, 'and I can say this now: the night before I went out with a friend of mine – I hadn't even been mentioned in the papers – and we had a few drinks. So when Jimmy called me to the hotel and said I was playing, I wished I hadn't been out the night before. But at least I didn't have time to get nervous.'

The twenty-year-old local lad scored twice as United ran out 3–0 winners. 'The first goal was sheer luck,' he says. 'It was from a corner, and all I wanted to do was make it look decent. It was a windy night, the goalkeeper made a bad mistake, and the wind caught the ball and sent it straight in the net. I certainly wasn't trying to put it in. But I was a hero.' Afterwards, in the dressing-room, Harry and Bill sat together, quietly.

Two days later, Duncan Edwards died in his sleep at 2.15 in the morning. His loss after such a long struggle was an even bigger blow for Matt. Edwards had been dialysed five times, but the damage to his kidneys was too great, and his circulation had been failing. 'Bulldozer with heart of gold' was the headline the following day. Wolves' and England's Billy Wright recalled the mighty power of the 21–year-old star, who could be devastating in whatever position Matt chose to switch him to in a match. England manager Walter Winterbottom knew more than most that the loss went beyond Old Trafford. 'He played with tremendous joy and his spirit stimulated the whole

England team,' he said the day Duncan died. 'It was in the character and the spirit of Duncan Edwards that I saw the true revival of British football.'

In Munich, Matt's condition was slowly improving, but the question of how to tell him about the deaths hung around the hospital like a black cloud. 'The doctors wanted him to get stronger before they told him anything in case depression set in,' says Sandy. 'One of the doctors asked my mother what she thought they should do, and she said, "When the time comes, I'll tell him." The time came when he asked my mother who was dead and who was alive, because he hadn't heard them talking about big Duncan, he hadn't heard them talking about Roger.'

Matt later recalled the moment himself. 'I had drifted in and out of consciousness for days. Something, when I was awake, told me there had been a terrible accident, but the nuns and doctors said nothing. Then I came to one day and Jean was there, leaning over me. She said nothing either. Jean has always been my strength. I said, "What happened?" She still said nothing. So I began to go through the names. She didn't speak at all. She didn't even look at me. When they were gone she just shook her head. Dead . . . dead . . . dead . . . dead . . . dead . . . dead . . . dead . . . dead.'

'When I went back out,' says Sandy, 'he still looked like an old, grey man, although some colour had come back. One side was completely smashed – ribs, bones, his foot. He came out of intensive care and was put into a room with a balcony. It was a beautiful day and the nurse said he should get some fresh air, so we moved the bed round, but as soon as we'd put it on to the balcony, he cried, "No, no, take me back in." He felt he was up in the air. I stood in front of the bed and told him it was all right, he was on the balcony, but he insisted on being taken back in again. Not long after that, though, I sensed that he'd got the football bug again, because he'd say things like, "They got a draw you know." ' Yet Matt's passion for the game he loved was hard to rekindle at first. He wanted nothing to do with football ever again.

The extraordinary groundswell of sympathy that engulfed United in those first weeks was captured by writer, Keith Dewhurst, who reported on the next FA Cup game, away to West Bromwich Albion. 'United stayed the night before the game in an old-fashioned hotel at Droitwich,' he wrote, years later in 1971. 'The bedrooms were full of massively gloomy furniture. David Meek and I were the two travelling reporters and we were a bit nervous, because it was the first time we'd been away with the club. All the same, we did not think it inappropriate when on the way to the match the radio on the team bus played 'The Ride of the Valkyries'. Outside the ground there were thousands of people with no hope of seeing the match, just milling about and staring. It was simply an occasion out of the normal run. United led 2–1 for much of the game and in the dramatic exchanges before West Brom's late equaliser the crowd surged more than once across the barriers. They did not know which side to applaud most. They certainly wanted neither to lose. They were moved and made brothers by the spectacle of mortality defying death and time.'

The match programme for the replay at Old Trafford carried a sad solemn tribute to Duncan. 'We who thrilled to his awe-inspiring demonstrations of seeming invincibility, coupled with a joy-of-living that infected his comrades whenever and wherever the going was tough, will always remember Duncan. Let the words of Robert Browning be his epitaph:

> One who never turned his back but marched breast
>   forward,
> Never doubted clouds would break,
> Never dreamed, though right were worsted, wrong would
>   triumph,
> Held we fall to rise, are baffled to fight better, Sleep to
>   wake.

Before the game, the crowd listened to a recording of Matt's voice: 'Ladies and gentlemen. I am speaking in the Isar Hospital in Munich, where I have been since the tragic accident of just over a month ago. You will be glad, I'm sure, to know that the remaining players here, and myself, are now considered out of danger, and this can be attributed to the wonderful treatment and attention given us by Professor Maurer and his wonderful staff, who are with you today as guests of the club.' (In May Professor Maurer was to go to Buckingham Palace to receive the CBE.)

United won only one more League game that season but the FA Cup had become a crusade, Jimmy's makeshift team making it through to the semi-finals where they beat Fulham 5–3 after a replay. They were back at Wembley again, just as skipper Roger Byrne had predicted the year before, although poignantly, he wasn't around to say 'told you so'. Billy Meredith sent a telegram, 'Wishing you and the boys every success.'

The accident investigator published his report. Captain Josef Reichel of the German Federal Aviation Board said there was no indication of engine failure. 'The first two [attempts] were broken off because the compression indicator wavered. The technical maintenance service of BEA explained this wavering by the altitude of the airport. Therefore the captain attempted a third take-off attempt. The fact that the aircraft did not rise off the ground at this attempt was probably due to icing on the upper sides of the wings.' Years later this analysis would be declared incorrect, and the slush on the runway would be blamed.

On the afternoon of 18 April, Matt arrived home by car with Jean. Thirty children and neighbours surrounded the sleek black Humber as it pulled up in Kings Road. Four workmen had left a bunch of flowers propped up against the green garage door and a supporter from Sale left two bunches of grapes. Always the courteous football ambassador, Matt got out of the car, acknowledged the well-wishers and addressed the reporters and photographers, 'Are you all right, lads? How have you been while I've been away?' As he struggled up the path on his crutches, Sheena ran out to meet him. Callers had brought bouquets; there were flowers from Joe Mercer, then manager of Sheffield United, and Ray Wood and his wife, Betty; a magnificent avenue of flowers lined the hallway and spilled on to the mulberry carpet of the living room.

Matt's convalescence was painful, physically and psychologically. 'He stayed at home in bed for a while,' says Sandy. 'The doctor called every day at the beginning, and I'd go and help my mum to dress and undress him because he still couldn't put his slippers on, or his dressing gown and pyjamas. But he was a quick healer, considering what he'd gone through.'

'A long time after he came home Matt was a sick man,' says Paddy McGrath. 'His nervous system had gone. When he saw me in the garden he came and put his arms round me and then he broke down.'

Matt was terrified at the thought of going back to the ground, but he forced himself.

Irene Ramsden

Whenever he made a speech, no matter where he was, he always thanked his laundry lassies. He always had time for you. When he came back from Munich the very first time, when he was on crutches, he went in one of the rooms and we saw him. There were such a lot of people around him we didn't like to intrude, but he spotted us and called us to him and gave us a kiss and a hug.

The staff gathered to hear a few words from the Boss in the medical room, but Matt broke down and was helped away; it was asking too much.

'I just looked at that empty field,' Matt later recalled, 'and in all my life I have never felt such a terrible vacuum. And so I cried, and afterwards I felt better for the tears and because I had forced myself to go back there. It was something I had to do, something I had conquered.'

'When Jimmy had taken the team to the Norbreck in Blackpool, Matt asked me to drive him there,' says Paddy, 'but on the way I had to stop the car a couple of times because he kept breaking down. For a long time after, what used to upset him was that he'd get Mark Jones's little lad or Roger Byrne's wife coming in, perhaps wanting the kids to be ball-boys, and he could see the fathers in the sons. It used to upset Jean, too. He'd had these boys as kids – they were only fourteen or fifteen years old when he got them. He once said to me that they would have done to football what the Harlem Globetrotters did to basketball. They'd have been too good for any normal competition – they'd have had to play exhibitions.'

With typical self-sufficiency, for the most part Matt was grimly, privately forebearing about the pain he felt. He might admit to Jean or Paddy that he'd had a bad day; they wouldn't discuss the crash. The boys, his beloved boys, he'd frequently talk about. For years he felt he could see them still in the shadows cast at Old Trafford, bubbly Eddie Colman, carefree Duncan Edwards, ebullient Tommy Taylor, tousle-haired David Pegg . . . locked in perpetuity as extraordinary talents only half fulfilled, half finished. Matt kept an album with pictures of them all. He had always bottled things up. His release was always either the escapism of the golf course or that of a night out and a singsong. His shoulders were big enough to handle others' problems; they had to be strong enough also to bear his own burdens.

Today it might be called post-traumatic stress disorder, or denial. For Matt, it was simply coping, the only way he knew how. The early loss of his father, the snatching of his own four tiny sons, a life peppered with hardship; all had been trial runs for moments like this. There were floods of tears, there was torment; there was terrible guilt and self-doubt. The quest for European glory had begun at his insistence – had his own ambition and egotism been the catalyst for this disaster? Why hadn't he intervened at Munich to abort the third take-off attempt? Why had he survived, he who had already lived a full and fruitful life, while the youngsters he'd reared, their lives still to be lived, had perished? The purposeful, immortal Boss, a man born to lead, who had rewarded his boys' fierce devotion with loyalty and prestige, for once lacked the answers.

Matt's return from the brink came about in typical fashion. He and Jean were sent away to Interlaken in Switzerland to escape the claustrophobic sorrow of Manchester. 'Towards the end of our stay there, Jean said to me casually, "You know all the lads would have wanted you to carry on." I thought about it for a few days and realised she was right. Women are so much stronger than we are.' The women of Bellshill cut their teeth on such calamities, and Jean Busby, Matt's nurse, his strength, his confidante, helped her man reclaim his purpose in life through her resoluteness.

Matt himself emerged a different person. He'd always been a tower of strength and reassurance, a rock, but after Munich there was a hint of melancholy ever-present in his eyes – except two special moments when the consummation of long-harboured dreams momentarily eradicated the trace of tragedy.

Physically Matt was no less wrecked, but as the figurehead of United and the public barometer of their recovery, he felt compelled to conceal his suffering. The crutches went at the earliest opportunity, then the stick. He would run downstairs and force the crushed foot – as Gregg remembered it, turned back on itself by the impact at Munich – into a boot for a kick about with his players. 'It's his wonderful spirit,' noted Jean. 'He has this tremendous determination to get better, completely better, again.'

The Bishop of Chester's words eleven days after the crash were to provide succour for his spiritual wounds too: 'There is a responsibility laid on these young players, professionals, who are watched by over a million people each week, admired, glamorised, idolised, imitated. They set a standard which, unseen perhaps, unquestionably leaves a mark on the whole moral standards of our society . . . the ultimate discharge of any team like Man United is a duty to become a byword for those who play a good game wherever in the world football is played.'

Matt Busby

I'm not saying I'm the greatest Christian who ever lived, but I attend to my duties and go to Mass and confession, and the Church is a great solace to me. I want to be, and try to be, a better man than I was before the crash, but I don't think I am.

Matt was just well enough to go to Wembley, against Professor Maurer's advice. Jimmy led out the team, all wearing badges depicting the phoenix rising from the ashes, a symbol of the club's determination to realise the words of Harold Hardman in the Sheffield Wednesday match programme. 'Just go out and follow Jimmy's instructions,' Matt told the team. After three minutes, Nat Lofthouse pounced and Bolton were one up. United were playing as individuals, not a team – a family. Ten minutes into the second half came the moment for which the 1958 final will be remembered. Twelve months earlier, the challenge on Ray Wood had dictated the course of the match, and as Harry Gregg jumped for a high ball and seemed to have gathered it, in came Lofthouse to bundle both ball and goalie over the line.

The goal would never stand today, when even a hostile look at a keeper seems to warrant a caution, but on this occasion the referee pointed to the centre spot. It was another opportunity for commentator Raymond Glendenning to roll out his favourite expression for United's calamitous Wembley appearances: 'Just one of those things . . .'

Like most of the players, though, Harry Gregg found a solace of sorts. 'The football had helped me keep my sanity. The more I could get involved, the quicker I could put the crash out of my mind. But after Munich everything was an anticlimax, even shaking hands with His Royal Highness, which should have been an honour and a delight.'

The team returned to Manchester without the Cup, but with something more precious – a strange kind of glory. 'We came in from the station and I've never seen so many people,' remembers Bill Foulkes. 'They all seemed to be crying. We were on top of the bus, and I thought, "I can't stand any more of this." In Albert Square it seemed like a million people just standing there, not moving, no noise. As captain I had to get up and say a few words, but after that I had to get away.'

Bill Foulkes

After the crash I was captain until the end of the season, but I asked Matt to let me relinquish the captaincy the next season. At first he wanted me to carry on, but I told him it was taking too much out of me. He saw that it was, and said, 'All right, have a good rest. Come out of the team as well, go off to Harlech, play a bit of golf.' But I couldn't; I played a round then I was back. He said he'd play me in the reserves: 'Why don't you play centre-half?' He was the shrewdest man I ever met – he'd remembered I'd played centre-half before. He said, 'Just feel your way around,' and a few games later he played me at number five, where I stayed till I finished.

Incredibly, there was still the European Cup to play for, and on the Wednesday after the Cup final, United beat AC Milan 2–1 in the first leg of the semi. In their wisdom, the FA had insisted that Bobby Charlton, who by now was carrying most of the hopes of the club on his young shoulders, would have to miss the game, as he had to play for England the day before in a friendly against Portugal.

There was no question of flying to Italy for the return leg, and the next day the team took the train to London. They stayed the night there, crossed from Dover to Calais and endured an eighteen-hour journey to Milan. Matt did not make the trip and neither did Bobby, as he was required to fly with the England party to Belgrade for another World Cup warm-up match.

United reached Milan without any balls for practice. It had been Jack Crompton's view that the poor display at Wembley was down to too much training with balls. The players protested and John Charles, the first major UK soccer export at Juventus, provided them with an Italian match ball to practice with. Though they lost 4–0 to Milan and crashed out of a tournament they were tipped to win, United produced a feistier display than they had in the Cup final.

Matt Busby

There were many difficulties to overcome, but the hardest thing of all was coming round to flying again. For a few matches after Munich we went abroad by sea and train, but obviously that couldn't go on for too long. We all had to deal with it in our different ways. For myself, I arrived at Old Trafford one morning and had a talk with our chairman, Louis Edwards. I said, 'Could you give me a hand?' We drove to the airport and, I must say, drank a lot of Scotches. Then we bought two returns to Rotterdam. And flying has been no problem for me ever since.

Yet Matt was still sick to his soul and Jimmy's heart was broken. Though the cream of their young team had been destroyed, Matt was committed to one last pitch at his life's ambition. Find the right sort of men, create the right atmosphere and the football would flow . . . there was time for one last heave for the ultimate goal.

The month after the Milan game, Matt was appointed CBE. He was a prophet with honour. The brutality of the crash had helped, in an unexpected way, to transform Manchester United,

Matt Busby and his achievements before and after into the objects of worldwide admiration. God knows, it was not how Matt intended, but Munich was ultimately life-affirming.

Jimmy Murphy

(Matt's assistant from 1946, hired after a chance meeting. Assumed temporary control of the team in the aftermath of Munich. Manager of the 1958 Welsh World Cup team. Died in 1968, having made a vital contribution to United's success.)

People wonder why I've turned down top jobs to stay with Matt, but our association is founded on mutual respect. Matt respects everybody with whom he has dealings, all the way down from the boardroom to ground and laundry staff. That is just one of his qualities. The others include wonderful intuition and extreme patience. His foresight was proved when he led English clubs into Europe and when he broke up the 1948 side to give youth a fling. My greatest reward was at Wembley in 1958, when the Boss came back from Munich, still a sick man. He said, 'Thank you Jimmy, you've done a wonderful job. I'm proud of you.'

Reconstruction

Matt Busby

Going away isn't escaping you know. I've never come to terms with what happened. I never will. Time isn't the great healer. There hasn't been a single day in the last 25 years that I haven't thought of them. (Talking on the eve of the 25th anniversary)

It's frequently been suggested that Matt inherited a team, raised a team and bought a team, but in truth there were four great teams during Matt's reign: those of 1948, 1957, 1963 and 1968. In 1958, a nucleus of the 1957 first-team survivors remained: Bobby Charlton, Bill Foulkes, Harry Gregg and Denis Viollet. Just as when he assumed control at a bombed-out Old Trafford in 1945, the pragmatist in Matt knew his 'grow your own' policy would take too long. This time he would have to buy his family. At least he knew that Louis Edwards and Harold Hardman would back him on that point.

The days when a whole team could be secured for a princely £10 were long gone. This was a Football League populated by players who wanted to be rewarded for their talent. They were products of the rock 'n' roll years, 'angry young men' and wild ones, in the years of teenage rebellion and social change. The compliant, even servile, soccer player was becoming a thing of the past. In 1961 the maximum wage was abolished, bringing a free market to soccer; clubs and players could carve out their own deals. Matt's aura still charged the atmosphere of Old Trafford for the juniors at the club – and there was plenty of promise still there, though some had to be bloodied before they were really ready. The players Matt and Jimmy bought over the next few years to rebuild their shattered team were men of that age and disposition. There was a new mood in the game as a whole, and new heroes arose who were discontented with the old platitudes that the British way was the only way to play and that, like our policemen, our beer and our cars, our football was the best in the world.

At times, Matt and Jimmy's methods seemed archaic. United under Matt had always played with a style that liberated the individual player's skill, Matt's team talks often consisting of a simple 'Go out and enjoy it, son', 'fizz it around', or 'win the ball and get it to Bobby'. But this was a scientific age, in which Harold Wilson would shortly win an election on the back of a pledge to harness 'the white heat of technology'.

Britain wanted progress, and through the tactical awareness of managers like Jock Stein, Bill Shankly, Joe Mercer, Malcolm Allison, Tommy Docherty and Don Revie, it was being delivered. For the first time the Boss faced players who were their own men, with their own ideas about how the game should be played. Matt had once been an innovator, redefining the role of team manager, breaking down barriers between himself and players, taking English club football into Europe for the first time, unfettering the classic English wing play with a 4-2-4 formation; he also adopted the innately Italian technique of defending on away legs of two-leg matches in Europe, and, to a lesser extent, the League. Matt remained a forward thinker and philosopher about the game he adored after Munich and into the seventies, but his ideas now were largely administrative, strategic.

He even admitted himself that the crash made him more lenient in his treatment of players. 'I was never soft before, you know. I may have looked it but if players were naughty, I could be twice as naughty with them.' He was still the Boss, though.

Irene Ramsden

There was a rest room built for the youngsters to go in for the afternoons and have a game of cards or whatever, but no gambling was allowed. Matt never used to go in there in the afternoons, but one day he did and of course the money was on the table. He just put his foot under the table and kicked it up in the air. He really kept the youngsters in line.

The plane crash injuries and the psychological scars kept Matt on the sidelines of the training sessions. He had always maintained an aloof air, but for the first time the original track-suit manager was largely confined to the office these days, pulling all the strings from behind his desk. Jimmy Murphy, another feeling his age, was less concerned with the senior players too. Jack Crompton, Johnny Aston and, after his enforced retirement through injury in 1959, Wilf McGuinness filled the gap. Crompton, feeling there was too much emphasis on ball skills and not enough fitness training, introduced weights and other muscle toning devices. Johnny Aston, father of the lad who signed apprentice forms in 1962, left his sports shop in Clayton to become youth team coach, while Wilf and Jack became the day-to-day inspiration to the players. They would report all the goings-on to the Boss, but it wasn't quite the same.

Matt was forced to give up his tutelage of the Scottish national side. It was an honour also accorded Jimmy Murphy, who coached the Welsh team, and both went to the Sweden World Cup in June 1958 for more proof of the fallibility of the British game. (England and Scotland departed after the first stage, but Wales, under Jimmy, lost 1–0 in a quarter-final to the eventual winners, the brilliant Brazilians.) Matt was at least able to enjoy the performances in the early rounds of his beloved Hungarians, the Argentinians and Brazil's awesome Garrincha. A young fellow called Pele also caught his eye. Meanwhile, his coaching of the Scots was to have a more practical application, for he witnessed at first hand the quality of a player who was to become one of his finest purchases: Denis Law.

Bryon Butler

He got inside players. It was a natural thing. Probably one of the great arts of management is getting players to play for you because they want to play for you. That's to a great degree tied up with respect. People did have respect for Matt. Some managers lead, some managers push, some managers whip, some managers demand. Matt managed to get the best out of people in another way. Not that he couldn't drive, not that he couldn't command; all these things he could do, but he drew the best out of players in the best possible way.

In September 1958, the rebuilding process began when Albert Quixall was signed from Sheffield Wednesday for £45,000 – a British record, which showed that if the frugal Matt wasn't used to splashing the cash, he was a quick learner. Maurice Setters would follow, and David Herd, Noel Cantwell, Tony Dunne, Denis Law and Paddy Crerand. The 1957 team, who came so close to the League and Cup double, sported three bought-in players; the 1963 Cup winners featured seven.

Noel Cantwell

(Genial Irishman and mainstay of the early sixties team, eventually became coach at United.)

I enjoyed Matt's company a lot. My first recollection was after signing from West Ham, when I was in his car and asked him, 'How do we play?' He was amazed. 'I just paid £30,000 for you. "How do we play?" We play football.'

At Matt's United you blended in. You were a footballer, and that was it.

Quixall was firmly in that United tradition established by Busby; there was an air of glamour about him. Young, blond and handsome, he played with panache and verve. His penchant for the unorthodox, instinctive variation made him Matt's kind of player – a player in Matt's image, in fact. At 25, he was old enough to guide the raw kids thrust forward before their time. Ernie Taylor and the querulous Stan Crowther had done their job, but Matt needed a younger man to inspire the youngsters. Quixall came expensive and proved his worth only after a debut season which produced just four goals in 33 appearances, but he played for United until 1964, scoring 56 goals from inside-forward and winning an FA Cup medal.

Remarkably, United finished runners-up in the Championship. Wilf McGuinness and Bobby Charlton were primary reasons for that success, Bobby netting 29 times – his biggest haul for the club. 'It showed the strength in depth we had,' Wilf says, 'that we could finish second the season after something like that happening – all those good players who hadn't been able to get into the first team.'

In December, Wilf McGuinness, one of the mainstays of Matt's revival plans, broke his leg. Without scanners and modern medical equipment, there was no way of knowing that he had been playing for weeks with a stress fracture of the shin. Poor form, hardly surprising under the circumstances, had put him in the reserve team, and he had been having painkilling and cortisone injections in an attempt to win back his place. He went in for a tackle in his usual full-blooded way, and his leg snapped like a twig. A 7–3 defeat by Newcastle signalled the need to fill the gap left by Wilf, and Matt went to Dundee United for Ron Yeats, their giant centre-half. The club would not part with him (he later became part of Bill Shankly's great Liverpool team) and instead Matt signed Maurice Setters from West Brom, who had been on the transfer list since the beginning of the year, turning down offers from Everton and Manchester City. United being more to his liking, he signed within ten minutes of meeting Matt, for a fee of £30,000. A hard man, tough and aggressive, he was the perfect player to plug the gaps in a profligate defence. He stayed with United until 1964, eventually becoming big Jack Charlton's assistant in his various managerial jobs and recently helping shepherd the Irish team through the World Cup in America.

The rebuilding continued with the arrival later that year of the Irish international full-back, Noel Cantwell from the 'Academy' at West Ham. Another £30,000 buy, he joined Setters in shoring up the defence and later became club captain, leading United to the FA Cup in 1963.

David Herd followed in the summer of 1961. Matt had had designs on him since 1951, and had nearly bought him from Stockport County before hesitation allowed him eventually to slip away to Arsenal in 1954. Matt had been pursuing him there for two years until one day he rang Highbury, expecting the usual reply, only to be told that he could have the Scottish international for £38,000. He did not need telling twice.

Harry Gregg

In the early sixties there was a certain amount of in-fighting. Some players came to United from clubs where more attention was paid to the coaching than to ability, which was the last thing that was needed at Old Trafford. That caused one or two ripples – there were one or two who were full of their own importance, who thought the clubs they came from knew more about football than Manchester United, which was utter stupidity. So there was a bit of a rough ride around then, and it was a very rough ride when we almost got relegated. There were one or two people who were mixing it. There was a time when we weren't getting enough of the ball in training, and there was an article calling us 'spoilt party-wallahs', plus there were one or two cliques. We were playing Arsenal one time at Highbury, and staying in the Royal Lancaster Hotel, and I was sitting by myself, when one of the players came in with a journalist – they didn't see me – and he started slagging off everybody. I went to see Matt in his office, locked the door behind me and said, 'Boss, I'm calling a meeting of all the senior pros.' But he was very clever. He said, 'No, Big Man, I'll call the meeting, you start them talking.' So we had the meeting to clear the air, and we had three that season. Matt had a rough ride that season.

In the summer, a skinny lad from Belfast arrived. George Best came over with his pal, Eric McMordie. 'He came here from Northern Ireland,' remembered Matt, 'got homesick, went back and tried again. A little elf, so brilliant that there was nothing to teach him.' Matt was more excited about George's prospects as a pro than anyone's since Duncan Edwards.

Paddy McGrath recalls the faith that was to follow a rocky road in later years. 'Matt said to me early on about George, "I've got a young Irish lad, very frail, and I've told Jimmy Murphy not to try and teach him anything, let him get on with what he's doing. He's the most naturally gifted player I've ever seen.' George had the mixture of sublime skill, flamboyance and spirit – a touch of arrogance – that Matt adored. He once told George he was the best tackler at the club; even as a junior the Belfast boy gave a good account of himself against the pros in five-a-sides. He could ride tackles that would have deposited less lithe kids over the wall and in the cricket ground.' Paddy McGrath marvelled at his impishness: 'Paddy Crerand told me that when they were playing Partizan Belgrade and George had got three or four men kicking him, he just jumped up and stood on the ball.'

George was incredible with the ball – a magician. The sorcerer-apprentice was to become the source of Matt's greatest joy and pain in his last years as manager. He went to work for the Manchester Ship Canal Company as a tea-boy, training at the Cliff on Tuesday and Thursday nights with the juniors and amateurs.

George Best

(United and Northern Ireland winger, the greatest player to emerge from the British Isles, but a troubled genius who tested Matt's patience and ultimately undermined Matt's authority. Nevertheless one of Matt's great finds and great friends, too.)

When I was a kid I used to hide from him, I was so much in awe. I lived in Chorlton where he lived. I used to have to catch a couple of buses to get to the ground and every so often he used to drive past in his car and pick me up. I used to hide at the back of the queue so he couldn't see me, because I didn't know how to handle it. But then he became a pal.

Comedian Jimmy Tarbuck was the guest of Manchester United: 'Arsenal were playing Manchester United. I went with Tommy Steele. We walked in, and he introduced us to this waif in the corner – skinny kid, scraggy hair, three-button suit and looking to all intents and purposes as though he needed a good feed. He said, "You want to see this kid play." His name was George Best.'

George Best

The nice thing was he loved great players. He had a lovely method of doing things. He decided who he wanted and where he wanted them to play and that's what he'd have. He went out and bought Paddy Crerand – he wanted him as a playmaker, bit of a calling these days. He wanted Denis when he came back from Italy because he loved him so much, and he went out and got him. And always in those days the youth team was important, too. He treated

*the youth players like they were superstars. For kids trying
to get into the team that was amazing.*

Bobby Charlton, writing in *International Football Book No. 3*
(1961): 'He is a wonderful man, and how I wish that I could
be a man like him, were that possible.'

Harry Gregg

*Matt bought Maurice Setters after a 7–3 defeat at New-
castle [January 1960]. Maurice was a very strong, hard
player. He was the only man I ever saw Matt lose his cool
with, on two occasions.*

'But he turned it round,' says Harry Gregg. 'He signed Denis
Law, and there were some good players coming through. It
broke the Boss's heart to sell Denis Viollet, but no player was
bigger than the club. And I think he regretted selling Johnny
Giles. But no one at Old Trafford ever asked for a transfer, so
when Johnny asked for a transfer, he was gone in less than 24
hours.'

The Law-man's tale says a lot about Matt's single-mind-
edness, as well as his increasing alliance with Louis Edwards.
Edwards it was who backed him against Harold Hardman in
the boardroom battles of the early sixties; Edwards who convinced him that the expensive gamble on Quixall was worthwhile. Quite apart from anything else, United had been left
with financial difficulties by Munich, being under-insured on
players killed or retired by the crash. A benefit game organised
by Real Madrid helped, but the early sixties were not notable
for success.

The summer of 1962 saw the return from Italy of most of
the expatriate colony, including pioneer soccer emigré John
Charles and Jimmy Greaves. Denis Law, whom Matt fancied
to replace the recently sold Denis Viollet, was having a torrid
time at Torino. He detested life in Italy where the football was

defence-minded and the life for the players repressive. They were handsomely paid and treated like superstars, but their lives belonged to the club, with monasterial training camps in the hills before every game. Torino were also awkward about allowing Denis to turn out for Scotland. With Matt showing interest, Law finally walked out and flew to a Caledonian refuge, refusing to lace his boots again for the Italian club. They could hammer out the details of his transfer to United, and that was that. Torino promptly handed Denis's playing contract to Juventus. If he maintained his stance UEFA might ban him from playing altogether.

Matt and Harold Hardman tracked the Torino officials round Europe, becoming so fed up with being messed around, as factions within Torino played a tug-of-war with Denis's contract, that they nearly gave up the chase. On 7 July, there was a cable from Torino authorising the sale, although there was a mystery over who had sent it. It turned out to be one group of directors who wanted to sort the club's finances. They were heavily in debt, still owing Manchester City £40,000, and the financial windfall proved irresistible.

Denis flew down from Scotland. The day he arrived, an eight-week drought ended in a rainstorm that swept the country, so that Stretford was under three feet of water as Denis sprinted from the plane at Ringway to the traditional Manchester welcome – a deluge. The following day Matt flew in from holiday in Spain, and on 12 July, Denis signed for a fee of £115,000. It was calculated that Law was worth four times his weight in gold – and so it proved. Two years earlier he had also attracted a record fee, when Manchester City had paid Huddersfield £53,000 for him. Matt had given Law his first Scottish cap, against Wales in 1959, and a series of impressive displays in his national colours had convinced Matt that United must have him. Even earlier than that, Matt had taken United's youth team to play Huddersfield Town on a mucky evening at Heckmondwike, when the frail little blond lad from

Aberdeen had caught his eye. After the match, he offered Andy Beattie £10,000 for him.

He was Matt Busby's most expensive signing, but also his most inspired. Together with the established presence of Bobby Charlton and the emergent genius of George Best, he defined the United way of playing football. A few months after he arrived at Old Trafford the Beatles made their first record and took Britain into a brave and gaudy new world. United were the team whose image and talents fitted best into the exploding pop culture. Law established an immediate rapport with the fans, who christened him the King, the older fans likening him to Billy Meredith. He stayed at United for ten years, scoring 236 goals in 393 games, including 34 FA Cup goals in 44 games and 28 in 33 European games. During the 1963–64 season he scored 46 times altogether, and netted 39 a year later as United took the title.

Paul Doherty

I don't think even he knew the extent of what he was creating. I think it would be more difficult with the kind of liberated man you've got around today. His friends say he used to tell them, 'Just go out and enjoy yourselves.' That cavalier thing. If you are good at man-management – and he was excellent – with the kind of men that were around in those days, you could achieve great things. He could go out and buy the best and say to them, 'Right, let me see the best.' Matt certainly liked a streak in a player – Denis Law for example, who was an excellent player for him. They would respond to him. If you've got quality workers and they like you, then you're going to get a quality performance. And that's what I think he did.

A few months later, another element in the team Matt Busby was creating arrived at Old Trafford. Paddy Crerand had been dropped by Celtic for the second game in a row. Matt had an understanding with Celtic that he would have first refusal should Crerand wish to leave Parkhead. 'I was told by a reporter that Manchester United had signed me. It was one of those things that happened to a player in those days. Luckily I'd always supported them anyway so I was delighted. It wasn't that I necessarily wanted to leave Celtic at the time – it was just that I happened to get pushed out a little bit, and I didn't think Celtic were going anywhere, because they'd let Jock Stein go, which I thought was a big mistake.'

Paddy Crerand

(Classy Glasgow-born midfielder and hero of the triumphant 1968 team; often described as Matt's 'adopted son'. Scottish international and close friend of the Busby family. Occasional football pundit.)

He did no negotiations – he did his own negotiations, and I didn't get a word in edgeways. But he was a very fair and honest man, and treated everybody as an individual and a human being. He never ever spoke to you as if you were schoolchildren. A lot of people in football treat players as if they're kids, but he was never like that. Everybody was a man. It was a different world coming to play for Matt Busby. He knew everybody. To be fair, I think Alex Ferguson's a bit like that. Maybe it's a Scots trait – you like to speak to everybody and know what's going on. Matt knew everybody: all the kids, wives, everything. It was always a great big family.

Paddy eschews the usual line about the 'Green' Mafia at United. 'People used to say that because of Jimmy and Matt, but to say United was a Catholic club is like saying everybody in Russia's a Communist because the government was Communist or everyone in Britain's a Tory because the government's Tory. That would never come into consideration when Matt was

The end of a long wait: Mark Hughes and Sir Matt pose with the Premiership trophy

Two greats share some special memories.

Sir Matt with Alex Ferguson, the man who continues his vision at Old Trafford.

Sir Matt and Jean in 1983 with the FA Cup.

Sir Matt reunited with Bobby Charlton, Eusebio and other stars of the 1968 European Cup Final.

Young fans pay their respects to the father of Manchester United.

A sea of scarves and floral tributes in memory of Sir Matt.

Tributes for the great man underneath the Munich clock at Old Trafford.

The Old Trafford flag at half-mast.

Players, fans, officials - all united in silence for the father of football.

The funeral procession.

The seat that will always be Sir Matt's.

talking about players. Some of the great players who played for United weren't Catholic – nobody ever bothered to ask.'

Paddy Crerand

Matt and Jimmy were such clean-living people. They always went to Mass and Matt never used bad language, which is incredible in football. Matt was always a hero in Glasgow, among Celtic supporters anyway, maybe because of that, and Celtic supporters are always a bit pro-United anyway, because of Matt Busby – coming from Bellshill, and having been a Celtic supporter when he was a kid. it's just that he was actually a good-living man. It didn't play any part in me going to United.

Paddy arrived in Manchester five years to the day after Munich. 'My first impression of him [Matt] was memorable. He's big and you could tell he really *was* someone,' recalls Paddy. 'He was very friendly. He met me at the airport with Denis Law and his wife – I'd known Denis from the Scotland team. That was typical of Matt – always so considerate.' The sum of £56,000 was more venture capital than struggling United could really afford, but it proved an investment as inspired in its own way as Law's.

Crerand combined elegance and aggression, with a talent for the killer ball that splits a defence. But if Matt was building another team of creative individuals, it could still be one betrayed by self-interest. 'In one of my first games I tried a 35-yard shot and hit the bar,' chuckles Paddy. 'Denis turned round and said, "You c***! We're the strikers, you give the ball to *us* to do that!" But Matt was great. If you were playing and trying something a bit ambitious and it wasn't quite happening, he'd come up to you and say, "I can see what you're trying to do. Keep trying and it'll come good." '

Paddy went on to play 392 games for United (eventually joining the coaching staff and becoming assistant manager to

153

Tommy Docherty). At his best, that resolute presence provided all the midfield steel and scheming Matt needed. Before a game he'd tell Paddy, 'Get the ball, win the ball.' The others were urged, 'Give it to Paddy or Bobby.'

'Alex Ferguson plays 4-2-4, with the wingers chasing back,' says Paddy, 'and that's just how it was in our day.' The two became great friends and allies. People, including the Boss, came to regard Paddy as Matt's adopted son.

John Aston

(Father Johnny was a United player whose career was curtailed by injury, and youth team coach after Munich. John, a winger, played exceptionally well in the European Cup final.)

> *After Munich, Matt was less of the track-suit manager, but he was still the figure of authority. When he came into the dressing-room it always fell silent. It was a tremendous mark of respect. You didn't carry on with the banter; you waited to hear what he had to say. The sheer weight of his personality came through. But his success didn't have a lot to do with tactics, and by the time I was in the side he didn't have a lot to do with the day-to-day training. The club was starting to buzz again. They'd bought Denis, and they won the Cup in 1963. What Busby did was re-introduce what I call the star system, where tactics weren't so important as employing the best players. He tried to find players with character – he liked strong personalities. So it was always difficult for players like me, competing with these strong characters. It was like market forces, survival of the fittest.*

Matt's management style had changed. He continued to suffer back pain, and the club paid for a holiday for him at the end of every season to recuperate. While he was the same avuncular figure to his players, he was also becoming increasingly powerful within the club, assuming many of the duties that a general manager might be expected to perform, such as negotiating over perimeter advertising and even making out the directors' rota for attending Central League games. He also negotiated with the FA over the use of Old Trafford during the World Cup. Matt was developing a taste for business.

Instrumental in the creation by cheque book of a team to emulate the 1957 fledglings was Louis Edwards, who he became increasingly involved in the club's affairs once he joined the board. He represented the club at many of the Munich funerals, became involved in the insurance negotiations and was soon the most active of the club's directors. He was keen to encourage Matt to buy the players he needed, going to Sheffield to help secure Albert Quixall's signature and helping in the tortuous negotiations with Torino to buy Denis Law. In the early sixties he began to buy up shares, and by 1964 he had effective control of the club. It suited Matt to have his old friend at the helm. In December he was proposed as vice-chairman, and when Harold Hardman died in June 1965, Louis was elected unopposed to replace him.

Matt's new team took time to gel. With two games to go in the 1962–63 campaign, they needed a point against Leyton Orient (managed by Johnny Carey) to stay up. Although Orient opened the scoring in the eighth minute, Charlton and Law hit back, and an own goal sealed things. Paddy Crerand remembers joining at a bad time for the club. 'It was bad winter, and they hadn't been doing very well in the League, they were down near the bottom. We played City at Maine Road one day and we got a penalty that was a bit dubious to give us a one-each draw. Unfortunately City went down after that and we stayed up.'

The freezing weather stalled the season for months. It had been a winter of discontent for United.

For now, though, they were safe, and there was still the FA Cup to play for, Second Division Southampton having been overcome in a gritty semi-final at Villa Park. Before the Cup final, the United team stayed at a hotel in Weybridge, and the night before, theatre-loving Matt arranged for the team to visit the Shaftesbury to see *How to Succeed in Business Without Really Trying*. Their opponents, Leicester City, were favourites: fourth in the League, eighteen points ahead of United and with the best defensive record in the First Division, they were anchored by the presence of Gordon Banks in goal. 'I'd never seen a Cup final. I went into the dressing-room before the game and got changed into boots, socks, pads, but I didn't put a strip on because it was a very warm day. I walked down to the bottom of the tunnel at a quarter to three and listened to the crowd singing "Abide With Me", but I don't think Matt was too impressed because he didn't know where the hell I was.'

Matt's new United side was just beginning to display its finer points with greater consistency, however, and in a sense the final, won 3–1, was a turning-point. Denis Law was the inspiration, feinting and darting round the pitch, leaving Leicester mesmerised in his wake. Paddy Crerand and Johnny Giles carved up the fabled Leicester defence.

'We had a great time, but it could have been even better – we could have had even more success. We finished second a lot of times, and got beaten in so many semi-finals. United had already lost the 1962 semi-final, and we lost the 1964 semi-final, the 1965 semi-final, the 1966 semi-final and the 1970 semi-final. I always wanted to go back for another final, because it's like people tell you – the day goes by so quickly, you don't get time to appreciate it. You'd have to do it a couple of times to appreciate it.'

More importantly, the victory lifted United out of the post-Munich doldrums and its worst sequence under Matt. 'Winning the Cup made a big difference,' says Paddy. 'It gave everybody a big lift. We were a different team the following year – we should have won the League, but Liverpool beat us by four points.

Meanwhile Johnny Giles had played his last game for Matt.

156

He was a modernist; anxious to learn about technique and disappointed at the vagueness, the simplicity of methods at United. There was no great mystery at Old Trafford: you're a good footballer, you're playing for United, go out and play. To Giles, this was dated football, paternally organised, too abstract. 'I was a United romantic, an optimist, and I still am,' reflects Wilf McGuinness, 'whereas Johnny Giles was a realist. Johnny was a pal, a team-mate, younger than me, just. Along with Bobby and Shay we'd play golf at Davyhulme. Then I broke my leg and I didn't have the time then because I was coaching. I read in the paper, "Johnny Giles up for transfer", and immediately I assumed he'd been put on the transfer list, because nobody asked for a transfer from United. "John, I can't believe it," I told him. "But don't worry, he might change his mind." And he said, "He might change his mind, but I won't." More mysteriously, Matt's intuition for a players rightful position seemed to desert him with regard to the tenacious young Irishman. He played him mostly as an out-and-out winger, short spells as inside-right proving ineffectual. Johnny Giles became one of the few players to ask Matt for a transfer, going quietly in the close season to then Second Division Leeds United for £37,500. Letting him go was Matt's greatest regret as a manager. But Giles made his mark in Revie's fold – as an inside-forward.

George Best

It was an amazing period. I went there as a kid. My team was Wolverhampton Wanderers, because at the time they were the team in Europe playing the Russian teams. But Man United were always your second favourite. Then in 1958, after the crash, everybody wanted to take them into their hearts and you became a supporter even if you didn't want to. Old Trafford, the theatre of dreams, it's so special now, but it was big then. When you think that in my first game we had 50,540 against West Brom. We played

Chelsea on a Monday night in front of 43,000 and there were 20,000 locked out every game we played. It's getting back to that again now. Apart from the fact that he'd got a great side together, I think half of them came down because Matt was in charge. If he'd have gone somewhere else and sat on the bench, they'd have got 50,000 extra there. Very few people can do that.

The new era of hope was ushered in when Ian Moir's thigh strain let in George to enter the fray against West Bromwich Albion after scintillating form in the reserves. It was September 1964. 'I was two years in the B team,' George recalls, 'and he told me I was making my debut on the day of the match when I turned up at the ground. So I didn't have time to think it over and get nervous.'

'Boy Best flashes in Red attack', the *Manchester Evening News* claimed, even though George had been clobbered several times and picked up an ankle injury. Wilf and Jimmy's concerns about George's strength weren't assuaged. 'The next time I got a look in was after Boxing Day,' says George. 'I'd been out so long I thought I was never going to make it as a player. I'd gone home to Belfast for the holiday and he sent a telegram asking me to get back for the next game.'

That chance came about as much in desperation as anything. Four days before Christmas, United had tumbled to Everton 4–0, and on Boxing Day they crashed 6–1 at Burnley, for whom a winger named Willie Morgan scored twice. Matt sent for George, and in the return fixture against Burnley two days later, United won 5–1, George coolly scoring the third. By April, George was an international, playing against Wales just fifteen games into his career with United.

United were chasing three lots of silverware – the League, the FA Cup, and the Cup-Winners' Cup – but were out of two cups in five days. The FA challenge again collapsed at the semi-final stage when United lost 3–1 to West Ham. In Europe they had dispatched the Dutch side, Willem II, 7–2, then overcame

Tottenham 4–3, and in the quarter-finals they seemed set to advance after whacking Sporting Lisbon 4–1 at Old Trafford, courtesy of a Law hat-trick. The second leg, however, was a disaster. Lisbon delivered a knockout 5–0 defeat on the same night that Cassius Clay took the world heavyweight title from Sonny Liston. Five down after an hour, they contained Sporting for the rest of the match, but were never able to rise from their lethargy. Afterwards they sat in the dressing-room for half an hour, speechless, while Matt uncharacteristically raged at them, calling their performance an insult to the people of Manchester. It was a measure of Matt's priorities and how much he wanted a European trophy. That was what drove him on.

'A lot of us hadn't played in Europe, apart from the older ones seven or eight years before. We went over there with our usual attitude – to attack,' says Paddy Crerand, 'and we were three down in about ten minutes. But our goalkeeper [David Gaskell] left a lot to be desired on that particular day – he let in some dreadful goals. That was a horrendous experience – we'd had it won at Old Trafford – but it was also a good experience. We played in a lot of games in Europe after that and we never did anything like that again. We approached Europe completely differently – it's all about concentration and playing tight. We came back and beat Tottenham 3–2 the following Saturday. We were so angry with ourselves, for giving it away so stupidly.' Six of that crestfallen side went on to play in the European Cup final three years later. In the stormy aftermath, Matt's decisiveness was once more displayed as Maurice Setters was handed to Stoke for £30,000; Nobby Stiles claimed a regular first-team place.

They were crazy times for George Best. 'I remember one week I played on the Saturday in the First Division against Arsenal, Monday night against Swindon in the first leg of the Youth Cup, Wednesday night against Uruguay in Belfast, the second leg against Swindon on the Thursday – and we won them all.'

Shay Brennan

(Irish international and a real character at the centre of United's European champions team. Another youth team product. Ironically known as the 'Bomber'.)

> *I might not have been the greatest defender, but I could pass a ball. All they wanted me to do was get the ball up to people like Georgie Best and Bobby and Denis. They didn't want me to go on an overlap – why take the ball off players like that? That was the Boss's secret – the players he picked. He picked good players and let them get on with it.*

The sixties' teams were different to those before Munich: full of zeal and braggadocio, but harder in the tackle, occasionally brittle too. They might just as easily lose 4–1 as win five nothing. Matt had always set out to entertain – let in four as long as we net five – but this inconsistency and fragile spirit troubled him. After Matt stood down in 1969, it was to be a feature of United's play for the next twenty years as they became a 'cup side'.

The more physical side of United's play was intriguing. Hardness has always had its place in football; Matt was a tough tackler and always admired such attributes in his players. But the man who once rebuked Bill Foulkes for dirty play with the words, 'Always remember, we play football', was overseeing a team that, in a game that was becoming increasingly nasty, could – and did – bite back. Nobby Stiles epitomised that streak, while Setters and Crerand could look after themselves. In the ten years between 1958 and 1968, Matt's team accumulated twenty sendings-off, but United were by no means the worst offenders. It was a trend: the treatment meted out week in, week out on his boys – Law, Best, Charlton – was quite appalling. The 'modern' approach of some rival managers seemed to be to kick skill into touch. It's doubtful Matt turned a blind eye; more likely that he recognised that the game had changed irrevocably and that if he was to achieve his life's work, some principles would have to be massaged. He couldn't just be kicked off course.

Paddy Crerand

He was so strict about discipline, about keeping the good name of the club. You can never be 100 per cent right all the time – somebody's going to get sent off from time to time, or do something daft off the pitch. That's part of life's rich pageantry. But he was very strict as far as the clubs name was concerned, although he'd never bollock you in front of anybody. You always felt embarrassed that a man like that should give you a dressing down. He'd never demean you, but he'd make you feel a bit ashamed that you'd done something that wasn't proper.

Violence was becoming a part of football. In the 1965 FA Cup semi-final, United's opponents were Leeds, who did little to refute their reputation as a team rugged enough to mix it with the hardest. For their part, United had the short-fuse quartet of Law, Crerand, Setters and Stiles. It was a bout worthy of Ali–Frazier. Round one took place at Hillsborough before 65,000 fans. The X-certificate semi-final, the papers dubbed it. Jack Charlton and Denis Law – United's captain and Matt's personal representative on the pitch – had to be pulled apart, Denis's shirt hanging off his back. It was all a far cry from the cultured air of Johnny Carey or Roger Byrne. Only two players were booked, though, a situation which merely encouraged the simmering ill temper. The replay was a tense affair. Leeds scored in the last minute, and as the referee was leaving the pitch he was knocked to the ground by a United fan.

On his retirement, Matt wrote to his best friend in the press, Hugh McIlvanney: 'The way things are going alarms me deeply. Hard men are nothing new in football. In my young days there were quite a few killers about, men who went in for rough play and intimidation . . . What is new and frightening about the present situation is that you have entire sides that have physical hardness for their main asset. They use strength and fitness to neutralise skill and the unfortunate truth is that all too often it can be done. George Best survives only because his incredible balance allows him to ride with the impact of some of the tackles he has to take. Because of their heart and skill, he and other outstanding players in the League can go on giving the crowds entertainment. And it's true that there are still a few teams who believe the game is about talent and technique and imagination. But for any one, you'll find ten who rely on runners and hard men.'

Paddy Crerand

The team talks were always simple. Matt never believed you could create anything by talking about it; he never believed you could score goals saying, 'Do that, do this.' He believed you could defend, stop teams scoring against you. He was a great believer in the idea that if it broke down you'd all come back and help one another. The United team I played in had a very similar style to the team they have today – more or less 4-2-4, but the minute anything breaks down the two wingers come back and fill in in midfield, making it 4-4-2. Lots of teams play 4-4-2 today, but they don't play with two adventurous wingers. We did then, and Alex Ferguson's team do today. George Best was a great defender – when he first got in the team at outside-left, Tony Dunne must have thought it was brilliant because he didn't have to tackle wingers, and he was always looking for the intercepting balls more than anything because the guy had to get past George first. It was the same with John Connelly. Everybody worked very hard for one another, up and down the pitch – it was great to play in. All Matt had to do was give you a shape,

*because he knew what everybody was going to do. That
meant we could have a bit of frivolity, a bit of laughter –
he always liked a happy dressing-room. And when Matt
was in that dressing-room, nobody ever used bad language.*

Another aspect of Matt's approach became more pronounced,
too. As Noel Cantwell remembers, the old ways still held sway,
but there was a new caution. 'Our tactics were very simple. We
always played attractive football, simply, on the floor. "Pass it
to a red shirt and we'll be okay," he used to say. We weren't
deep into tactics. However, he liked defenders to defend as a
first priority, the idea being that if you defend well enough
you'll win.'

Initially established as a technique for European away legs,
this defensive tactic was applied in the League on occasion
too. Matt liked to keep a clean sheet; he sometimes gave the
impression that he was happier at not conceding a goal than
he was at scoring one: it meant the defence was doing its job.
Some of the players now believe that the techniques had the
effect of stifling United's play. They were too cautious, and
suffered accordingly. Perhaps that, too, was a trait reflected in
Matt's character, for one of his greatest gifts was patience. It
was, for his son Sandy, perhaps Matt's greatest asset. 'He had
a way of when you had a problem, he'd pat your hand and
say, "Be patient, relax, it'll all come right in the end." And most
of the time he was right.'

Jimmy Tarbuck

*He was an imp. He was a delightful man. He hated
pomposity; would prick pomposity in a lovely way; would
quietly pull the rug from under other director's feet after
a game when they got pontificating about football, about
which they knew bugger all. He'd just look at you and
wink, and he'd come out with a classic of football knowledge. He was like your dad or your favourite uncle. You*

could confide in him, you could have a drink and a beer with him; you could have a bloody good laugh with him. You could talk football and he'd listen diplomatically – wouldn't look bored – and then he'd put his points.

There's no doubt that Matt was a man who loved football and the people who play it. From his own experience, he considered that the game, at its best, moulded young men, providing strength of character, consistency and reliability as well as camaraderie. Win or lose, the Matt of the sixties retained such qualities, as well as the extraordinary dignity and charisma that had led to his depiction as the 'father of football'. After the game, implacable Matt would head upstairs for his customary glass of whisky and become a generous host. Real Madrid might have shown him the value of treating the opposition courteously, but it already was an innate part of Matt's make-up. If United had won 4–0, he never gloated, but would look for positive points to hearten the vanquished. Should it be the other way round, he would again sing the praises of the opposition players who did the damage. As one manager put it, 'He seemed to be able to take an inordinate amount of defeat.'

George Best

He always treated people exactly the same. To him, there were no superstars or tea ladies; you were all the same, which was amazing. He was as much at ease with the groundsman, old Fred, as he was with anyone else. He sat with them all – the Pope, the Queen, he sat with kings, he treated them exactly the same. You can pretend you feel the same, but actually to be able do it and feel at ease, that was one of his great qualities. We all have our heroes and to be with them we clam up a bit but he never did. He was relaxed in anybody's company.

Manchester United were chasing rainbows again, and with the sixties at their most swinging, Matt began to enjoy his football again.

'He couldn't go anywhere,' says George. 'Manchester for him – for all of us in those days – at that time was a village, so close and tight. Imagine for him. He ended up, like I do, going to the same places all the time because you know you're not going to be hassled.' Those same places were where Matt felt most at home, surrounded by his family – actual or adopted – out of the limelight, not telling jokes but guffawing at those told; and then maybe a singsong: 'I Belong to Glasgow' or 'The Gooseberry Song'.

Paddy Crerand

There weren't many places in Manchester where you could get a bit of peace if you played for Manchester United. It was such a fanatical city. We'd go to the Cromford Club, owned by Paddy McGrath, Matt's big pal. If you were in there, Matt would inevitably come in with Jean, and he'd always buy you a drink and sit down and talk to you for ten minutes, and then he'd bugger off. We always went into a great Italian restaurant in Faulkner Street called Arturo's. Five out of every six Saturdays I'd be in there with Denis, Maurice Setters, Noel Cantwell, Shay Brennan, and George would often come in with Mike Summerbee. Matt would often be in there, and he'd come and have a drink with us, then go back to his pals.

Matt's family had become even more important to him after the crash and, with younger members now augmenting the Busby fold, Matt spent more time with them. They loved his gentle, affectionate nature. But his other family was rarely left out and Jean still kept the United womenfolk on their toes, organising their social events. 'The Busbys are very, very close-knit,' says Paddy Crerand, Matt's 'adopted son'. 'He's got seven granddaughters, and the players were at every single one of their christenings. The christening would always be on a Sunday, but come eleven o'clock you were out, whether you wanted to or not, because you'd have a game the following Wednesday. Often I'd leave my wife there until two or three in the morning. They were always great parties. Paddy McGrath would be there, Johnny Foy, who was a dear friend of Matt's, Eddie Clarke. They'd be talking about the 1948 team, and you'd sit there listening.'

Matt's life had changed. He was comfortably off. He was beginning to feel his age, and while his role at United was more administerial, he still controlled the team from his desk. Although ill health continued to dog him, life had its compensations. His religion had taken on a greater significance for him; Jean was even more fundamental to his life; and there was golf – the sanctuary. Matt was spending more and more time at Mere and other courses. He was a public figure, a symbol of perseverance and good prevailing over adversity. He was fêted by Harold Wilson, new Prime Minister and leader of the Labour Party he'd always supported, but the private man loved going to Monte Carlo, where he found another refuge from the public gaze, save for the odd Englishman stopping him for an autograph. Around Old Trafford he still wanted to be one of the boys, to kick a ball around, and with his old friend and partner, Louis Edwards, installed as chairman, the future looked healthy. Although the idea of a move 'upstairs' was tempting, there were spectres that needed to be laid to rest. There was the European Cup to be won; then those lads he still thought about, still saw dancing in the shadows of Old Trafford on his daily walk around the ground; then he and his lovely boys could find peace.

The fruits of the debate about English football's standing in the world were beginning to show as the mid-sixties became the pinnacle for a nation's game so humiliated in recent years. For the next four years United would play with a style that epitomised everything that was good about it. Yet still no British club had won the European Cup, although 1965 represented a milestone. Bill Shankly's Liverpool were getting into their stride, with the talents of St John, Hunt and Callaghan, while Don Revie's Leeds United team featuring Giles, Bremner and Hunter, was making waves with a well-organised blend of dashing skills, thundering tackles and bloody-mindedness. Manchester City would soon be a force through Bell, Lee, Summerbee and Young, and Chelsea, 'Docherty's diamonds', were a stylish side, boasting Tambling, Venables, Osgood and Cooke.

George Best

At the end of the day he was the top man. The other managers used to call him for advice – Shankly, Jock Stein, can you imagine? That's a testimony to a special man.

Don Revie was an admirer of Matt's, even if his more stifling, technical approach was at odds with Old Trafford's flamboyant fold. 'I felt quite green about the managerial side of the game when Leeds gave me the job,' he said, as his team were on the ascendancy. 'I turned to Matt Busby for guidance. Some men in a number of professions might guard their secrets from others. Not Matt. He went patiently over the ground with me and answered question after question. He demonstrated his wonderful gift for making the man who seeks his advice seem like the most important man in the world. Later, when things weren't working out too well, he put his hand on my shoulder and said, "It'll turn out all right, son." '

To the footballing public the decade belonged to two charismatic managers: Matt Busby and Bill Shankly. Over the years the enmity between Liverpool and Manchester United has evolved into a snarling beast, an endemic clash between two of industrial northern England's rival metropolises. In the sixties, though, just as the Beatles and the 'Mersey beat' were establishing their credentials at the hub of world pop, the competition between Liverpool and Manchester was adversarial but rarely embittered or aggressive. Both clubs had teams and managers who inspired universal admiration.

Ian St John

These were the days before crowd trouble, when Manchester United and Liverpool fans could go to a game and it would be rivalry rather than violence. It was wonderful. When I was with Liverpool at Old Trafford, they were always great games, all great stuff. I used to stay over in Manchester for a party. The lasses would come and we'd stay over with Denis, George and Paddy. You know Shanks' gag about Matt: 'Matt has got a bad back. I tell you, it's two bad backs! And not much of a midfield either.' But I remember once, in an Old Trafford game, Matt's beckoning Shanks, like, 'Hullo, welcome. Eh, come up to the office Bill.' Before a game Matt would like a little glass of Scotch or something; Shanks, of course, had tomato juice, or tea or something – never drank. A little later, we're getting our boots on and Shanks comes rolling into the dressing-room, his face flushed red – you could see Matt had slipped something in Shanks' cup of tea. And he's saying, 'This is the place to play boys!'

The bond between the two Reds was immense. Rivals on the pitch, they were the best of friends off it. When Liverpool played in the 1965 Cup final, some of the United lads watched the game in a pub, and when St John headed the winner, Paddy Crerand recalls the United boys rushing out to send the 'Pool players a telegram of congratulations. The empathy between two great teams began on high, for Shankly had long been an admirer of his fellow Glaswegian. He was manager of Huddersfield in the late fifties when Denis Law was there, and Denis remembers Shanks once sidling up to the dressing-room mirror brandishing a trilby – a trademark of Matt's. He slipped the hat on his head, tilted it to a jaunty angle and inquired: 'D'ye no' think I look like Matt Busby, boys?' Shankly was another who frequently sought Matt's advice.

Both shared a common conviction about how the game should be played and run: it was a simple game that should be played as such and enjoyed for what it was. They were both tough when necessary, and both were amongst the lowest payers after the abolition of the maximum wage in 1961. 'I think that those old managers, once they had retired, thought they'd been too strict on us,' says Ian St John. 'But it was difficult for them because of their background where you don't want to spoil someone. Money was not the motivating factor in anything. Your performance should have been the thing and the money would sort of come along, but the point is they'd never been used to big money – they weren't used to small money! It was going against the grain to be paying out to play football, to play the game that you played for the love of it in a way. They were very strict with us in that respect and it was hard-going to chip away to get yourself a decent wage. In fact, when I left Liverpool in 1971 I was still on a maximum of £100. I never got more than £100.' Johnny Haynes of Fulham, in the Second Division, was earning £100 in 1961, when the United and Liverpool players were on a basic £25 per week, plus £10 appearance money, plus a 'crowd bonus' of £2 per 1,000, starting at 28,000. Despite that, both managers were able to maintain reasonably happy ships.

George Best

It was different then. It was the sixties, it was the music, the fashion, flowers in your hair and all that. From my point of view, Matt couldn't handle it because he'd never seen anything like it before.

Man-management – negotiating for wages included – was Matt's strongest suit, and his aces were always his personal aura, his resolve and the atmosphere of mutual respect he generated at the club. Few disputed the earnings – to Matt's face. In his entire tenure of Old Trafford, George Best was the only player who failed to respond to Matt's coaxing and who wasn't immediately transferred. But no one challenged Matt's team selection.

Willie Morgan

(United winger of late sixties, early seventies, last signing of Sir Matt's management at United.)

> *Lady Jean was very easy-going, liked a laugh. All the Busbys were ordinary, nice people. That's the great thing about Matt – he was such a simple man in his outlook, very ordinary, very humble. A lot of people play at being humble, but he just was – he was just a nice, big guy. The only thing you had to do was avoid the Friday mornings: you had to get past the Referee's Room. He'd be waiting in there if he wanted to drop you. Paddy marked my card; he told me to sprint past the Referee's Room. I thought it was idiotic, till eventually, after I'd been there a few months, one Friday morning I was strolling past, and he called me in and went through the routine: 'Have you enjoyed coming here, have you settled down? Kids all right, house okay? How d'you think things are going? How d'you think you're playing?' 'All right,' I said, and he let it go. I thought he was just being nice. The following week he did it again. 'You're looking a bit tired. Why don't you take the weekend off, take the wife out.' I said, 'Thank you very much,' and left the room, as we all did, thanking him for dropping me. But he commanded so much respect. It's hard to describe without sounding corny, but I looked on him as a father-figure. He just had this tremendous aura, this charisma. He was just a wonderful human being.*

George Best came to know Matt's office better than most,

with its 'guest' seat slightly lower than Matt's, emphasising his imposing presence; its nostalgic pictures of Highland stags on the wall; its pregnant silences like those in the room of a doctor about to impart bad news. George's picture is remarkably similar to Willie Morgan's. 'His method of telling you you weren't playing on a Saturday was great,' says George. 'You'd get summoned to the great man's room and you'd just sit there. You didn't look at him; the head was down. And I'll never forget around his office he had all these stags – "The Stag at Bay" and stuff – and I used to sit there counting them, because I didn't want to look at him. He didn't say you were dropped, he'd say, "How d'you think you played last week?" You'd say, "I thought I did all right, Boss," and he'd say, "I'm giving you a rest." He wasn't one of those managers who said, "You're dropped because you were crap last week." You used to come out and you used to be thanking him: Thanks very much Boss for not playing me on Saturday. That's the way it was; that's greatness.'

It was a rare approach in a game over-populated with brutes and inadequates. 'I used to talk to Bobby Johnstone and Ken Barnes,' says Paddy McGrath. 'When they were playing for City, they'd come in the Cromford and say, "The wife tells me I'm dropped – it's in the paper." Matt would never do that.'

Mike Summerbee

(Manchester City hero and winger of the sixties and seventies. England international and friend of George Best, Matt and Paddy Crerand.)

From the very early days when he took over at Man United he had that sort of strong character. It was something that attracted players to come to Old Trafford. He was similar to Joe Mercer . . . he was easy-going, but when he stamped down, people jumped to it. He was brought up that way. He knew hardship, about loyalty and respect. He was also a great family man. I was with him in Tenerife once and when we met up for a meal you should have seen it. The restaurant just stopped. He gained so much respect for what he did and the way he conducted himself. It doesn't just come from being a nice guy; his word was his command and when things weren't going right he could lay it on the line. He knew what me and George were like but when he cracked the whip the hairs came up on the neck. I think he adapted. The rigours of Munich were getting to him but things never slowed down. I remember at a recent Swindon game, I got out of the car and he was mobbed. He always wanted to sign every autograph but later on he couldn't. I think after he retired he might have wanted his brain picked – he was a walking encyclopedia of football. If I had been a top manager, I know I would have a chair in the room for Sir Matt. I was privileged to be in his company.

In 1965 United were champions again, for the fourth time under Matt's reign – albeit by the narrow margin of 0.686 of a goal. Denis Law scored 28 goals, David Herd twenty, but just as important were the unsung stalwarts, like Shay Brennan and Tony Dunne, as effective a full-back pair as any in United's history. United's newly frugal defence conceded only thirteen goals at Old Trafford. For ten years Brennan and Dunne were the immovable objects at the heart of the United team and the Republic of Ireland squad.

Paddy Crerand

I thought 1964–65 was the best team we had at Old Trafford: John Connelly, George was a fixture by then, Bobby Charlton, Denis, David Herd was centre-forward – he doesn't get enough credit for the things he did. And how we didn't win the European Cup in 1966 I will never know. We were by far the best team in Europe. Injuries and a little bit of misfortune cost us. We went over to play Partizan Belgrade with some serious injuries, and maybe

172

the Boss took chances with one or two players. If we'd
had a big squad he wouldn't have played them.

Matt and United were again gunning for the European Cup.
Real Madrid's empire had fallen and Portuguese giants Benfica
were now the team to beat, powered by Mozambican-born
Eusebio. For the most part, though, the Spaniards' free-flowing
football agenda had been replaced by an overwhelming fear of
defeat that brought with it tight defences and a safety-first ethos.

United clashed in the quarter-finals with Lisbon's European
kings. They were formidable opponents: winners twice and
finalists on another two occasions in the last five years. At Old
Trafford in the first leg, 64,035 saw a thrilling game in which
Charlton and Eusebio were in majestic form. As the crowd
drew their breath at the end, it was 3–2, Eusebio nearly hitting
a third for the Portuguese. The consensus was that a single
goal's difference would not be enough to take to Lisbon.

One goal was indeed not enough for United, and amid a
wall of sound in one of soccer's great citadels, 75,000 in the
flower-decked Stadium of Light watched stunned as United
forsook their defensive ideas and tore into Benfica. 'We'd won
3–2 at Old Trafford, and people were saying it wasn't enough,'
recalls Paddy Crerand. 'Then out there, in the dressing-room
before the game, I was messing about with the ball and hit it
against a big mirror and smashed it. The place went deadly
quiet and I started laughing. We went out on to the pitch, then
had to come back in because Eusebio was being presented with
the European Player of the Year award, and the kick-off was
delayed about half an hour. It was nerve-wracking. Matt told
us to keep it tight for twenty minutes till the game settled down,
till the crowd had settled down. The game hadn't been going
long when Tony Dunne got a free-kick about 30 or 40 yards
out. Now, Tony couldn't get a great deal of distance with his
kicks, so I said to George, "Get to the near post," because I
didn't think Tony would reach the near post. And George
headed it straight in the back of the net. We were three up in

about fifteen minutes. We were magnificent. The only performance I've seen that was better was Real Madrid against Eintracht Frankfurt. Everything went right.'

George – at his coquettish best – John Connelly, Paddy
Crerand and Bobby Charlton made it 5–1 on the night. It was
possibly the most complete display in United's history, a night
on which every single player was at the top of his game. Spirits
were high; misfortune was another place. 'I scored the best own
goal you've ever seen,' says Shay Brennan. 'But I'm lucky –
they don't show that on the highlights, they just show the goals
we scored. Any other night and I'd have kicked that ball into
the stand, but we were playing so well, I got cocky. I volleyed
it back to Harry and it went into the top corner.' The night
belonged to George, the first of many he was to claim as his
own. It was to be a watershed in his life: the sombrero he
sported when the team got off the plane the next day betrayed
a new approach by the shy Belfast boy. 'El Beatle' was born,
and life was never the same again. 'George was the first player
the media went wild about,' says Paddy of that night. 'And it
just went on from there.' David Sadler, George's room-mate as
a junior, saw his rapid change, almost overnight, into a man-
management challenge that was to become one of Matt's few
failures. 'When I was at Mrs Fullaways with George,' he recalls,
'we didn't have a wild time. We'd just socialise normally – play
cards, go out to play snooker or bowling. He was only
interested in football. But Lisbon changed all that – things were
never the same for George. The thing was, this had never been
done before, footballers had never been like film stars, and
George didn't know how to cope with it.' As Geoffrey Green,
the former *Times* writer put it, 'Busby wanted George to dance
with the angels, but it wasn't to be.' George was made of mortal
flesh and blood.

'Ah, George . . .' Matt would ponder, when the vexed question of the wayward genius cropped up in conversation. 'He
was a first-class example of everything until he was 22, but
then he got in with a bad crowd. I hated the company he was

with, I kicked up a stink about what he was doing with his life, but this time I didn't win. He should have been the first millionaire footballer, but I suppose I was softer on him than I should have been. I had lost the other lads and that maybe made me more lenient with those who came afterwards.' Sandy recalls the time when the 'Best and his Birds' press romp was at its height and Matt called George into his office for yet another heart to heart. He declared himself concerned at the succession of dolly birds. 'Why don't you just find yourself a nice young lady and settle down?' he suggested. 'Next thing,' says Sandy, 'it was all over the papers with this Swedish girl. "Oh no!" me dad said, "I didn't mean the first girl you met." But he loved the little fella. He said George never really let him down. He said geniuses do crazy things every now and then. There were a lot of things George did for Matt that never got out. He was a charitable fella.'

George Best

He said it perfectly for me once. We did a dinner once and someone asked him a question about me, 'Could anything have been done . . . ?' And he just came out and said, 'All the pleasure George gave me, I can forget about all the other stuff.' When I sat down and thought about it, while I was there, they won a cup in 1963 when I signed professional; we won the Youth Cup in 1964, which they hadn't won since the fifties when they basically owned it; I played for Ireland. We won the League 1965, 1967, won the European Cup 1968, I was European Player of the Year, I was British Player of the Year, I was United's leading scorer for six years in a row – as a winger – and one season I actually topped the First Division goalscoring. When I look at it like that, I thought maybe he's right, maybe I did have a little hand in what they achieved. And the European I scored in the final, scored in the semis when we beat Madrid 1–0. And basically he summed it

*up when he said that. Little compliments too. I used to
pride myself on working on the parts of my game I thought
were weak. I was a skinny little thing and he said he
thought I was the best tackler in the club. All the time I
was doing it for him.*

The semi-final couldn't have been of greater contrast to what
preceded it. If football is a funny old game, Matt couldn't see
the humorous side in Yugoslavia, now part of Serbia. Partizan
Belgrade won the first leg 2–0. 'El Beatle', injured and playing
with his leg heavily strapped, was being so badly battered at
one stage that he jumped up and stood on the ball.

After the Benfica game, Matt had turned to his wife and
said: 'I've a feeling this is it, havent you, Jean?' and indeed, the
Belgrade field reaped a bitter harvest. 'I'm sick. Sick we've lost
our greatest chance,' he said.

Shay Brennan

*He was like a father. He knew I was gambling, and he'd
always ask me how much I was doing. He'd try and get
me to keep it to a minimum. When we lost to Sporting
Lisbon he called it his worst night in football. But he still
didn't come in accusing us individually; just a quiet word
a few days later, telling you where you'd gone wrong.
Which was the best way – youre a professional, you know
when you've made a mistake.*

It was Matt's lowest point since Munich, and he groaned to
Paddy Crerand, 'We'll never win the European Cup now.' 'No,
Boss, we'll win in two years' time,' Paddy replied. Publicly, at
least, Matt had not given up hope.

'This is not the end. This is the beginning,' he told the
papers. Privately he described it as the worst night of his footballing life. He was close to quitting. And he was out of Europe
for another year.

Glory

Bobby Charlton

The point was, if the crash had happened during an FA Cup run, we would have chased after that. But it took place in the European Cup and things wouldn't have been right until we'd won that.

Europe remained the albatross around Matt's neck throughout the next season. Jean had already seen the toll the last few years had taken on her husband. The injuries sustained at Munich still dogged Matt, though with typical self-deprecation he would never show it. His new duties as manager were occupying more and more of his time, and he wasn't getting any younger. It was around that time that Jean suggested, 'Matt, I think it's time you looked around for a successor. It needn't be now but I should start thinking about it.' Surely, as happened throughout his life, Matt was thinking, planning. Jock Stein was a friend of Matt's, a Glaswegian and a believer in the beautiful game. He'd been in contact with Matt, asking advice, discussing aspects of the game, and was a natural inheritor of the Busby mantle. In 1967 his Celtic aces became the first British team to lift the European Cup, pipping United by one season. But the appointment could wait while there was still one last chance; one last heave for the boys.

Bill Foulkes

You could always go to him – he'd always advise you, do what he could to help. I admired his vision. He's got to be the greatest manager ever, and a wonderful human being. He was strong, ambitious, a very forward-thinking man. He was a real leader. And winning wasn't everything: you had to win, but most of all you had to play well. You must entertain.

Between buying the two Burnley wingers, John Connelly in April 1964 and Willie Morgan in October 1968, Matt made only one purchase, in the summer of 1966, but it was the signing that more than any other, he believed, brought the League title back to Old Trafford, and it showed that Matt's desire for success sometimes overrode his sentimentality. Harry Gregg had been a hero at Munich. Now, although his touch was probably deserting him, it was his manners that were his undoing.

Harry Gregg

I left in 1966. It came about because of my big mouth. I'd just signed a two-year contract with the largest wage I'd ever had at Old Trafford, and two months later it was goodbye and God bless you. We went on a pre-season tour. We always picked the easy games, like Bayern Munich, Hamburg – we never had an easy game in our life – and Munich beat us 3–0. Then we went to Hamburg, and he dropped Bill Foulkes, Noel Cantwell and even Paddy Crerand, who we used to say was his adopted son. Then we played an Austrian Select and Nobby was sent off, and there was near enough a riot. I looked up the park and saw their centre-half running at George Best, so I started to run and I heard Matt's voice: 'Get back in your cage!' and I shouted, 'F*** off!' We got a bad hammering, but Paddy

Crerand told me afterwards, 'Greggy – all the trouble, all the rows, the Boss never flapped, but when he saw you running up the park he nearly fell down the steps.' At the same time Denis had fallen out with the Boss because he hadn't signed a new contract. Now, after every game the Boss always came up to the players who smoked, gave each one a cigarette and lit it for them. That day he didn't. He was up and down the dressing-room saying to himself, 'Not fit to wear the red jersey, not fit to wear the red jersey,' and the Law-man said to me, 'That's me he's after Greggy,' and I said, 'No it's not, it's me. There'll be no cigarettes for us today.' I got on the aircraft the following morning, and a press man came down to the back of the plane, and said, 'They're in for Bonetti or Stepney.' I played two more League games and they bought Alex. I said, 'Look Boss, I'm not the sort who walks the corridors, that's not my style.' He said, 'You're the last man I'd see walking the corridors. But Alex has started badly – hang about for a month.' So I hung about for a month then I went to Stoke City.

Alex Stepney had begun his career with Tooting and Mitcham, before joining Millwall. Tommy Docherty paid £50,000 for him to go to Chelsea, making £5,000 profit when he sold Stepney to United four months and one game later. 'Matt just told me my wage,' says Alex. 'He said, "We do not give back-handers, you're on a good wage, with good bonuses. If you accept those terms not one player will know what wage you are on. No player at the club knows what the other is on." ' Stepney would go on to play 535 games for United and win an England cap.

An incident in the game against Burnley in September typi-fied the style and endeavour that Best and Law brought to the side. The ball appeared to be going out for a corner, but Best pursued the lost cause, shadowed by a defender, and knocked it over his head into the six-yard area, where Law rose to send it into the roof of the net; in the second half Best picked up one of those surgical passes from Paddy Crerand, slid and twisted through a thicket of defenders, was brought down but chipped it to the Law-man from a prostrate position. Denis, with his back to the goal, scored with an outrageous overhead slammer. For a generation of youngsters, performing a scissors kick was known as 'doing a Denis Law'.

On the second-last Saturday of the season, United went to Upton Park – the 'Academy'. They weren't intimidated. 'We played brilliantly that season. The 6–1 win at West Ham stands out. We needed to win to take the title, and Matt told us the usual thing, play tight at the back. Then we scored direct from the kick-off. We were three up at half-time, and Matt said to us, "Keep it a bit tight, you're only 2–0 up." He hadn't seen the first goal. He was a bit late getting to his seat, and when West Ham kicked off after the goal, he thought that was the start of the game. They had a smashing side – Geoff Hurst, Bobby Moore, Martin Peters.'

Newspapers raved about Matt's new braves, declaring the first 30 minutes the best football seen since the war and the current team the equal of the Busby Babes. For Matt, it was yet another 'greatest hour'. The team was still mercurial, boasting more than its share of temperamental wizards – certainly more than Matt had in any other of his teams – but the quota remained within the parameters of the now classic Busby blend of schemer, striker, ball-winner, ball-juggler, of power, skill; the perfect balance of positive and negative, thunder and lightning. Matt and Jimmy would watch from their customary seats in the stand. If Matt ventured down to the touchline, you knew something was wrong and redoubled your efforts to stay on the park. Matt stayed put an awful lot that season.

In a game that was becoming increasingly dominated by defences, United won matches in breathtaking, magnificent style. John Aston's emergence as a dashing winger was crucial. The son of Johnny Aston, he came through the legendary 1964 Youth Cup-winning side and made his first team debut in 1965.

'With youth teams,' he says, 'if you get one player who goes through to the first team, you've done well. In our side we had George Best, David Sadler, John Fitzpatrick, Jimmy Rimmer.' And though George was seen by many as the star of the European Cup final, Aston toiled away out of the limelight in an equally vital role.

The hunt for the European Cup was back on – possibly for the last time as far as Matt was concerned – and this time it was serious. In the Championship, United were close, but no cigar – City were top dogs there and it was just a sideshow to the main event: Matt's holy grail.

Paddy Crerand

When Celtic won the British Team of the Year award after they'd won the European Cup, and Matt made the presentation to Jock Stein, Jock said, 'I hope I'm here to present it to you next year,' meaning he hoped we'd win the European Cup, and that's what happened.

In April, United faced old adversaries Real Madrid in the first leg of their fourth European Cup semi-final, having dispensed with Hibernians, the Maltese part-timers, followed by FK Sarajevo and then Górnik Zabrze of Poland, who offered the stiffest competition of the entire campaign. United were shading it 1–0 until the closing seconds of the first leg, when Junior graduate Brian Kidd, David Herd's replacement, back-heeled in to give the Reds a more comfortable safety margin. Matt's lads were harrassed all the way in the away leg in front of 105,000 in a raging blizzard, but held out to win on aggregate.

In the Old Trafford leg of the Real semi, Best cracked the ball into the roof of the net for the only goal of the game. Once again, the 'smart' money said it wouldn't be enough: Real may not have been the force of old, with only Gento left of the fifties' masters, but new aces like Pirri and Sanchis could cause trouble enough.

However, United played Newcastle United without Denis Law, whose knee had given out causing him to miss the rest of the season, and they still managed to win by the margin of 6–0. George got a hat-trick, Brian Kidd a couple and there was one from David Sadler. During the week, Matt went to Madrid to see the Spain v England European Nations Cup match, with six Real players in the Spanish side.

United flew to Madrid, the club with whom they enjoyed an old friendship. At a banquet to celebrate Real's usual League title, the 72-year-old Santiago Bernabeu, the man who had tried to persuade Matt to coach Real, said: 'Manchester United must be greeted, treated and respected as the greatest club in the world and as our friends for many years. Nothing must go wrong while Manchester United are here. If we lose to Manchester United, then we shall have lost to a great side. We have met them on many occasions and it is time their luck changed.'

The two teams had developed a friendship unusual between football clubs. In 1958, Real had offered free holidays in Spain to Munich survivors, and had tried to lure Matt to Madrid as manager. During the post-Munich years, Matt had tried to prepare his players for the eventual return to European competition with a series of friendlies against the best foreign sides. At that time, Real could command fees of £12,000 to play a friendly, but they agreed to play cash-strapped United for less than half that. They visited three years in succession from 1959, and each match was treated as a grand occasion, with banquets and exchanges of gifts, while the players were instructed to treat the games as serious affairs. So it was fitting that United should play Madrid as they strove towards Matt's El Dorado.

The team stayed in a mountain retreat thirteen miles outside the city. On the morning of the match, the Catholics in the team went to Mass, where Nobby put a 400 peseta note (about 12s, then worth rather more than it's current 60p equivalent) into the collection box. 'Bribery,' said one of his team-mates. As he got on the coach the next day, a bottle gashed Nobby's hand.

Paddy Crerand

We were 3–1 down at half-time, but Matt reminded us we were only 3–2 down on aggregate. We thought we were going to lose 6–1; we thought, 'Were not getting a kick at all here.' But he talked to us and talked to us, and it must have got through, because we went out and battered them. It was a totally different game. The Spanish died, and we just charged.

For the first half-hour United employed their customary away tactic: a five-man defence, with only Best and Kidd up front. But with 40 minutes gone, they were 2–0 behind on the night after goals from Pirri and Gento. Zoco put through his own goal to give United a glimmer of hope, before Amancio made it 3–1. At half-time the United dressing-room was despondent. Matt, sensing that the European albatross would forever hang round his neck, was pained and crestfallen, and as they left the pitch, he turned to Jimmy Murphy and groaned, 'We've had it Jimmy.' Yet such feelings were never transferred to his players. His face bore a warm smile as he told them how tired Real were looking – and in football, the more tired you look, the more heartened the opposition become. He reminded his team that they were only a goal behind, and that the new ruling of away goals counting double meant one goal would steer Manchester into the final. 'We must go out and attack,' he told them. 'If we are going to lose, it might as well be by six goals.' In the second half, Sadler pushed up as United set about Real and he was rewarded with a goal that came off his heel. 'I remember the silence most of all,' he says. 'At first I thought I must have missed.' The Spaniards sank while United soared.

Shay Brennan

There were 30,000 United supporters there, but you couldn't hear them. I made a terrible mistake for one of the goals. I misread a ball and got caught in two minds as to whether to pass it to Paddy Crerand's side or kick up the line, and I left Gento and he went through and scored. So I wasn't feeling too great. We seemed to have no chance – if I could have had a bet at that point, I'd have bet on Real Madrid. But we got level, and Bill scored. It was one of the most important goals ever scored for Manchester United. But what was he doing up there?

With twenty minutes to go, Matt had been equally concerned to see his limping centre-back, Bill Foulkes, way out of position.

Bill Foulkes

I should never have been on the field, really. I had torn ligaments and I couldn't stop, I couldn't turn. We'd played really well, I thought, but we'd been completely outplayed by a brilliant team. We'd been hammered. But then they stopped. They played a containing game, which took the pressure off us, and we started to create, we started to come out. George hadn't had a kick in the first half, but things started to happen. The ball was played in, hit David on the shoulder, and went in. So Nobby and Tony said to me, 'Right Bill, we'll keep it tight,' and I wasn't happy at all – my knee was getting bigger and bigger. The atmosphere was really strange: they weren't playing, we were holding on to what we'd got. Then we got the ball on the halfway line, and I didn't see anybody making any moves, so I ran from the back. I shouted to Pat and I could see the shock on his face because it was me. The cover came off George; I kept running and Pat gave the ball to George. He went past one, he went past two, I kept moving up. I was only jogging, I can tell you. I was the only red shirt in the box. George feinted to drive it to the near post, the goalie went to block it. George flipped it to me, a perfect pass, and I just hit it in the opposite corner. They all came after me, and I was waving them away – I was terrified about my knee. Then for twenty minutes we didn't give them a kick. I only ever scored one other goal from free play, and that was from George, too.

United were in the European Cup final. In the dressing-room, Matt cried and the players showered fully clothed, seemingly too dazed to notice they hadn't taken their kit off.

Paddy Crerand

The reception we got outside afterwards was horrendous. They stoned us, threw bottles at us. We stayed till the following morning. We went out that night and Madrid seemed to be packed with United fans. I don't think we went to bed, actually. We went to a nightclub, Stone's it was called, packed with United supporters. There was a group on, an English lad, Carl Douglas, who made a record a few years later called 'Kung-Fu Fighting'. It was a wild night. Paddy McGrath ran a plane from the Irish Club in Manchester, and four or five of the wives went out. We went to their hotel to meet them after the game, and Sandy Busby was there – extremely happy and a little the worse for wear. We flew back the following day, and Louis Edwards, God rest his soul, was standing at the bottom of the gangplank telling the reporters, 'If you're sober when we get back to Manchester you're not getting off.' We flew on to London for the Player of the Year award and George Best won it.

The day after the semi triumph, as Matt got off the plane in Manchester, he commented: 'Like Satchmo says, it's a wonderful world.'

The following Monday, United headed for their secluded hideaway in Surrey. It was announced that they would receive a bonus of £1,000 per man for winning the European Cup, a sum that had been written into their contracts at the start of the season. Those who had played in every game of the campaign so far – Stepney, Dunne, Crerand, Foulkes, Best, Sadler, Charlton and Kidd – had already earned £1,000 from the graduated system of payments, starting with £50 for beating Hibernian in the first round. Matt had always held that if performers on the stage could earn £1,000 a night, then footballers deserved it too – it just happened a year or ten later.

Shay Brennan

We stayed out of the way in Egham. Matt was very calm. A few of us went to Mass on the day of the game – I was a good Catholic then. On big days like that, you're sent to bed in the afternoon, but Nobby and I liked to bet, and the Derby was on the same day. There was no television in the room, so Nobby and I sneaked down to the television lounge. I backed Sir Ivor, 5–4, and had a good bet on it, so I had a great day – won the European Cup and backed the winner of the Derby. A nice little earner.

It was English football's biggest night. Europe, once meaning-less stuff to an indifferent press, was flavour of the month. The papers were loaded with human interest stories in the build-up to the big night, coincidentally to be staged at Wembley. Children were allowed to miss school for the day if they could produce their match ticket. Twenty-four parents, wives and team-mates from the Munich disaster were at Wembley, includ-ing Jackie Blanchflower and his wife, Harry Gregg, Johnny Berry, Bert Whalley's widow and Albert Scanlon. A group from Orbiston, including Matt's proud mother Nellie, also made the trip.

The home crowd was confident of victory: odds on United were 7–4 on or 11–10, depending on which bookmaker you dealt with. Matt, who himself liked a flutter, would have gone along with such figures. He'd been to see Benfica defeat Juventus in their semi and was happy with what he saw. 'They're for us,' he declared. 'They're our style. This is going to be our year.'

Another of Matt's great qualities, crucial to his team's success, was evident here. Although the Cup meant so much to him, Matt showed no sign of tension, and instead threw himself into buoying up his lads: 'You're brilliant; you must be, you're playing for Manchester United.' He wasn't impervious to nerves, but he always appeared so.

Though United were confident, Benfica presented a formidable barrier. They had scored 76 goals in their 26 League games, 42 of them by Eusebio, and had conceded only nineteen, although they had nearly fallen at the first European Cup hurdle. Eusebio just scored four minutes from time to equalise against Glentoran – George Best's favourite team as a child – to win through on the away goals rule.

Wembley was filled to capacity, a seething, ecstatic arena from the touchline to the top of the twin towers. The attendance meant that United had been watched by just under three million spectators that season.

The first half was a dull affair, neither side sparking, but after the interval, the game blazed into life, as Bobby Charlton headed David Sadler's cross past the Portuguese keeper. Benfica surged everything forward, chasing the equaliser. It came ten minutes from the end of normal time through Graca. As extra-time loomed, twice Eusebio broke loose, only to inspire wonderful saves from Alex Stepney. The Mozambican's best effort occurred after he swept in from the right and hit the ball with immense power. Fortune favoured Matt's braves. 'Eusebio left Nobby, who was marking him in our half, and came running out. The Wembley grass was quite long, though, and held the ball up. I suddenly realised I might be too far out and he was going to go for one of his spectaculars, so I just stood up to face him and luckily he hit it straight at me,' Alex says. 'I smothered the shot and thought the ball felt soft. It either burst when he hit it or when it hit me – either way it took away some of the sting. But the marks still there on my chest – I've had 'Mitre' written on there ever since.'

Bill Foulkes

I never for a minute thought we were going to lose that final. Even when Eusebio went one on one with Alex, I thought, 'He's going to miss.' I think we were playing for Matt and for the boys. I've never spoken to Bobby about it, but I think he felt the same.

When the whistle blew, Matt and Jimmy exhorted them to further effort. 'I told them they were throwing the game away,' Matt said. 'They were giving the ball away and hitting it anywhere instead of using it. I said they must hold it and start playing football again.' The players, understandably perhaps, recall Matt's words about the opposition more readily. 'They're finished,' he said. 'They've had it.'

Which they had. United left Benfica in their wake with an extra-time display worthy of European champions. A long clearance from Stepney found George, who left Enrique and the Benfica defence fumbling, rounding the goalkeeper for perhaps the most famous goal in English club football. Two minutes later Brian Kidd, the Collyhurst lad, headed against the bar before sending the rebound looping over the keeper's fingers for the perfect nineteenth birthday present. The elder statesman, Bobby, sealed victory with the fourth.

'I always though we'd beat Benfica,' Paddy Crerand recalls. 'We'd beaten them 5–1, we'd beaten them 3–2, and playing at Wembley was a big help. I had a little doubt when it was one each, and Eusebio went through on Alex. The first half was a bit scrappy – there were a lot of nerves. But in extra-time we ran amok. John Aston was magnificent. David Sadler should have had a hat-trick – he missed chance after chance. And George maybe should have passed it once or twice.'

The unusual heat was a problem. 'It was a hot night,' says

Paddy. 'You couldn't breathe in the stadium. After 90 minutes Matt just said, "Keep the ball, let them do the running." And they had to do some running in the first fifteen minutes of extra-time – we absolutely slaughtered them. And don't forget they'd played at Wembley more often than three-quarters of our team. They played against Milan there in 1963, and about seven of their side had played in the World Cup semi-final two years earlier.'

In the event David Sadler didn't really have cause to rue his profligacy. 'I missed three really good chances in the second, but I always think that if I hadn't missed those we wouldn't have had extra-time, so it worked out okay.'

'I'd never seen the game until we did a video for the 25th anniversary,' says Shay Brennan. 'and I was amazed how good a game it was. Johnny Aston should have retired after that game. He had an amazing game.'

Bobby Charlton fell to his knees. Nobby Stiles performed a cartwheel. Matt was in tears.

Bryon Butler

If I remember one picture of the man it will be that period – the moments, the minutes after the European Cup final. He had a smile then that went twice round his face. That smile, that marvellous smile. It was also for the team that perished at Munich. You had the impression that they were there somewhere up in the rafters of the old stadium looking down.

United had won the European Cup. Typically, Matt went to the Benfica players first, before making for Bobby. At this moment of ultimate vindication Matt was surrounding himself with the people he trusted. Hugh McIlvanney was the only member of the press allowed into the United dressing-room immediately after the final whistle; Matt had always relied on the *Observer* journalist not to write rubbish like some others would. Alex Stepney was amazed to find his older brother, Eric, in the dressing-room, having 'blagged' his way in. Matt also singled out the fellow Munich survivors, Bobby and Bill Foulkes. The three shared unspoken perspectives on the victory that no one else could fully appreciate or understand. Hugging Bobby, Matt said, 'This is the greatest night of my life, the fulfilment of my dearest wish to become the first English side to win the European Cup. I'm proud of the team, proud for Bobby Charlton and Billy Foulkes who have travelled the long road with me the last eleven years.'

Bill Foulkes

I was so relieved. It was like pressure had gone from me. I felt so relaxed, I was floating. I wasn't jumping around. People have accused me of being stonefaced, but I was ecstatic in my own way. It was different for the younger lads – they wanted to have a party. The ones who'd been at Munich wanted to do it more quietly. It didn't hit me until later. We went back to the hotel, had a party, went to bed. I said, 'See you in the morning,' but there was no way I was going to be there in the morning. I came back with my wife and sons in the car – we drove back at six in the morning, so I wasn't on the coach that brought the cup back.

There was a reception at Wembley. Bobby was very emotional, with no appetite for exuberance. He and Shay Brennan sloped off and sat in the stand. Everybody had gone except for some workers taking seats away for the greyhound racing. Football is like that. Defeat requires bucking up, solidarity, a different kind of strength and brashness; victory often leads to a slump, an anticlimax, a time for other thoughts.

Nobby Stiles

(Competitive youth team graduate, another hero of the 1968 triumph, the terrier who provided the bite in the United team.)

I can remember the Boss saying that he thought it would take ten years to rebuild the team after the crash. Exactly ten years later, in 1968, we won the European Cup. That's got to be more than foresight.

Afterwards there was the dinner-dance at the Russell Hotel, featuring the United 'house band', Joe Loss and his orchestra. Matt was a friend of Joe's from way back – his one-time singer, Frank Rogers, having been a driver on Matt's army team Italian convoy in the war. 'All the players were fagged. Bobby Charlton went straight to his hotel room and never came down,' remembers Sandy. 'Every time one of the players came into the room, Joe Loss would get the band to strike up "Congratulations". Eventually my dad entered the hall and seeing as how he loved to sing – and Joe knew he did – he was convinced to do a song.' They asked Matt what he wanted to sing. There was only one tune appropriate for the bitter-sweet feelings Matt experienced that night. 'Play Louis Armstrong's "Wonderful World",' he laughed, and launched into Satchmo's song of hope, beauty and togetherness, reflecting precisely the qualities Matt saw in the game he loved.

Alex Stepney

(London-born goalkeeper bought from Chelsea in mid-sixties. Hero of Matt's European Championship campaign.)

It was wonderful. That was the pinnacle. That was every-thing. Ten years after the crash and he'd achieved what he probably should have achieved ten years earlier. And he just took over the evening. I think he'd had a few. He was a better manager than he was a singer! I can remember him singing the Louis Armstrong and everyone joining in, applauding him. He was such an ambitious man but held it within himself. No one thought he would ever pack it in. After that achievement, I suppose he found the pressures were worse than he expected.

Alex Stepney and Nobby Stiles was among five lads under strict instructions not to have a late night – they were on England duty in the Nations Cup the next day – but they were among the group that headed off for Danny La Rue's club and rolled in at 5 a.m. 'Alf never knew,' chuckles Alex. While the younger lads partied, the older players, the survivors, drew a quieter pleasure, relief their overwhelming emotion. George has only a vague rememberance of what he did that night, but a clear sense of what Matt had done. 'I was still a young man of 22,' he says. 'I enjoyed myself after the Wembley game. I seem to remember Matt just locked himself away in his hotel room for a while and thought about what he had achieved. It was awesome.'

Shay Brennan recalls having breakfast before hitting the sack. Bobby collapsed in his hotel room, as he had done after the game in Madrid. Afterwards he said how sorry he felt for the Portuguese: 'They didn't know how much it meant to us.' In the early hours, Matt was heard walking along the hotel corridor, crooning, 'What a Wonderful World'. David Sadler wondered where United could go from the pinnacle they were occupying.

David Sadler

(Versatile late sixties/early seventies midfielder/forward who won England caps in 1968 and 1971. Now runs the United old boys' society.)

At times I used to want to protect Matt, because he seemed frail. But he always made you feel special. In his time he must have seen hundreds of people, but when he saw you he made you feel as if he wanted to see you, and even if there were twenty people around, it was you he wanted to see. He had a marvellous knack of dealing with people, and we just grew to love him. I say 'we', and it's one of those times you're confident you can speak for other people. The players who played for him, without exception, even the players he sold, they've all got stories to tell about him, they've all got such affection for him. It's uncanny really.

The M1 motorway was thronged with fans that steamy night. The last of the fans returning from London by train did not arrive at Piccadilly until four in the morning. The next day, United's victory train, a nine-coach special, pulled in at Platform 11. The party boarded a twenty-year-old red and white open-top coach that proceeded at 3 mph in a convoy of seven coaches and a security van, with the police forming a five-deep chain. Matt had always loved the fans, had always found time to spend talking to them; now he was overwhelmed by their affection for him and his team.

At the civic reception at the Town Hall, Matt addressed those present and expressed his gratitude: 'I said last night was the greatest of my life, but I don't know whether tonight is the second best or the greatest as well. I feel very deeply for the enthusiasm which the crowd outside has shown to the boys.'

Irene Ramsden

I don't think even he realised that he was as big a man as he was. I always remember when he was made Freeman of the City in 1967, one of the young lads said, 'Does that mean he can go in the top shop now and get free ciggies and a paper?'

Abdication

Sandy Busby

My kids loved him, adored him. He never came through with the blasé 'I'm Matt Busby', he was just grandad. They didn't call him grandad, they called him Matt. I started that off, because when he got into his sixties I never wanted him to grow old, and I started calling him Matthew.

In December 1968, Matt Busby announced he would be standing down shortly. Bill Foulkes was shocked. 'I rarely spoke to Matt – I was in awe of him, even though I was in my thirties – but the day he told us, I said, "What? You're not going to retire. What the hell for?" I thought he left too soon. It put the club in limbo.'

Whether or not Matt had already made his mind up to quit as manager of United before the 1968 European Cup final – win or lose – his team's indifferent spell running up to Christmas that year probably decided things for him. Yes, there was the trophy to defend, and the World Club Championship to enjoy, but Matt was approaching 60 and the stress of managing United in a different age was beginning to show.

Paul Doherty

I don't think he changed one dot in the whole period of the experience I had. He was never a media, a television figure. He just had a manner with him that probably wouldn't survive today, because the press is more provocative and more intrusive. Busby had a great ability to let you get as close as he wanted you to get. In the sixties they used to write about football. Nowadays the press can get beyond that. They don't wait. They don't have the courtesies that existed and they would not stand somebody putting up a barrier and saying, 'I don't want to talk about that.' But he certainly wasn't comfortable with television. I think he must have recognised that TV could expose people quite cruelly if it wanted; the naughty question going in, the uncomfortable aspect of being unable to answer it showing on the face. So he was extremely careful and selective about what he did. He set the parameters about how far you could go. You knew that here was a man who was prepared to tolerate so much; and if you took the liberty of going beyond, he would not complain at the time but he would never again agree to talk to you. It was a delicate balancing act. I think he became a better television figure when he got older, because he was a grandfather image. As a younger manager he was clumsy with TV. He never said, 'Why can't I project myself better?' Nowadays they go on charm courses, but he never bothered.

And there's little doubt that the 1968 team was a talented but mature one, full of internationals but short of legwork. Willie Morgan was to be Matt's last purchase as a manager. 'The Saturday I signed, they were playing Chelsea at home. They lost 4–0 and I wondered what I'd done. I made my debut on the Wednesday evening against Tottenham – I faced Cyril Knowles – and we won 3–1. It was still a very good team then. I won't say I joined the wrong team, because it was great, wonderful, and to be bought by Matt Busby was an honour in itself. In my opinion he is the best manager there's ever been. The vogue at that time was managers and players retiring early.

It's changed now, but then, when you were 30 you were finished. But Matt could have gone on indefinitely really, because his style of management was very simple. It was purely man-management, and judgement; there was no tactics, no coaching, he relied on the skills of his players. When he did retire, it was a disappointment for me because I'd made the move because of him really, and he retired within two years of me joining. On reflection I joined an aging team. But I went on to become friends with Matt, and to captain the club.'

Alex Ferguson

Sir Matt retired from management when he thought the time was right. I don't think he would have stepped down unless he was completely happy in his own mind. He had been in management for a long time – 25 years at the helm of Old Trafford – and I imagine he was ready to take things a bit easier.

Matt's business interests were growing too. In September 1968, Matt bought the 21-year lease on the year-old Red Devils souvenir shop, for £2,000 with a rent of £5 a week. This was instead of the fixed sum that would accrue from a testimonial match, and the shop rapidly became a lucrative venture, eventually passing on to Matt's son Sandy.

Frank Gidley

(Manager of Matt's Manchester United Souvenir Shop 1966–79 and distributor of the matchday programme up to 1994. 59 years at the club.)

It went from success to success. We started in a wooden hut next to the ticket office with three open windows, and when it was passed to Sir Matt in the second year we moved indoors and became bigger and better. He never interfered with the running of the shop. Sir Matt was a wonderful man, very caring. Always the same person; family and otherwise he was the same person. He always insisted we were taken care of financially and he always wanted to look after us as much as possible. As for himself, he never took a souvenir once in his time, not once.

Over the next few years Matt was installed on seven committees including the FA and Football League – organisations whose eccentric decision-making he no doubt wished to quell – as well as other interests like the Central Lancashire New Town Development Corporation.

While Matt diversified, others looked for potential successors. 'There was talk of Jock [Stein] coming at one stage,' says George Best. 'It looked almost certain, because Sir Matt wanted Jock to be the one to take over. It didn't materialise for whatever reason. Only the two of them know the full details. That's a problem. Taking over from someone like that is very, very difficult.' Others – names suggested included Revie, Allison, Clough – may well have been intimidated by the idea of Matt remaining at the club. In the meantime, Matt was still in charge for the next challenge, the World Club Championship against Estudiantes to decide the best club team between Latin America and Europe.

The previous year, four Celtic players and two Argentinians had been sent off in the play-off in Montevideo, between the Scottish team and Racing Club. These matches were explosive: to this day Argentinian football is dominated by exploitative directors and their 'persuasive' gangs.

United received a huge welcome when they arrived in Buenos Aires, where they had a rugby team, friends of a director's son, to act as minders, interpreters and public relations officers. A hectic programme was proposed for the visitors, with a polo match, a barbecue with the mayor and a round of cocktail parties. Matt, however, gave his players sleeping pills and an early bedtime. Whether or not the giddy social programme was designed to sap United's stamina, the next day the Estudiantes players did not show for a cocktail party. The club president, Mariano Mangano, was diplomatic and apologetic. Not so the coach, Osvaldo Zubedia, who said, 'This is a game for men. I see no point in teams kissing each other.' There was little diplomacy from the players, either, one of them suggesting that 'this will be an opportunity to vindicate Argentine football, following England's win in 1966'.

The war of nerves reached its climax in the match programme, where Benfica's coach, Otto Gloria, who had also been in charge of the Portuguese team in the World Cup two years earlier, wrote a scathing pen picture of Nobby Stiles: 'A defensive man without a fixed position. A dangerous marker, tenacious and sometimes brutal. He takes recourse to anything to contain his man. Very badly intentioned. A bad sportsman.' The fans could hardly contain their hostility. The Welsh rugby team, who were touring with the company, had planned to watch the match, but were advised against attending for their own safety – having had a brush with trouble on a train when a bunch of locals mistook them for United.

Paddy Crerand

Matt was a great believer that you should play games like the World Club Championship, creating friendship all over the world – remember FIFA has more affiliated teams than the UN. But that was the last thing that happened. We were treated horrendously over there. The referee was a disgrace. We couldn't walk the streets of Buenos Aires, we had to have a police guard wherever we went. We landed on a Sunday, and there were ten or eleven Catholics amongst us, and we had to have a police wagon to take us to Mass with sten guns. And Estudiantes were filthy.

United lost the match 1–0, coming out of it battered and bruised. Throughout, they had been kicked, pinched and spat at. 'The night they spat on sportsmanship' was the headline in the *Daily Mirror* the next day. Charlton had a deep stud puncture, the club doctor judging that he had been lucky not to have sustained a broken leg. Stiles had a boxer's cut over his eyebrow after a head-butt from Carlos Bilardo, who went on to manage the Argentine World Cup-winning side eighteen years later. Early on in the game, the referee had warned the pair not to stick so close to each other, and Stiles was sent off for only the second time in his career, dismissed for 'gesturing' after being blown up for offside, when he had quite clearly run from his own half. In a rare moment of open criticism, Matt was moved to say of the linesman, Esteban Marino of Uruguay, 'He does not know his job.' Sendings-off in a World Club Championship match were punishable by three-year suspensions, but the disciplinary committee, headed by Stanley Rous, thought Nobby's offence so trivial that they did not even bother to hold a formal meeting.

For the return leg, Estudiantes brought a wreath to commemorate Munich. Matt said he hoped for the 'match of the century'. But again it was the antithesis of what the father of football believed the game to be about. Estudiantes continued to hassle and harry, and the match began disastrously as Denis Law limped off and the Argentinians went into the lead through Veron. United chased the game until, in the last minutes, the game erupted. George Best was sent off after reacting angrily to another foul on him by Medina. Willie Morgan put them back in the game three minutes from time and Brian Kidd put away Morgan's cross for what seemed to be the winner on the night, only for the referee to blow for time as the ball was on its way in. Britain had had enough of the World Club Championship.

Four months later, in January 1969, on the day that Bobby Charlton was named England captain by Sir Alf Ramsay for the next day's international against Romania at Wembley, Matt announced that he would be standing down as United manager at the end of the season and would become general manager.

The board tried to dissuade him, but to no avail, and the search for a successor began. It would not be Jimmy Murphy, for at 57, he was only a year younger than Matt. Matt was tired; emotionally drained. Few people have deserved a rest as Matt did.

Ken Bates

(Former chairman of Oldham, chairman of Chelsea since 1982.)

I have a particularly fond memory of Matt. When I first took over Oldham in 1965, he gave me some good advice, and despite me being a greenhorn he treated me as an equal. Years later, when living in Monte Carlo, walking down the Avenue Princess Grace, I saw him coming towards me. Matt loved Monte Carlo, taking his annual holiday there, always staying at the Beach Plaza near my apartment. To cut a long story short, we arranged to have dinner with our respective spouses. That night, on the way to collect him, I told my wife not to expect a great evening because Matt was very serious and his wife was the same, although they were a lovely couple and he was kind to me when I first started in soccer. Coming down in the lift Matt told his wife Jean not to expect a fun evening: I was a very serious young man but was kind enough to invite them out so, in effect, 'do your duty'. We drove to Menton and dined on the pavement outside a fabulous French restaurant where English was conspicuous by its absence. It was the Queen's birthday. Before the first course we had everybody toasting Her Majesty's health in Dom Perignon – and drank them dry. It was a riotous evening and driving back was a hazard because the Frogs kept driving on the wrong side of the road. In those days the Beach Plaza had a rooftop disco and it finished around three in the morning with me in danger of putting Jean Busby through the plate

glass window with the more daring of my dance routines.
Good job we were a staid foursome – God knows what
would have happened if we had been on the wild side.
Matt Busby was as human as the rest of us, but he will be
remembered long after lesser men are long forgotten.

Matt had been manager of Manchester United for 23 years,
during which time the team had won five League Championships, two FA Cups and the European Cup. They had been
runners-up in the League seven times, beaten FA Cup finalists
twice and beaten semi-finalists five times. Eleven times they
scored more than a hundred goals in a season in all competitions; in 1948 and 1949 they scored 103 and in 1957 the total
was a staggering 143, including 24 in the European Cup. The
next season they scored 126, the next 103, 109, 100. The great
sixties' team scored 127 in 1963–64, 128 the next season and
123 the season after that and 110 in the European Cup-winning
season. He had built three teams to dazzle and enthral Manchester, England and Europe.

Following the European Cup final, Matt was knighted,
adding to the CBE he had been awarded in the aftermath of
Munich. He celebrated his return visit to Buckingham Palace
by nimbly booting a football on a stroll through St James's
Park with Jean. 'I don't know what it is . . . about a football,'
he laughed. The Queen asked how he felt on the night of his
European Cup triumph. 'Marvellous, Your Majesty.' 'It must
have been a wonderful night,' she said. 'We were all delighted.'

George Best

He was so down to earth. It's a wonderful quality to go
down to Buckingham Palace with the Queen and be as
much at ease with her as he was down the pub with the
rest of us. When he walked in a room the whole place just
lit up – he had that from day one until he died. It was

amazing. When you think of the great players he had under him, you ask them all, and they all say exactly the same.

Matt was a public figure now, hugely popular, the seventh most popular man in Britain according to a 1969 poll. He mixed with celebrities, played as much golf as he could and enjoyed his life outside football.

Jimmy Tarbuck

The highest compliment I can pay him is that whenever I was in his company, I always felt better afterwards. I have to emphasise this – you glowed inwardly afterwards. He wouldn't allow you to call him Sir Matt, and yet I used to take great pride and pleasure in introducing him to my friends as Sir Matt Busby. He thoroughly deserved his knighthood. He had a lovely life because he was so much loved. Whenever I went to Manchester he loved to play golf. A keen golfer, quite neat until he got on the green, then bloody awful. He was a notoriously bad putter. I was playing at the Mere one day with Matt and Joe Mercer and it was, 'Good shot, Joe,' 'Oh, good shot Matt.' Joe was at Manchester City and Matt, of course, was at United. 'Well played Joe,' 'That was a fine shot, Matt.' Then Matt had a two-foot putt and he said, 'Jimmy, the boys at the club, Bobby and company, usually give me these.' I said, 'Yes, Matt, but they're looking for a place in the team on Saturday, I'm looking for your fiver!' He promptly missed it.

Another time Matt was playing with Jimmy Tarbuck and Kenny Lynch. Matt's tee-shot hit into the ladies' tee marker just a few yards ahead and the plaster marker smashed to pieces. 'Oh no!' wailed Matt. 'That's another lost shot.' 'You should think yourself lucky you didn't hit Lynchy,' said Jimmy. 'That would have been seven away.' Willie Morgan, another keen links man, became a great friend of Matt's at a time when the Boss was disengaging himself from the daily grind of management.

Willie Morgan

In all the eight years I was at Old Trafford we played golf hundreds of times and he never discussed football at all. He was a good golfer. He actually got a hole-in-one at Mere Golf and Country Club in the early seventies, at the twelfth hole, a par three. He hit a three wood and he loved that. He got his hole-in-one tie. At that time he played off about a twelve handicap. He sometimes had a touch of the yips on the putts – he tended to run the ball past the hole a few times – but we had a lot of great games. Some time during 1969 I began playing with him and Paddy Crerand and a guy called Martin Flint, who was Matt's partner – a couple of bandits, both of them. We started playing on Sundays for 50p and Matt and I began playing Monday afternoons after training. We'd play two or three times a week. Then we ended up buying places in Tenerife together. He bought one first, then came back and told me about it. I don't know where he thought I was going to get the money from, but I did nevertheless. So we then spent a lot more time together. Matt used to spend Saturday evenings with Jean, Paddy, Denis, myself, Alex Stepney. There was a lot of camaraderie. He was always a Labour man – as we all were from Scotland. When we were on holiday, after I'd finished playing football, then he'd talk about the old times, how he gave Sean Connery a trial, meeting Howard Keel, who he remained friends with right up until his death. He spoke about the members of his family who'd gone to America, his brothers and sisters.

On 9 April 1969, the 31-year-old Wilf McGuinness was named as Matt's successor, with the title of coach. He had full day-today responsibility for the team, with Matt in charge of overall policy. This proved to be an unsatisfactory state of affairs, for while Matt was supposed to be there as a father-figure, dispensing advice where necessary, his presence was inhibiting for Wilf. He had to make his own mistakes; that is part of a manager's education. He wanted the uncertain domain between his own job and Matt's, such as contracts, signing and new players, ascribed to him. Since breaking his leg at the age of 22, Wilf had served a long apprenticeship on United's coaching staff as asistant trainer with the reserves. 'I was very confident,' Wilf says. 'I'd captained England at every level except the full England team and I was the union delegate at United. I was noisy. I made people take notice, even when it had nothing to do with me. In team talks, if Matt said, say, to Albert Scanlon, "I want you to do this," I'd say, "Do you mean, Boss, that you want Albert to . . .", so I'd make sure that Albert knew what he meant. Matt reacted very well when I did that, but the other players started yawning. But I'd get my point over.' Wilf had recently been made trainer of the England Youth team and was part of Alf Ramsay's set-up for the 1966 World Cup.

'When I managed United myself,' says Wilf, 'the only improvement I wanted to make was better-organised defence when they had the ball. When we had throw-ins and corners, we could have the upper hand if we rehearsed a couple of moves, a couple of trick free-kicks, switching the play at throw-ins, catching the opposition out. We had a pattern: stay wide – we'd never bunch if we could avoid it – change the play. I thought we should have things up our sleeves, but the United idea is when you get the ball to have freedom of expression, and that's always been the way.'

Wilf was admirably qualified to succeed Sir Matt, but before he bowed out, there was security in the top flight to ensure and the European Cup to defend.

Willie Morgan

We got to the semi-finals of the European Cup, and we were robbed yet again. Over there they played very well – they had a great striker, Rivera. Then over here, Denis knocked it over, it went two feet over the line. I followed it in over the line, then turned to get hold of Denis, who'd set off, celebrating. Their guy slid in and hauled it out and the referee waved play on. I've no doubt that the referee was bought. That was a big disappointment for me, because I joined just after they'd won the European Cup and then the team started breaking up.

Television evidence later showed the referee to be in the wrong, and even the Italian newspapers acknowledged that Milan had been fortunate in the extreme. The Stretford End exploded and missiles were hurled, holding up the game. After the hiatus, United had lost their rhythm, and it was an easy task for Milan to hold on. United's reign as European champions was over.

In Wilf's first season in charge, United finished eighth, and the following season looked even worse. By the end of November 1970 they were near the bottom of the table and there were tensions and quarrels in the dressing-room that Wilf, who had always found the line between players and coaching staff difficult to negotiate, seemed unable to handle. In addition, his coaching style was alien to a team used to being given its head and told to go out and simply express themselves. Wilf wanted inspiration, too, but allied to organsiation. The blackboard began to appear in his team talks, which was a sure way of turning the players off. He also rubbed up many senior players the wrong way; they were used to the gentle father-figure, rather than the thrusting young gun who felt he had to assert himself to gain their respect. 'Wilf was too young,' says Willie Morgan. 'He was very immature, to say the least. He came in with a very pompous approach – "I'm the boss" – and he's in charge of all these great stars, and he wanted to prove he could control us. That was his undoing.'

Matt returned briefly when it was clear that Wilf's appointment had been a mistake. Sandy says his father was depressed by the failure, for Wilf was his man, and Matt had always held that the mark of a decent club was its willingness to give a manager time to prove himself.

Paddy Crerand

Matt wanted to retire in 1969 – he'd had enough. He had to go into hospital for an operation in 1970. We got to the semi-final of the Cup and lost after three matches to Leeds, and after that he wanted out. It was a psychological blow to everybody that Matt wasn't the manager any more. That more than anything was the reason we ended up being relegated. When we lost the Cup semi-finals in 1969 and 1970, we were still a young team – it was only Bobby Charlton and myself that were of any age. The rest of them were in their twenties – Jimmy Rimmer, George, Jimmy Ryan, John Aston, John Fitzpatrick, Carlo Sartori; they were all kids. When Matt left it was a culture shock. Matt always believed he shouldn't interfere with any manager who takes over, and he didn't. Maybe if he had it would have been different. It was all rubbish that you couldn't be at Old Trafford because he was there. He was only there as a figurehead. If he'd wanted to interfere he'd have stayed as manager, wouldn't he?

Many felt sympathy for Wilf, a friend who was perhaps out of his depth and appointed at the wrong time. Meanwhile, the ditched boss had to be philosophical.

Wilf McGuinness

I felt if we'd got three or four players we could have bought, it would have helped me a lot – or if there had been better players coming through from the youth side – but other clubs were trying harder to get players, so we suffered. George Best did brilliantly for me, but Denis was injured a few times, and Bobby – we were all getting older. We had weaknesses, and when I think of some of the players I did play, it showed we needed strengthening. I didn't feel pressure at the time, I know people talk about my hair falling out, but I didn't feel hurt. The only hurt I felt was leaving. I thought it was the end of the world. We did fall out – not while I was doing the job, but when I left. But that was the thing about Sir Matt – when he thought something had to be done, he did it. I remember Denis Viollet was 31 when he left. He was the captain of United. One day he was there, the next day he'd gone to Stoke City. I thought, 'What's happened? That's a bit quick.' But I'm sure it hurt Matt to tell me to stand down. I could have stayed at the club, but once you've been at the top you don't want to move back down. He was like a father to me, and that's why it hurt at the time. When it happened, the Busby family were great. Sandy was magnificent, and Sheena and Lady Busby, but it didn't stop me wanting to hurt the club back. I didn't, because I was still United deep down. But I wanted the club to feel the hurt I felt.

Matt's return was a brief and involuntary cameo. It was probably the biggest mistake of his career, for from that moment until he stood down as a director in 1982, Matt was accused of meddling, labelled 'the Boss who never retired', a situation which clouded every manager's stay and every potential manager's decision in that time. The press had been receptive to Matt's avuncular manipulation in the past, but now the knives were out. The next appointee was 'Father' Frank O'Farrell, the highly regarded Leicester manager, a tactician, a football philosopher, 'Perhaps the best signing I've ever made,' as Matt said at the press conference. O'Farrell, the players' choice as well as the board's, was hailed as a new beginning for United, and Matt moved upstairs, becoming a director. However, once it seemed the Irishman was adopting a remote role – perhaps too close to Matt's duties, which he had only recently relinquished for a place on the board – and that his sideman Malcolm Musgrove was trying to play the game on the blackboard, things quickly went awry. O'Farrell made mistakes, not least signing too many strikers when the defence clearly needed shoring up. 'From an all-out attacking team, we became defensive,' says Willie Morgan. 'Frank's policy was not to lose the ball, don't take people on if you don't have to. George and I were knackered.' O'Farrell, though, inherited a squad riven and aging, robbed of the vital flowering of its juniors, and it floundered, becoming a mockery in the football world with feuds and outbursts filling the new, scandal-mongering tabloids. Matt's enduring softness towards the wayward genius of George Best was a big problem, both for him and United. Matt loved George like a son, and was too tolerant of his no-show defiance and occasional disappearing acts. He'd ring up the likes of actor-comedian Kenny Lynch, with whom George shared a flat, and Kenny would find himself either protecting George or as much in the dark as the Boss; George had become pathologically unreliable and Matt felt it his personal duty to correct matters.

George Best

I went on one of my disappearing acts because I was having so much hassle; I had guys coming to me in the street and was getting in fights because I wouldn't take it, I wouldn't walk away. They were always the first to complain. So I decided I was going to become a beach bum. I went to Spain and they did all the photographs and I said

*'I'm here because I'm not going to play any more.' While
I was there, I was ill with thrombosis, so I flew back, had
my doctor meet me in Manchester and they put me straight
into hospital. What had happened was that the clot had
moved and luckily settled in my calf, but it had been 50–50
whether I'd have pulled through or not. They took me to
St Joseph's hospital, which was where all the players were
treated. The first visit I had was from the Boss. I'd been
away for six months or whatever. He just poked his head
round the door and said, 'I heard you were here. Just came
in to say hello. Look after yourself.' And he walked out.
Then he actually came back into the room and he said,
'You know you should be playing again, don't you.' And
I said, 'Yeah, course I know.' When he walked off, I cried.
He was a great man, he didn't have to do that. You've let
him down, gone off and not said goodbye, and he's the
first person to walk through the door. To me that summed
him up perfectly.*

Frank O'Farrell's reign was humiliatingly compromised by
several episodes as George slumped into a haze of Miss Worlds,
alcohol and nightclubs. Matt, Louis Edwards and Frank – an
infuriated bystander – tried to negotiate with the self-destruct-
ing star; the next manager, Tommy Docherty, was similarly
blighted. George squandered his talent at United and Matt felt
partly to blame. He played his last game for the Reds on New
Year's Day 1974.

Such public laundering of private grievances was anathema
to Matt, but he was stuck between a rock and a hard place,
not truly believing anyone could carry on running the club in
the way he wanted, yet not wanting to meddle with a role he'd
relinquished. His duties in his little office down the corridor
from the manager's involved, as he put it, 'answering letters'
three or four days a week. Nevertheless, at half-time during
one match, Matt had to be physically restrained from approaching Frank O'Farrell and remonstrating with him about his

tactics and the players he was using. 'Matt always stressed that you don't know what's going on at Manchester so you've no right to an opinion,' says Paddy Crerand. 'Whoever was manager at Old Trafford at the time Matt was there had complete control of the club. Matt never ever ran a feud because I know for a fact that all the time that Frank O'Farrell was at Old Trafford and, I think, Dave Sexton, Matt Busby was at the training ground once. He also went down with his wife once when Jean was receiving treatment from the physiotherapist, for a bad back.'

Docherty was a feistier character all round, but he was undone by his affair with physiotherapist Laurie Brown's wife, details of which were also splashed in the papers.

The truth is that Matt couldn't let go; not when the club he loved was being driven like a ship without a skipper on to the rocks. It was a sign of the times that the typically generous and humble offer that the 'door to his office was always open' became a hostage to fortune, used by countless sports writers and football pundits as a metaphor for Matt's inhibiting presence at the club.

Paddy Crerand

United lost 5–0 at Crystal Palace when Frank O'Farrell was manager. Jimmy Hill was working for London Weekend Television's The Big Match, *and was talking while the cameras were focused on Sir Matt and Louis Edwards. Jimmy Hill said, 'These are the guilty men at Old Trafford, these are the ones that have got the club in this state,' and all that sort of thing, which Matt got very angry about. Frank O'Farrell being the manager, Jimmy Hill didn't lay any blame at his door. Five days later, we were all at a football dinner in London and Jimmy Hill came up to us – we were all sitting with Matt having a laugh. Matt never used bad language and nobody used bad language in Matt's company: he wasn't that type of man. Jimmy Hill came* *over to the table and started to talk and Matt just happened to say, 'Jimmy, I'd rather you didn't speak to me.' So Jimmy started getting het up about it and started having a go at Matt. Then he said strange things like, 'You let Brian Moore into the holy of holies in Old Trafford and not me.' Such childish stuff! Matt didn't acknowledge it, but all of a sudden Paddy McGrath just started swearing: 'You f*** ing wanker, how dare you talk to this man and how dare you say this and do that; you f***ing tosser, you couldn't even play!' That barrage went on for about two minutes while everybody sat still. I was laughing. Matt never said a word – mind you, he was having a little smile as well. All the girls were shocked – particularly Paddy's wife, Jean. Jimmy Hill said, 'I didn't come here to be insulted,' and marched off. Jean was furious and said to him afterwards, 'That's terrible language to use in front of the ladies and in front of Matt. It's disgusting. You should apologise.' Paddy said, 'Well, I'm very, very sorry. I'm very sorry, Matt.' And Matt just looked at him and said, 'I wish I could have explained myself to Jimmy Hill in precisely the same way.'*

Matt had become a victim of his own aura. He was, amazingly, becoming *persona non grata*, an easy target amid United's struggle to hit back at criticism. Malcolm Allison wrote what most friends of Matt and admirers of his record were thinking of slamming the criticism of The Boss: 'It is ridiculous that the knowledge, the basic wisdom of Busby apparently had to be ignored. It's amazing that the club feel they have to say Busby hasn't been to the training ground for eighteen months!'

Alex Ferguson

They say some managers at Old Trafford were reluctant to go to him for help and guidance. I could never understand that. I just came around the corner a little too late in that sense. I would have loved to have been at United when he was younger so I could have absorbed all that knowledge.

Some areas of the media still regarded Sir Matt as the football visionary he remained, though. Throughout his time as a director, Matt was a forward thinker providing provocative ideas for the game's officials to respond to. In 1976 he set out his plan to revolutionise an English League that had slumped into an over-cautious, not to say dull and declining spiral. His three-point plan was to extend the season to ten and a half months, allowing for blank weekends prior to internationals; to introduce a League system which rewarded goalscoring with extra points; and, to avoid the over-technical, tactical approach of the FA's coaching doyen Charles Hughes, a policy shifting the emphasis towards individual skills. A year later Matt, always a fan of European football, called for an end to the ban on foreign players. The man who tried to sign Ferenc Puskas never let up.

Matt still had so much to offer the game.

Alex Stepney

The best story about the man as the man was when Tommy Docherty was manager and we went on an end-of-season tour to the Far East and Australia. Matt didn't go himself. There was a shortage of money – not for the older ones like myself, Willie Morgan, but the younger ones like Arthur Albiston, Jimmy Nichol. Me being the elder statesman, players were saying, 'Look we've got no money, we've been away four or five weeks.' We were staying at the Hilton in Tehran and Hong Kong, where Coca-Cola was a lot of money and beer was a lot of money for these kids. It was a case of 'You're not getting any'. We got a message through to Sir Matt and he flew out and came into the hotel reception: it was like Popeye coming through the revolving

*doors with a pipe blowing, smoke coming out, the lot. He
just walked over to me and Willie Morgan and he said,
'Right, you two boys, I want you to arrange a game of
golf for tomorrow. I'll meet you down in the foyer in the
morning.' Funnily enough, the following evening, envel-
opes were handed out to all the players and Matt flew
back. That was him. He didn't want an upset, bad publicity
for the club. The club and his family was his life, wasn't it?*

There were, ahead of Matt, times of joy and sadness, both
public and private. His health was increasingly a problem, and
in 1970 Matt had a hernia operation. In 1980 Louis Edwards,
the genial cohort in so many of Matt's plans, died of a heart
attack. The same year, shortly before he planned to pay a visit
to his beloved Monte Carlo, Matt was out shopping with Jean
in Chorlton, when he was taken ill and drove himself to the
United hospital, St Joseph's. He wasn't a very good driver at
the best of times, and the fact that he was able to make the
journey is quite incredible, demonstrating his robustness, even
at 71, for he'd suffered a stroke.

Two years later Jean was diagnosed as having Alzheimer's
disease. This was the biggest blow to Matt since Munich –
probably more so even than that fateful day almost 25 years
earlier. Matt and Jean had shared everything. They were first
loves, 'one of those great matches', as Paddy Crerand put it.
The condition Jean developed is a pernicious and evil beast,
which gradually robs the victim of his or her old ways; makes
one vulnerable where once was fortitude, reliant where once
was determined independence. It muddles the memory, extingu-
ishes the lights. Over the next five years Matt saw the most
important part of his life reduced to a shell. Jean was no longer
the same person by the time she died in 1988, and Matt was
devastated. He tended to her selflessly while she was alive, held
her hand in the nursing home for three or four hours at a time.
After she had gone, and Matt was living in Sale with his daughter Sheena, he would visit and tend her grave every day, every

afternoon. Sandy and Sheena were distressed to see Matt apparently giving up his own life. Matt cut down the visits to two or three a week. 'He'd just pace up and down smoking his pipe by her graveside,' says Sandy. 'I used to go out there and he'd see me, but it was as if he was in a dream.'

By the time Ron Atkinson succeeded Dave Sexton as manager in 1981, there was no argument about Matt's presence cramping anyone's style. He was now grandfatherly. He told Ron that the door was always open, and occasionally, unlike some of his predecessors, Big Ron would take advantage of the offer. He was a reassuring presence. In March 1983, when old rivals Liverpool defeated United in the League Cup final, Matt had kind words: 'Don't worry, son, we'll be back in two months.' And they were, slamming Brighton 4–0 in the FA Cup final replay. After that game, Ron had the coach stop at a pub run by a friend of his in the Midlands, whom Ron had dubbed 'Sir Matt' because of a passing resemblance. When Sir Matt himself strolled into the bar, it was a source of delight and awe for all those present. Matt still retained that special place in people's hearts.

Ray Wilkins

(Skilled midfielder who arrived after Sir Matt's retirement, but who was helped by kindly words afer a lingering injury sustained at Bournemouth. Now player-coach at Crystal Palace and sometime TV pundit.)

Sir Matt was immense. No question about it. Manchester United is Sir Matt Busby. He was the figurehead of all figureheads. What he had a fantastic knack of doing was bringing players who could play to Man United and, within a system, giving them their head. Now if that's tactically naïve then so be it. He picked the best players and played them in the right position – not a bad little tactic that, is it?

In 1989 Jimmy Murphy died. It's been said in some quarters that Sir Matt – now president of the club – failed to visit his old spar in hospital and that in some way this was a terrible slight. The truth, according to Sandy Busby, is that Matt and Jimmy were both so poorly that doctors advised against the reunion. Matt and Jimmy had shared so much together, there was little they could have added to an incredibly successful relationship spanning nearly 45 years. Soon afterwards, Matt's blood cancer was diagnosed.

Martin Edwards

> *He used to come in every day. He was off for a few days before he was taken ill, but I saw him within a few days of him dying. He used to come in for his lunch and to look at his mail. Somebody would always go with him, sometimes me, but he normally went with the secretary, Ken Merrett, or his assistant, Ken Ramsden. Or he might go with Brian Kidd or Norman Davies, and sometimes I'd join them. Most of the time the talk was about football. Towards the end he'd just listen really, and nod, but you never quite knew how much he was taking in, or not. He slowed down, but people didn't realise how ill he was. Up till the age of 80 he was magnificent, but there was a slow deterioration after that.*

It was Alex Ferguson who, more than anyone since Matt's tenure, had brought back the family spirit – and success – to an ailing club in the late eighties. A fellow Scot, a man keen to know everything going on at the club and in people's lives, a thoughtful man of principle and a considerate, private man, he could be Sir Matt's contemporary double in some ways. 'Sir Matt was extremely supportive when I arrived at Old Trafford,' says Alex. 'To be honest, I was in awe of the man because for such a famous figure he was so humble and unassuming; a wonderfully warm man. No, he didn't offer any suggestions regarding the running of the team but the welcome he gave me was marvellous and he helped me to settle down at the club. "If you ever need me, you know where I am," he said to me soon after I arrived at Old Trafford. I never forgot it and I never will. He also spoke of the hazards and difficulties of running a big club like United. "Always do what you think is right," he added. He was always very helpful to me, particularly in those first years.' In return, Alex kept an eye on Sir Matt when he was at the club to make sure he was okay.

Paddy McGrath

I used to go in a couple of times a week to United for lunch with him, but when he got in his eighties, he never went out without either Sheena or Sandy. He couldn't drive so well then. When he was younger he liked a night out, he liked a drop of Scotch, he liked a glass of wine. He would stop out, but not to the extent of being silly; he'd go home reasonably early. We've had some very pleasant times together. People would ask if I could get Matt to sign something, I'd ring him up and say, 'Matt I've got a pal of mine,' and he'd say, 'Oh come round, he's very welcome; we'll have a cup of tea.' My son is his godson, and his wife has just had a little boy, and they called him Matthew.

In 1993, Matt was present to witness the proof of United's revival under Alex Ferguson as they lifted the Championship – albeit of the new Premier League – for the first time in 26 years. 'He was a man of few words in his later years, but he was as thrilled as the rest of us that the title had returned to Old Trafford after such a long time,' says Alex. 'I remember he joined us in the dressing-room after the last home game against Blackburn Rovers and all the lads had their photograph taken with him and the Premier League trophy. He enjoyed the occasion as much as they did – nothing was too much trouble.

There was a shine in his eyes that night, he was so happy. It was great that he had seen his beloved United win the title again.'

Shay Brennan

The last time I saw Sir Matt was at a dinner, where the present United side were on one side of Alex Ferguson, and we were on the other. After the dinner, people queued for autographs, and Matt's was 30 yards long. There were two in front of me, three in front of Nobby. Even Bobby and Denis and the present players only had a few. Everyone wanted Matt's autograph.

When United retained the title and won the double he never achieved the following year, there was only sadness that the father of football wasn't there to witness it again, his eyes sparkling for a third time.

Paddy Crerand

I probably saw him more during the last six or seven years than at any time in his life. He was living with his daughter, Sheena, just beside me in Sale, and I'd see him practically every day then. He'd often go for a walk and, you know, there'd be a traffic jam wherever he walked. The former players' association has four or five dinners a year, and golf days, and Matt would be at every one of them. Everybody called him Boss, with affection and great regard, great esteem. Ask any player – they all loved him. And don't worry, he's kicked them all up the backside somewhere along the way.

Towards the end Sir Matt was very poorly, but there were still flashes of the younger man, and his family, especially the grandchildren, were very dear. Shortly before he died in hospital, his great mate Paddy McGrath, the prize-fighting rogue from Blackpool, Matt's oldest friend, paid a visit. 'I last saw him about two weeks before he died,' says Paddy. 'Then he went into hospital before Christmas. I didn't realise how serious it was and I asked Sheena if I could go. She said they'd be letting him out before Christmas. After Christmas he went back in and I asked Sheena again, but she said, "They've told us he's got four days to live. At the moment it's just the family going to see him." He woke up after three days. Sandy took all the grandchildren in to see him. He held all their hands, and he died the following day.'

Willie Morgan

I spent New Year's Day with him. I took a bottle of whisky round. We got it opened, had a few wee tots. He'd just had the first little operation on his leg, but he was great. We talked about when we were going back to Tenerife. So his death was a big shock. We were making arrangements to have a get-together at my house the week after. The last time we played golf was last year. He played very little golf the last two years, and he'd only go out and play a few holes. The thing about him was that, if you look at, say, Richard Nixon, he was a disgrace, then he dies and he's a hero. But everything that's been said about Matt since he died was said before he died. That's the greatest epitaph that he could have.

The Epitaph

Sandy Busby

*When the doctor came round to write the death certificate,
she stepped into the room where he was lying, then turned
round and put her hand over her mouth. She was obviously
upset. Tears were welling in her eyes. She said to Sheena
and me, 'I'm very sorry. It's just that he really was such a
lovely man.'*

Sir Matt died in his sleep on Wednesday 20 January 1994, at the
Alexandra Hospital in Cheadle. He was 84. A spokeswoman
explained: 'Sir Matt has had blood cancer for a number of
years.' A recent illness – the last of many – had debilitated him
beyond recovery, even for his tough old Lanarkshire consti-
tution, and 'his condition gradually deteriorated'. The grim
reaper, denied on a snowy runway 26 years earlier despite the
administration of last rites, would be cheated no more.

There had previously been two occasions when the city of
Manchester had stood still, and Matt was instrumental in both.
On a cold February in 1958 the citizens had been shocked by
the horrific events of 'the crash'; in total contrast, hundreds
of thousands had rammed the streets to welcome home the
triumphant European Cup team in May 1968. Now, a quarter
of a century on, the old cotton town's inhabitants were jolted
once again at the death of a figure who had seemed as constant
and immortal as the city itself. As the news filtered through,

fans were drawn out of their homes, as if the pain was too much to bear in private. As with Munich, there was cathartic relief in making the pilgrimage to Old Trafford and decking it out with the red and white like some industrial temple. Ill-equipped though football grounds are – cold, functional monstrosities endowed only with familiarity and history in their favour – the stadium became the focal point for mute feelings that were impossible to articulate in any other way. Still bearing the monument to Munich – the clock frozen at the time the plane crashed on the runway – it looked happier to bear these spontaneous tokens of thanks, of sorrow, of honour.

First, there was a trickle – those who had instantly recognised that there was only one place to pay your respects, to share the burden, grieve and ponder. But by midday there were masses; tearful, abstracted, devoted. They all came: the old – most who had followed United since the dapper, demobbed Scot had first arrived, and some City or Liverpool fans who remembered him as a pre-war player for their team; and the young, children to whom the Busby dynasty was simply vivid history handed down. Delivery vans interrupted their rounds to detour and drop off mementoes at the ground. Priests, respectful of Sir Matt's 40-year service to the church, but also of his contribution to so many more lives through his sparkling occupation, also attended this makeshift chapel. They too recognised that a little piece of Manchester had died with the papal knight.

The Warwick Road along which Matt Busby strode pensively towards the bombed-out ground in the autumn of 1945 had the look of a match day. Renamed by Manchester City Council 'Sir Matt Busby Way' in honour of the adopted son and local hero (Sir Matt had already had locomotives and aeroplanes dedicated to him), its signs were decked with scarves. A few were ancient souvenirs bought during cup and league campaigns in the sixties and seventies. There were anonymous hand-written dedications, each with their own reflections and eulogies. Many made the connection between Manchester's twin tragedies:

'SIR MATT
AT PEACE WITH
"THE BABES"
GOD BLESS'

On the same day, the death of football's most unequivocally venerated father figure was the main item on the evening news. In a final gesture for the game he adored, the ambassador from Orbiston had uniquely elevated football above war in Bosnia and the political and economic scene at home. Under different circumstances the man who lived and breathed soccer would have admired such news values.

So as one voice the organs of the media mourned Sir Matt's passing and celebrated a life rich in drama and success. Frank McGhee, writing in the *Observer* under the headline 'Noble red knight', was shrewd in his observation that 'they will never need to erect a monument in Manchester to the man. He built one himself at Old Trafford from the cellars upwards.' The *Manchester Evening News* offered, 'Matt proved that nice guys do win.' People throughout the football world readily made themselves available for interview; tributes poured in. David Ward in the *Guardian* ventured that, having been its president in life, Sir Matt was in death 'its guardian angel'. In the *Daily Telegraph* Malcolm Allison – he of the famous fedora hat, and manager of Matt's City rivals twice in the seventies – proclaimed football's chivalrous knight a great competitor and a brilliant man. 'He brought European football to England. The Manchester United of today are a credit to him, and thankfully he lived long enough to see them win the Premier League. He could be proud of them.'

Denis Law averred the Boss was 'probably the greatest manager English soccer has ever seen. But more important he was a true gentleman to everyone. Whenever he walked into a room everyone sensed they were witnessing a great man who could illuminate their day.' Munich survivor Jackie Blanchflower was more emotional: 'He was the best manager there ever was. He was like a second father to me.'

Willie Morgan

I've had loads of great moments in football, but the fact that Matt signed me, for a record fee – I'll go to my resting place knowing that he did that, and that's enough for me.

On the Saturday after his passing, all British football matches – and many thousands around the world – observed a minute's silence in honour of Sir Matt. It's a measure of his transcendant appeal that the terraces stood almost mute across the country. The Everton fans, hardly what might be described as best friends of the Red Devils, won a Carling No. 1 Award from the Premiership sponsors for 'their exemplary behaviour' at Old Trafford that day. Swindon served one of their fans with a lifetime ban for yobbish swearing during the otherwise silent tribute at home to Tottenham. Saturday's *Match of the Day* closed with a shot of the seat that will never again be occupied. It bears a brass plaque with the the words 'Sir Matt' engraved upon it.

The next day, some churlish Leeds fans chanted the name of their own 'Matt' figure, Don Revie, and held up offensive banners at a disgusted Ewood Park. Worse was to come. In a macabre and tasteless act while Sir Matt's body lay in state at the undertaker's, a pall-bearer is said to have taken photographs of the body, removed name tags and clippings of hair with the intention of selling them to the tabloid press for immense personal gain. Tom Gibbons walked in front of the hearse during the funeral procession. But a few days later the *Sun* alerted the police to his scheme and he was arrested and advised to leave his home, so strong was the sense of outrage after news of his sickening behaviour broke. To older friends of Sir Matt the incident had another echo of Munich: he had complained to the authorities about the intrusion of photographers while lying critically ill in the Rechts der Isaar hospital in Munich.

The funeral on Thursday 27 January 1994 was an incredible affair, as much a celebration of a long and fulfilled life as a requiem for the sadness of his passing and the tragedies of his life. The route taken by the hearse carrying Sir Matt's huge mahogany casket was lined fifteen deep in places; the casual observer from out of town might have likened it to a victory parade until the thirteen black cars and three buses passed solemnly by. Old Trafford was surrounded by probably the quietest, most respectful and deflated Manchester crowd in the club's history.

There were more banners. Swathes of flowers. Resolute smiles through tears. The Munich clock was passed for the last time. The procession stopped for two long minutes loaded with significance.

Manchester knows only one type of weather for such occasions; a wild squall enveloped the cortege's slow progress, moderated by two police horses, towards the house of God at which Matt had worshipped for 40 years, the Church of Our Lady and St John's in Chorlton-cum-Hardy. It was closed to the general public, but so many people were invited – 90 players alone – to attend, the organisers had to make a roster. Matt's Catholic faith was strongly represented – an archbishop, two bishops and 23 priests were there to see off their Knight of the Order of St Gregory. Banners accumulated along the funeral route in the timeless Mancunian drizzle: 'Manchester United 0, Heaven 1 – this will be one of the great signings'.

Reds fans arrived from all over the country, all over the world. Followers of other teams also made the pilgrimage: this wasnt football business, it was personal – again Sir Matt, the soccer iconoclast, was breaking down the barriers.

Wreaths had arrived from Real Madrid, from the United staff whose lives he touched – a representation of the Old Trafford pitch with the words 'Wherever and whenever Manchester United play, you will be remembered – from the playing staff and directors'. And from the former players' association, fittingly, there was 'The Boss', spelled out in red and white carnations.

George Best

I went to the funeral service with his family. And the biggest compliment anyone's ever paid to me was from them when we were at the graveside. They said to me, 'You know, he said he thought of you as his son.' I just freaked out. For him to have said that to his own family was incredible. You look at someone like Bobby, who's been through the crash, Harry Gregg, Bill Foulkes, and for some reason I feel closer to him than maybe they do, even after the longer time they spent knowing him. It was a special feeling I had about him.

Two Saturdays later, a lowly club pinned the words of Matt Busby, made during his acceptance speech on being made Freeman of the City of Manchester (the first sports personality to be honoured in such a way), on their dressing-room walls. It was on the occasion of Diadora League side Aldershot Town welcoming Wimborne Town for a Fifth Round FA Vase match. And those principled words would be well remembered in any stadium where the game of football, with all its mystery, magic, beauty and tenacity, is played and enjoyed: 'What matters above all things is that the game should be played in the right spirit with the utmost courage, with fair play and no favour, with every man playing as a member of his team without bitterness and conceit.'

Such eminently decent principles made Sir Matt a natural focus for letter-writers. He would receive many each week at his small office in the United stadium. But in death the correspondence to the club and Sir Matt's relatives was overwhelming. Sandy Busby has a wardrobe full of tributes and cards of

224

commiseration from strangers who felt a kinship with his father. Many others were from those whose life had in some way been touched by Sir Matt's kindness. Some reveal the charitable acts Matt would perform without fanfare or applause. One says, 'To Sir Matt, for your help when it was most needed. God bless you', and it is signed simply with initials. 'Now what did my father do for that person?' says Sandy. 'Who are they?' There must be many more such examples.

Many more poured their hearts out in the faithful organ of Manchester football, the *Manchester Evening News*. The salutes included some from Bolton, Manchester City and Everton followers. All told of the broad appeal of a great football man. All pronounced Sir Matt the greatest manager of all time, even alongside Herbert Chapman, Bill Shankly and Jock Stein. One wrote, 'As a true blue Evertonian I should like to say what a privilege it was to be at Old Trafford on Saturday. It was a privilege to admire United's scintillating football and a privilege to pay our respects to Sir Matt Busby, whose teams always played to the style admired by all Evertonians.' Others wrote of his approachability – about the autographs he'd willingly give at any time, about his pioneering youth policy, about his European vision, his patience and reassurance. The most poignant, from a B. M. Nield, noted how fitting it was that Ryan Giggs, a quintessential 'Busby Babe' of the new school, should have scored the only goal of the game. 'Football was united in the loss of a great man, and I was proud to be part of the crowd, not one of whom uttered a single sound to spoil that 60 seconds of total, tranquil stillness. The silence was golden. As the ground emptied, the roar of the crowd no more, you could somehow still hear the faint and distant strains of the lone piper. And it was difficult to imagine Manchester United without "the Boss". His memory will last forever. Thank you Sir Matt.'

Old Trafford was to stage one more formal farewell to its greatest son. A memorial service, open to the public and attended by thousands, took place on a typically damp Sunday towards the end of April. Black ribbons, attached soon after his death, still fluttered on Sir Matt's seat in the stands, the stadium flags flapped at half-mast. An adorned stage at the scoreboard end saw a parade of Sir Matt's United 'family', including 1948 hero Charlie Mitten and his 1968 equivalent Bobby Charlton.

Paddy Crerand

He was a big influence on me, and he was a big influence on every player who played under him. On and off the pitch. A few years ago they made a TV series about the history of Scottish football, and they came down to interview myself and Denis, and they wanted to interview Matt, but he wouldn't do it. I said, 'You should do it – you're an influential part of Scottish football. You wont live forever.' He looked at me and just laughed. I said, 'You should leave it so people in years to come can listen to you talk.' And he said, 'You know, Pat, I think you're right.' And he did it.

The most emotional moment at the memorial service came when the team talk a hollow-voiced Matt had recorded in his German hospital bed in 1958 was played to the assembled throng for the first time. The hissing, cracking quality of the broadcast added to the poignancy and sense of perspective. It was too much for many, including some players present. But it was a time for commemorating Sir Matt – the man. Munich veteran Harry Gregg signed autographs: 'I'm delighted to be here,' he said. 'I am sure it will be a nice party. Sir Matt will enjoy a party'; veteran broadcaster Kenneth Wolstenholme recalled some epic moments and sports writer/broadcaster Cliff Morgan reminded the mourners – it was sometimes required, so great was his contribution to the game – that Sir Matt hadn't invented football. 'But he has sewn a piece of very different and very beautiful material on to football's robe of state.' Others felt proud to have touched Matt's life in some way.

Nobby Stiles

Being a United supporter anyway made it special, and it was just a pleasure to play under him, because he wanted you to play with style and do things the right way, and you felt fortunate to be a part of it.

The players, including the man who'd first tended to Matt in the wreckage of the 'Lord Burleigh', Harry Gregg, shared thoughts not of glorious moments that might reflect on themselves, but of Sir Matt's personal qualities, his humility, consideration, reassuring nature. That same day Blackburn's championship aspirations evaporated in a dismal 1–1 draw with QPR. United were soon to be crowned champions for the second successive season.

That, surely, was the finest dedication of all.

Alex Ferguson

Sir Matt was one of the nicest people I've ever met and I feel privileged to have known him. I know I shall never forget him. His contribution to football in general and Manchester United in particular cannot be underestimated. I doubt if we shall see his like again.

Receive him, O Lord.
Wash his eyes with light and let
him meet again those who went
before. Let the angels help him
to make a team that will give
divine pleasure to all the souls in
heaven, just as his boys gave joy
here on earth.

Sir Matt Busby

Sir Matt Busby, CBE, KCSG
Born 26 May 1909
Died 20 January 1994
[memorial service card for Sir Matt]

George Best

Everybody talks about the greatest in their own sport, and he was. There was no one better at anything he did – the way he lived his life, the way he handled people, the way he had them playing, the way he ran the club. I think it was down to the fact that he loved life. You see people who maybe don't appreciate it once they're no longer young. Matt should have been around for another hundred years because he loved everything in life that was good.

For The Record

Sir Matt's career:

1909	Born Orbiston, near Bellshill, Lanarkshire, 26 May.
1928	Joins Manchester City from Denny Hibernians. Plays more than 200 games for City.
1933	Wins only full peacetime cap for Scotland, v Wales. Plays in FA Cup Final v Everton (0–3).
1934	Wins FA Cup-Winners' medal v Portsmouth (2–1).
1936	Joins Liverpool for £8,000, remains there until end of war.
1940–45	Member of wartime British Army team. Manages team on tour of Italy, 1945.
1945	Becomes Manchester United's manager on £15 a week.
1948	Manages United to 4–2 win over Blackpool in FA Cup final.
1952	United win League Championship – first of five occasions.
1956	United win League Championship, and enter European competition for first time, reaching semi-finals of European Cup.
1957	United win League Championship, reaching semi-finals of European Cup for second time.
1958	Munich air crash decimates United team and nearly kills Matt.
1963	United win FA Cup by beating Leicester City 3–1.

1964   Reach quarter-finals of European Cup-Winners' Cup.

1965   League Champions again. Reach semi-finals of Fairs Cup.

1967   United reach semi-finals of European Cup and win League for fifth and last time under Matt, who becomes Freeman of the City of Manchester.

1968   United become first English team to win European Cup. Matt announces his retirement from managing early next year. Matt is knighted and receives Papal knighthood.

1969   Sir Matt becomes general manager.

1970   Sir Matt briefly returns as caretaker manager following dismissal of Wilf McGuinness, and prior to appointment of Frank O'Farrell. Subsequently relinquishes general manager role and joins board of directors.

1980   Sir Matt steps down from board of directors and becomes club president.

1994   Sir Matt Busby dies, 20 January.

United's season-by-season record under Matt Busby:

1945–46   FA Cup 4th round

1946–47   League 2nd; FA Cup 4th round

1947–48   League 2nd; **FA Cup Winners** (beating Blackpool 4–2)

1948–49   League 2nd; FA Cup semi-finalists

1949–50   League 4th; FA Cup 6th round

1950–51   League 2nd; FA Cup 6th round

1951–52   **League Champions**; FA Cup 3rd round

1952–53   League 8th; FA Cup 5th; FA Charity Shield Winners; FA Youth Cup Winners

1953–54   League 4th; FA Cup 3rd round; FA Youth Cup Winners

1954–55   League 5th; FA Cup 4th round; FA Youth Cup Winners

1955–56   **League Champions**; FA Cup 3rd round; FA Youth Cup Winners

1956–57   **League Champions**; FA Cup runners-up (losing to Aston Villa 1–2); European Cup semi-finalists; FA Charity Shield Winners; FA Youth Cup Winners

1957–58   League 9th; FA Cup runners-up (losing to Bolton Wanderers 0–2); European Cup semi-finalists; FA Charity Shield Winners

1958–59   League 2nd; FA Cup 3rd round

1959–60   League 7th; FA Cup 5th round

1960–61   League 7th; FA Cup 4th round; Football League Cup 2nd round

1961–62   League 15th; FA Cup semi-finalists

1962–63   League 19th; **FA Cup Winners** (beat Leicester City 3–1)

1963–64   League 2nd; FA Cup semi-finalists; European Cup-Winners' Cup quarter-finalists; FA Youth Cup Winners

1964–65   **League Champions**; FA Cup semi-finalists; Fairs Cup semi-finalists

1965–66   League 4th; FA Cup semi-finalists; FA Charity Shield Winners

1966–67   League Champions; FA Cup 4th round; Football League Cup 2nd round

1967–68   League 2nd; **European Cup Winners** (beating Benfica 4–2); FA Cup 3rd round; FA Charity Shield Winners

Sir Matt Busby

Three great Busby teams and what they cost:
(Where no price is indicated, either already at the club or brought through youth ranks)

1948 FA Cup Winners

Crompton
Carey (£250), Aston
Anderson, Chilton, Cockburn
Delaney (£4,000), Morris, Rowley (£3,500), Pearson, Mitten

Total: £7,750

1956–58 Double League Champions (1956 and 1957)

Gregg (£24,000)
Foulkes, Byrne
Colman, Blanchflower, Edwards
Berry (£25,000), Viollet, Taylor (£30,000), Whelan, Pegg

Total: £79,000

1965–68 Double League Champions (1965 and 1967) and European Cup Winners (1968)

Stepney (£52,000)
Dunne (£5,000), Cantwell (£30,000)
Crerand (£43,000), Sadler, Stiles
Best, Law (£115,000), Charlton, Kidd, Aston

Total: £245,000